Praise for *The Book*

"Steven Forrest's warmth and access. _ will immediately draw you to this gem of a book. With a twinkle in his eye, he shakes up our habitual thinking about the Moon and challenges us to see Her again with new eyes. Not only does he remind us that the Moon is much more than we imagined, he brings a distillation of deep practice and creative thinking to his writing on the lunar phase. He makes complexity fun and adds his inventive, evolutionary twist."
—Lynn Bell, Centre for Psychological Astrology

"This wonderful book explores the oft-ignored phenomenon of moon cycles in astrology. Steven puts a personal spin on all of his chapters that make his books consistently enjoyable and easy to relate to and understand for even the novice astrology student"
—Graham McNallie, Amazon

"Steven Forrest's latest publication *The Book Of The Moon* is likely to become is a modern classic. Here is an author who actually has something new to say and he effortlessly gets his ideas across in a most engaging fashion. *The Book Of The Moon* is modern in its approach and relevant for astrology today. This book comes highly recommended for both students and professionals alike."
—Alison Price, Starzology.com

"Steven manages to bring fresh insight to this foundational topic, breathing life into each of the lunar phases with his gift of poetic language and his skillful use of anecdote. He navigates easily between the more technical, astronomical material – the practical knowledge necessary for any astrologer to have under their belt – and the metaphoric arena of interpretation. I heartily recommend *The Book of the Moon* to students and professionals alike."
—DenaDeCastro, Sirius Astrology Podcast

Praise for Steven Forrest's work

"You carry the noble art of Astrology so faithfully: I have had several charts done in my lifetime but none of them - but yours - have escaped the astrologer mistaking so much of the chart as a sounding-board for his own ego. You have restored the divine art to its noble status."
—Robert Johnson, author of *We*

"Steve's book manages to disarm the skeptic, as well as debunk the charlatanism that surrounds popular astrology, with language that is as intelligent and cogent as it is poetic."
—Sting

The Book of the Moon

Also by Steven Forrest

The Inner Sky

The Changing Sky

The Night Speaks

The Book of Pluto

Measuring the Night (with Jeffrey Wolf Green)

Measuring the Night Vol. 2 (with Jeffrey Wolf Green)
Stalking Anubis

Skymates (with Jodie Forrest)

Skymates II (with Jodie Forrest)

Yesterday's Sky

ᚦHE BOOK
OF ᚦHE MOON

by Steven Forrest

Seven Paws Press, Inc.
Borrego Springs, CA

Published in 2013 by Seven Paws Press, Inc.
PO Box 82
Borrego Springs, CA 92004
www.sevenpaws.com

ISBN 978-0-9790677-4-7
LCCN: 2010908824

First Printing July 2010
Second Printing April 2013

Cover by Steven Forrest
Printed in the United States of America

CONTENTS

ACKNOWLEDGMENTS

My special thanks to Paige Ruane and Patrick Kearney of the Integrative Medicine Foundation for providing the generous grants which allowed me to write both this volume and the previous one, *Yesterday's Sky: Astrology and Reincarnation*.

I could not have done the exhaustive research which underlies this book without the resources provided by AstroDataBank, both in my full desktop research version and in their up-to-date on-line version. My gratitude to everyone involved in offering that act of generosity and support toward the astrological community. There is no better test for a theory than reality itself, and AstroDataBank provides that.

Carol Czeczot did a monumental job of line-editing the text, and did so during a time of personal grief. Thank you, Carol. You are the soul of the Beltane Moon.

Finally my thanks to the following friends and colleagues who were actively engaged with me in various ways during the writing process: the members of my Apprenticeship Program one and all, Scott Ainslie, Aysem Aksoy, Lynn Bell, Virginia Bell, The Blue Sky Ranch Fellowship, Ingrid Coffin, Cheryl and Garry Cooper, Mike Czeczot, Beth Darnall, Karen Davis, Dena DeCastro, Janette DeProsse, Robert Downey Jr., Rona Elliot and Roger Brossy, Michael Erlewine, Maurice Fernandez, Hadley Fitzgerald, Chris Ford, Bunny Forrest, Jodie Forrest, Kelli and David Fox, Rishi Giovanni Gatti, Tracy and Ryan Gaudet, Nan Geary, Connie George, The Metropolitan Atlanta Astrological Society, Martha Goenaga, Robert and Diana Griffin, Kathy Hallen and Fran Slavich, Amy Herring, Tony Howard, Baris Ilhan, Bill Janis and Shannon Glass, Robert A. Johnson, Stephanie Johnson, John and Judy Johnston, Lisa and Terry Jones, Rhiannon Jones, Barbara King, Michelle Kondos, Alphee and Carol Lavoie, Michael Lutin, Eileen McCabe, Chris McRae, Christine Murfitt, the Nalbandian family, Carey Nash, Rafael Nasser, Vinessa Nevala, Dorothy Oja, Betty Pristera and Jeff Krukin, Keron Psillas, David Railley, Dusty Recor and "Indian Joe" Stewart, Melanie Reinhart, Paul Richard, Evelyn Roberts, Lee Russell, Moses Siregar III, Cristina Smith, Susan Sokol-Blosser, Herb and Geoff Stone, Trudie Styler and Sting, Diane Swan, Tem Tarriktar, Kay Taylor, Gisele Terry, Glen Tig, Joyce Van Horn and Kathy Jacobson, Patricia Walsh, Bob and Gail Wilderson, Christal Whitt, Sanford Wolcott and Scotty Young.

For Virginia ("Bunny") Forrest,

the first Moon I ever know…

FOREWORD

Steven Forrest is a rare combination; he's a brilliant astrologer, a gifted writer and communicator, as well as an inspiring teacher. He also possesses a generous spirit and a profound compassion. Perhaps that's why his books, readings, and lectures resonate with so many diverse people and why his information penetrates so deeply; it reaches beyond the intellect and goes straight to the heart. It is a privilege to be able to share my experience of Steven's work and his newest book, *The Book of the Moon: Discovering Astrology's Lost Dimension.*

I initially got to know Steven through his first book, *The Inner Sky.* Reading it turned out to be a major turning point for me. I had always been fascinated with astrology; as a teenager I devoured the monthly Dell astrology magazine searching for answers and glimpses of hope. When I opened a natural foods restaurant in Greenwich Village in 1974, I consulted an astrologer for an auspicious date. In the '80s, I even had one on staff; he ate in exchange for readings for myself and the employees. In those days I merely wanted to know when the current crisis would end so I could get on with my life. I didn't understand that the crisis (or present transit) was the whole point—a precious opportunity to transform something within myself.

All that changed in 1988; I opened a second restaurant and was under tremendous pressure. Unbeknownst to me, transiting Pluto (in Scorpio) was opposite my Taurus Sun. One night a friend read aloud a passage from Steven's book, *The Inner Sky.* I was totally riveted and profoundly moved. An old life was ending and a new one was about to begin.

In *The Inner Sky*, Steven writes about the planets, signs and houses—the most basic and fundamental concepts in astrology—but he does so with such richness and reverence. I always viewed astrology as something distant and divorced from real life, a secret language known only to a special few. Steven translates that language into one that is accessible, engaging, and poetic. Thanks to Steven's book, astrology no longer felt remote, but instead something that was intimately and divinely connected to all of life.

I called Steven for a natal reading, then a transit and progressions reading. I'd had readings before but this was different; I felt truly seen, even though the reading was on tape and not in person. I was hooked. I never knew that astrology could be so deep and rich or that it could be a catalyst for personal growth. Steven is a master storyteller and, I suspect, a bit of a wizard. He brings the chart alive with parables, colorful metaphors, humor, and great humanity. He doesn't shy away from pointing out the issues that block your development or the work that needs to be done, but he does so in a style that is nonthreatening. In this way he makes it safe for you to connect with the parts of yourself that you've disowned or repressed. That is the beginning of true healing. It's also an art form.

During an astrology conference in 1989, I had a chance to meet Steven in person; it really felt like encountering an old friend. Over the years we kept in touch and in 2000 I joined Steven's Apprenticeship Program. I was already involved in astrology professionally and the program was a godsend—a rare opportunity to study with a master astrologer who freely shares his methods and techniques, as well as his wisdom. There are now several programs around the world, and Steven is inspiring a whole new generation of astrologers. It was during this period that Steven was developing his approach to Evolutionary Astrology, and it has been exciting to watch it progress to where it is today.

Evolutionary Astrology is not merely an astrological technique; it provides a philosophical framework for the kind of astrology that is based on freedom, choice, and a respect for people's innate ability to grow and change. Like holistic medicine, Evolutionary Astrology deals with the whole person. It doesn't just diagnose the problem; it aims to heal and do no harm. That's good astrology; it's also a good way for living one's life. Thanks in part to the Internet, astrology has never been more popular, and an approach such as Evolutionary Astrology, one based on integrity and responsibility, is greatly needed and extremely relevant. In that sense it is a method whose time has come.

About this book you hold in your hands: *The Book of the Moon: Discovering Astrology's Lost Dimension.* Each of Steven's books takes us on an extraordinary journey and this one is no exception. We all have a relationship with the Moon which, after the Sun, is the most familiar and observable object in the heavens and yet the most enigmatic. It is so intimately connected to our lives that we often take it for granted: as beautiful and ordinary as the sparrow or the smallest flower, as dependable as the seasons. Using not only astrology, but astronomy, history, science, and literature, Steven examines the Moon closely, yet none of the magic or mystery is diminished; in fact it is deepened. What Steven does is help us understand the Moon above as well as our own lunar nature, the part of ourselves that is timeless and eternal.

One of the most fundamental areas of astrology, yet one that has been greatly overlooked, is lunar phases. We are all familiar with the various phases of the Moon; nightly we observe the spectacle in the sky and feel it in our blood and bones. Whose heart hasn't swelled at the sight of a lush Full Moon or a slender, silver crescent emerging from behind the clouds? Yet most of us are not aware of the lunar phase we were born under and how powerfully it shapes our lives. This book will change that. Like an archeologist, Steven uncovers this valuable material and elevates it to its proper place. He travels familiar ground with fresh eyes and a courageous heart and offers a treasure trove of new insights and exciting revelations. Always the poet, his language is lyrical and soulful as befitting the subject.

This book is pure alchemy. Read it once; read it twice; read it not just with your mind but with your heart. Let it soak in. This is a book you will not easily forget. In fact, it will help you remember who you are.

Virginia Bell
March, 2010
New York City.

INTRODUCTION

THE INCONSTANT MOON

Maybe the moon may learn,
Tired of that courtly fashion,
A new dance turn.
—William Butler Yeats

The Moon shocks us. We round a corner just after dark and there it is, bright as a neon pumpkin. Weeks later, we glance overhead at lunchtime and it ambushes us again, looking like a pale ghost floating unexpectedly in the blue sky. The reliable Sun, by contrast, rises prosaically in the morning, arcs in dignified fashion through the sky and sets in the evening, as predictable as a traffic light. But we never know quite where the Moon will be or how it will look. The Sun may be brighter, but the Moon makes up the deficit by being mysterious, strange, and as full of surprises as a deck of cards.

Humans have been meditating on the Moon since the beginning of our time on Earth. As long as there has been anything we could call astrology, it has been central to all ideas and theories about celestial influence. How could it be otherwise? The Moon punches straight into the bull's eye of our attention. And in astrology, everything big and bright and punchy in the sky plays a pivotal role, while everything faint and obscure . . . is more complicated.

Let me set the stage for our long meditation upon the Moon by reflecting on how we choose what to use astrologically from the vast menu of objects and events the sky offers us. There is something very systematic about that elective process—and there are a few mysterious loose ends as well.

FAINT AND BRIGHT

Flickers too dim for the eye to see can have momentous astrological consequences. Witness the feeble glint of Pluto. By far the smallest planet, it is physically smaller than seven of the *Moons* in our solar system, and so dark and far away that it is 1,148 times fainter than the faintest star detectable to the naked eye. Some astronomers do not even call it a planet anymore—but when faint little Pluto came to the Ascendant in the most commonly used birth chart for the United States of America, the Twin Towers in New York were blasted to rubble. When it aligned with John F. Kennedy's Moon, he was assassinated.

In astrology, faintness does not mean insignificance!

On the other hand, faintness does not make something significant either. There are plenty of faint objects in the sky that have very limited meaning. The asteroids and the newly discovered planet-like bodies out beyond Neptune provide a good illustration: some of them are profound in their impact and some seem significantly less so. I plan to write a book with Melanie Reinhart, author of *Chiron and the Healing Journey*, about some of these new worlds, so I am going to give them short shrift here. But as of this writing, the tally of named asteroids is above fifteen thousand. And although all are dim, many are actually brighter than Pluto.

How do they work?

Asteroids with mythological names can be powerfully evocative of the realities of our lives, once we know the myths. Most of the bigger asteroids follow this pattern: Ceres, Vesta, Hygeia, Pallas and Juno, for example. Or Persephone and Titania. We can learn some Aztec mythology and perhaps make sense of Tezcatlipoca opposing our natal Moon. With a little creativity, we can often make meaningful connections with more modern asteroid names, such as Goldfinger, Springsteen, or Pink Floyd. We can have fun with Geisha, Excalibur, or Dudu—and again, maybe even generate some insights.

Very often the names of the asteroids click quite literally with the actual names of people in our lives. It is not unusual to find, for example, an asteroid bearing your partner's name in close aspect with your Venus. In my own chart, the asteroid "Jody" lies in 22 degrees of Sagittarius while my natal Venus is at 21 degrees—and I married a woman named Jodie. In Jodie's chart, the asteroid "Stevin" falls in late Scorpio, near my

Ascendant and closely trine her Venus.

But what are we to make of the asteroid Mork or Turtlestar? Or Superbus? Or Bandersnatch, Carp, or Dodo? What about Whipple? Very likely such names will not ring a bell, even for people with these bodies rising or conjunct their Suns.

So we have a muddle here. Faint objects are sometimes compellingly impressive in their astrological relevance—witness Pluto. Or seemingly purposeless, pointless, and irrelevant—witness Superbus or Carp. With faint objects, you just have to sort it out case by case. Sometimes you hit, sometimes you miss.

But what about the opposite principle? What about celestial objects that move along the ecliptic and are brilliantly bright and obvious? Are any of them unimportant to astrologers?

None at all.

Mostly, we are talking about the classical planets: Mercury, Venus, Mars, Jupiter and Saturn. And of course the Sun and the Moon—and, by the way, we will be capitalizing Sun and Moon throughout the book to emphasize their equality with the planets. These bright, obvious points of light in the sky are the basic tools of astrologers everywhere in all traditions. Bright comets could qualify here too—and, historically, astrologers were obsessed with them. Modern astrologers often ignore them, which is probably a big mistake.

The general principle is that in the living traditions of astrology, *obvious always equals important.*

With one glaring exception . . .

WHAT'S YOUR MOON PHASE?

Go among astrologers and casually ask any of them, "Where's your Moon?" You will certainly hear a sign of the zodiac. "Aquarius," says the fellow with bright eyes madly gleaming. "Taurus," says the woman in the mumu.

There is a good chance you will hear a house position too—"Gemini in the Eleventh," says the elfin-eyed girl glancing curiously around the crowded room.

Possibly you will get more detail than you bargained for. "Virgo," says the bookish-looking gent, "in the sixth house by Placidus but in the fifth house by Koch and Meridian, conjunct Venus, but square Uranus and sesquiquadrate the midpoint of Mars and Mercury . . . and bi-quintile to Tezcatlipoca, and—" Got that?

But there is something you will almost never hear, "My Moon is in the Waxing Gibbous phase."

Yet what could be more obvious about the Moon in the sky than its phase? A Crescent Moon and a Full Moon are entirely different beasts, visually. Why don't we hear about that? "Obvious equals important" seems to be a very reliable astrological principle. *Why is the lunar phase astrology's lost dimension?*

Immediately, astrological scholars might object. They will make reference to the well-known work on lunar phases done by the great Dane Rudhyar in his epochal 1967 book, *The Lunation Cycle.* There he devotes about forty pages to the topic. The scholars may also quote a volume that they may have never read: *A Vision,* by the splendid Irish poet, William Butler Yeats—a profoundly dense work on lunar phase published in 1937. They may follow the reference to Yeats with a mention of another book which explores the same terrain, published in 1988: *Moon Phases: A Symbolic Key,* by one of my favorite astrologers, Martin Goldsmith. Some may remember the hard-to-find 1974 book, *Phases of the Moon: A Guide to Evolving Human Nature,* by Marilyn Busteed, Richard Tiffany and Dorothy Wergin. Or Demetra George's *Finding Our Way Through the Dark.*

My point is not that lunar phase has never been discussed in the astrological literature. It has. My point is that *lunar phase has not caught on as a significant element of practical astrology.* A minority of present-day astrologers could name one or two of the books I just mentioned. Only a few of them could describe in any detail the actual contents of these works. And almost no one includes the Moon's phase in their interpretations. *Why?*

Lunar phase is dramatic. It is beautiful. And it hits us over the head whenever we look up at the sky. Why is it relegated to a minor footnote in modern astrological practice?

CH-CH-CH-CHANGES

Let me seem to change the subject for a few lines. The 1890s society my grandparents knew is almost as alien today as Shakespeare's England. The world my parents met when they were young feels nearly that exotic—no air conditioning? No television? Much of Africa and Amazonia still unexplored? A world population under two billion?

The changes witnessed by the past three or four generations are unprecedented in their scale and reach. It is easy to be awed by their technological dimension. But what about our collective attitude toward gender? Race? Gayness? Church? The environment? What about our attitude, for one American example, toward Turkey or Indonesia? When I was growing up, those countries seemed like other planets. Now they are places I go where I have friends who do not seem so radically different from me. I email them and they email me. Sometimes I know what they had for breakfast.

The list goes on. What about marriage? What about the expectations we hold of fathers toward their children? What about healing? And seeking spiritual or psychological counsel?

"Paradigm shift" is one of those terms that has become odious through overuse. And yet, has there ever before in human history been such a profound shift in *everything?*

Here, in a nutshell, is the case I want to make in this book: the current paradigm shift has finally opened a window on the meaning of lunar phase. Up until now, I believe that astrologers have been in the position of 15th century astronomers who tried to reason about what they observed in the heavens while simultaneously maintaining the assumption that the Earth was the center of the universe. Like them, we have been blinded by what we thought we knew. But the old system of belief, with its blind spots, is giving way to something new. A fresh way of being human is emerging. As the old paradigm dies, for the first time we begin *to see things that have always been there.* As usual with big mythic changes, this shift is not happening quickly. And of course it is a scary ride as we watch the old certainties hit the wall.

In Chapter Six, I will make my specific argument for the precise way the old, patriarchal, mechanistic belief-system has blinded us to the lunation cycle. I think I will prove that we astrologers have been terribly limited in our understanding of lunar phase because of cultural assumptions and prejudices. I will do my best to ferret out the new assumptions and show how they reveal insights into the lunar cycle that we have simply not been ready to see very clearly until now—insights that, at least for me, triggered a compelling fall of the intellectual dominoes. I think that you will find the same thing that I found, which is that as I shed some epistemological baggage I had carried since I was a child, lunar phase clicked into place.

I believe I will also make a good case that the roots of this "new" understanding are actually quite ancient—and still detectable in the cultural traces left by the so-called "pagan" people of pre-Christian, pre-Aristotelian, Europe.

Before exploring all that, I want to lay a foundation of basic lunar theory in the context of Evolutionary Astrology. This I will do in the next chapter. There we will learn some counseling-room perspectives on the Moon in general which will later be relevant to lunar phase. We will first investigate them in the more familiar terrain of the lunar sign and house.

In Chapter Three, I want to introduce some details about the mechanics of lunar phase, and also pay homage to the pioneers in this branch of astrology whom I mentioned earlier—Yeats and Rudhyar and the rest. They have much to teach us, despite their frequent immersion in the cultural blind spots to which I have been referring.

Finally, I understand that there is a certain audacity in what I claim to be doing in this book. I believe in what I am about to write. Otherwise I would not write it. But I also am acutely aware of making bold claims, dismissing some existing work, and then stepping into territory that is significantly uncharted. This is an age-old formula for spectacular pratfalls! I will surely make some. And I will probably make some enemies. But I pray I make some friends too—friends who will stand on my shoulders and see further than I have.

Thank you, readers, for coming on this journey with me. Thank you to my clients and students for letting the realities of your lives correct my mistakes. And thank you, once again, Integrative Medicine Foundation, for making it possible for me to write this book.

Now let's go to the Moon.

Part One:

The Mother
of All Mysteries

1

☾

THE ASTROLOGICAL MOON

Before we dive into the monthly cycle of lunar phases, let's understand the intrinsic nature of the astrological Moon itself. Like a diamond, it has many facets—sign, house, aspects, and some unfamiliar pieces we will be exploring in the next few chapters. Each one flavors the primal core of lunar energy, affording it a kaleidoscope of possible meanings.

What does the Moon mean? Ask any astrologer and most likely you will soon hear the word "feelings." And that is quite accurate. The Moon definitely resonates with the emotional body. But "feelings" is too narrow. It puts the Moon in a kind of emotional or psychological ghetto. Let's give it some room to stretch.

RETURNING TO OUR SENSES

You are gazing upward while lying on your back in the desert at midnight on the night of the Full Moon. Because it is the middle of the night, the Sun is just about as far below the horizon as it can possibly be. That means the Moon, always opposite the Sun at the Full phase, is riding high, near the top of its nightly arc. And so the world is bathed in supernatural light. (It is bright—on the night of the actual Full Moon, the Moon reflects 15% of the sunlight that strikes it. The night before or the night after, that figure is down to only 8%.) At this moment of maximum lunar brilliance, everything you see in the surrounding desert landscape is luminous. Ghostly cacti poke up among seemingly-diaphanous granite boulders. Shadows are cast. Dazzling, almost blinding moonlight is washing over you—and into you.

A scientist would assure us that this supernal luminosity is actually just sunlight reflected off the gray, barren surface of the Moon a quarter million miles away. But no one would ever mistake moonlight for sunlight. Obviously sunlight is more intense. But even in deep twilight when the sun's light is pale, no brighter than the Moon's; everyone knows that this lunar light has a special quality.

Still lying on your back under that desert Moon, still engaged with your primal senses, what do you intuit? What do you know in your bones? What do you know by the light of the Moon that you cannot know by sunlight? *Am I stretching too much to say that you know you are a magical being in a magical world?*

From a rational point of view, the last line is sweet romantic nonsense. But there is another viewpoint inside of us all, one that does not confirm the "reasonable" deductions of objectivity. All of us possess this second center of perception, as legitimate within its own frame of reference as deductive reason. This is the part of us that resonates with magic and wonder. This is the natural mystic in all of us.

Astrologers call this second center of perception the Moon. One of the great works of our present era lies in reclaiming it.

Equating the Moon with mere emotion ignores all this magic. Those psychological astrologers who limit their work with the Moon to that impoverished level are simply reflecting their training in the dominant paradigms of this Sun-addled Age.

Still, if we call the Moon our "feelings," we are not wrong. As human beings, we are capable of feeling love, fear, hate, joy, self-pity, expansiveness, generosity, vengeance, majesty, shyness, sanctity, humor, dullness, awe, acuity, despair, triumph, shame, silliness, rage, lightness, indignation, self-importance, humility, pomposity—the vast palette of affective responses that make us who we are as men and women. That is all lunar territory, and it is rich.

But we are also capable of "getting feelings" about the weird ways the spirit world penetrates this material one. We can feel that life continues beyond the death of the physical body. We can feel the presence of what we might call God. We are capable of feeling that someone will become a dear, familiar friend thirty seconds after our first meeting—and of being correct in that assessment. We might even "get a feeling" about which horse will win the Kentucky Derby. We can sometimes ask ourselves ultimate questions about our lives—and have answers float up from somewhere deep inside.

From where do they float up?

We might write a poem or a song or a book, and have no idea how the inspiration arose or where it originated. Again, from where do such inspirations arise?

What is this strange realm within us whose existence is impossible to question, but which is so far beyond our fathoming? *The part of you that knows what I am talking about is called the Moon.*

The history of the past two or three centuries has leached so much of this magic from our astrological understanding of the Queen of the Night. But that magic is a fundamental part of human life.

Compounding the confusion, many astrologers after 1846 began to assign much of the Moon's natural domain to the planet Neptune, thereby both muddling Neptune and robbing Luna.

Bob Berman is a science guy who writes a wonderful monthly column for *ASTRONOMY* magazine called "Strange Universe." He has not been friendly to astrology, but I doubt there is an astrologer in the world who would fail to purr at these words of his from the October 2009 issue (to his credit, he also capitalizes the "M" in Moon):

> *The Moon rings like an enormous gong. When unneeded spacecraft are sent crashing into the lunar surface, the Moon still shakes two hours later. By contrast, impacts on Earth dampen out in just a minute or two. Explanation: The Moon must have a solid core **like a giant crystal that transmits vibrations** (emphasis mine), unlike Earth with its liquidy, creamy nougat center.*

Let's release the Moon from the ghetto of mere emotion. That framework is too small to hold it. This gorgeous giant crystal circling our planetary home not only transmits vibrations from the universe to us on far more wavelengths than mere reason—but also on more wavelengths than those that convey our laughter and our tears.

THE LAWS OF THE INNER WORLD

Maybe you dream you can fly. Maybe you have a dream in which Tuesday is the day after Wednesday. You wake up laughing and baffled, or uplift-ed. But not surprised. We all know how dreams are. We are accustomed to that peculiar world. We have all spent a lot of time there.

People speak glibly of "reality." They forget that we actually live in two of them: the outer world and the inner one. The outer world is some-thing we more or less share with other human beings. We all agree that Wednesdays naturally follow Tuesdays, and that if humans leap from buildings they fall unpleasantly to the ground.

The inner world is more personal, and its laws are not so universal. Time runs strangely there, and a kind of left-handed logic applies to everything. This widdershins realm is the Moon's province.

When we speak of "the inner world," we have to be careful not to make it too lofty and spiritual, although those perspectives are part of it too. This second reality we all inhabit is utterly familiar. There is noth-ing exotic about it at all. We actually spend more time in it than we do in the outer world. Do the math—even during the day, it is always there flavoring our interpretations of our outward perceptions. And at night we surrender to it utterly, losing all connection with the outer realms.

Perhaps your Moon lies in Sagittarius. The laws of your inner world are biased toward your having broad, rich experiences. Everything else being equal, you see possibilities everywhere, both inside yourself and in the world around you. Left alone and free of outward requirements, the winds of the mind blow toward far horizons—speculations, destina-tions, existential notations. On the other hand, perhaps your Moon lies in Capricorn. Then you see a world defined by caution, responsibility, and consequences.

Now, wide-open Sagittarian possibilities are in fact part of the ac-tual fabric of outer reality, as are Capricornian reasons for caution and responsibility. But the lunar laws of the inner world bias the attention in one direction or the other. With the Moon in Sagittarius, we may see the possibilities, but be ambushed by the dangers. With the Moon in Cap-ricorn, caution could blind us to the merry idea that sometimes gambles pay off and boldness opens golden doors.

We take in the world through the lens of the heart.

This matrix—outer experience passing through the prism of our in-ner world—is what we actually see and experience in our mind's eye when we believe we are looking at "the facts." Rather hilariously sometimes, we project that matrix onto a subjective cerebral canvas which we then label "objective reality." This is how the Moon flavors our perceptions of the outer world. This is how the inner world defines the nature of the outer reality we experience. *Thus the Moon actually creates the inner psychic phenomenon we think of as "outward reality."*

This is why different people contemplating the same "reality" will usually disagree about it. They are all correct within their own frames of reference. If we bet the house, the Sagittarian Moon knows we might win a kingdom. And the Capricorn Moon knows we might just lose the house. They are both right.

(Notice, by the way, that when describing the Moon in Sagittarius a few lines ago, I put in the words "everything else being equal." And it never is! Astrology is complicated, and no skillful astrologer is happy saying very much about an individual based only on his or her Moon sign. Please take everything else I suggest about various Moon signs, here and below, with that same grain of salt. In astrology, holistic context creates the real meaning.)

HEART AND SOUL

Lucky me—here at the beginning of this project I have a vast wilderness of empty pages ahead of me. I am sure I will have no trouble filling them, so big a subject is the Moon. In fact, I know that whatever I write, it will not be enough. And later, after it is all condemned to the finality of print, I will think of all the things I forgot to say. I will get email, protesting "Thanks for the book, but there is something you never mentioned . . ."

The inner world is a stupendous subject. There is no fear of exhausting it. Unlike outward reality, it contains all possibilities in the past, present, and future—amplified by anything and everything within the scope of human imagination. Anything that might ever have happened or that might happen in the future. Singing pigs and beggars on fine horses. Hogwart's Academy open for business and taking applications. It is vast. But if someone asked me to define the Moon in a single word, I would say *heart*.

The Moon is your heart—the thing that balances your head. Or maybe I would say *soul*. But if I did, I would quickly add that I did not mean soul in any theological sense—some immortal principle of consciousness. I would mean soul as we use the word on the street, when we describe a soulful time or speak of a soulful connection with someone.

Heart and soul—in either case we recognize something humans have known since the beginning: that this is half of what we are. As we just saw, we all have two distinct centers of perception. They complement each other and often argue with each other too. "Logically, I know it looks like I should take the job, but my guts are telling me to wait." This is the familiar dialogue of heart and head, the Yin and Yang of our being. "Rationally, I know it looks like Hayden would make the perfect partner for me, but I just can't get Shannon out of my mind."

We have all been there. The head/heart balance is hard to find. Sometimes we trust our reason too much and live to regret it. Hunches, intuitions, feelings in our bones—lunar data—often seem to link us directly to some higher source of knowledge and understanding. And of course other times we trust our hunches and land on our haunches! Both are common events. But experience has taught us that the Moon is at least sometimes a better guide than logic and reason, which are the realm of the Sun.

If your Moon is in Aries, we could say you have the "soul of a warrior." Those are just a few words, but the poet inside us all can immediately run with the phrase. We imagine someone whose instincts are courageous, direct, and fiercely loyal. And, from a Shadow perspective, someone whose heart might be inclined toward anger or resentment, or interpreting situations in unnecessarily competitive terms.

Underlying these characterological observations about the Aries Moon is deeper water. This is a person who is in this world to *to learn* about that kind of courage, how to be less aversive to risk and more willing to frame life as an adventure. Beneath the surface phenomena of character, he or she is *growing* the warrior's soul. That, in simple terms, is the evolutionary perspective on an Aries Moon.

With the Moon in Gemini, your heart is *curious* and you have the "soul of a storyteller." With the Moon in Aquarius, you have the "soul of a revolutionary, or a genius, or an exile." These are all simple phrases, but connecting with them emotionally opens up a long, fruitful highway of lunar free-association. What might it *feel like* to have "the soul of an exile?" What is the good news? What is the bad news? You do not have to be versed in astrology to answer those kinds of questions. You only have to be human. The words that come out of our mouths vary from aeon to aeon and culture to culture, but the meanings behind these words have been with us since human time began.

YOUR MOOD AVERAGED OVER A LIFETIME

You have a friend whose mood is always serious. You might make a joking remark—except that he doesn't register that you are joking. He interprets the remark seriously and responds patiently to your "illogical" comment. When you explain that you were joking, he forces a little social smile and gets back to being serious. You have another friend who would take less than five minutes to turn it into a joke if you told him you had just been given a diagnosis of a brain tumor. That reflex is how he defends himself against life's seriousness. We all know both of these people. They are straight out of Central Casting. As with every one of us, the *underlying mood* of their lives shapes their perceptions of reality and their reflexes within it.

Everyone has good days and bad days. We win a contest or get a raise or hit five o'clock on the last day of work before vacation—there is an excellent chance we feel merry and bright. Our cat dies or a big, unexpected tax bill arrives, and we instantly sing the blues. This is not rocket science. Mood, when healthy, is not always happy. There are times for grief and sadness; those are not mood disorders unless they are chronic and disconnected from outward reasons. Healthy mood always mirrors outward reality, at least to some extent. Thus it runs the gamut between bright and dark, as does our existential experience.

The point here is that beneath these natural ups and downs, everyone has a kind of "cruising mood." The emotional compass needle, free of any extreme outward stimulus, always swings back to it. Serious or funny—those are the examples we just explored. But of course there is a long list of other possibilities. There are people who are naturally optimistic—or pessimistic. There are people who are never in the mood to meet anyone new—and ones who are always ready to party. Resentful—or forgiving. Assertive—or passive and accepting. Suspicious—or trusting. The list is practically endless.

This is another way of looking at the Moon. It is *your mood averaged over a lifetime*. It is where your emotional compass needle naturally points when outer reality leaves it to its own devices.

Maybe your Moon lies in Scorpio. Your mood tends to be *psychological*. By instinct you will look deeply into things, get serious and real. If no one will go there with you, you will reflex into moody solitude—which you may enjoy, even if others imagine you to be facing bleak emotional weather. The mood of your life is that of the *psychoanalyst* or the *detective* or the *shaman*.

Maybe your Moon lies in the opposite sign, Taurus. Now your mood tends more toward an appreciation of peace and simplicity. You will let a sleeping dog lie. Complicating things with a lot of psychobabble is not your predilection. You will do it if it seems necessary, but you don't have much patience for people who make a fetish of it. Your mood is that of the *wise animal in its natural habitat*.

Let's weave together some of these elements we have explored. What have we learned so far? The Moon is:

○   The mood averaged over a lifetime.

○   The heart and the soul.

○   The source of the laws that shape the inner reality—and which underlie the inwardly imagined and projected "outward reality."

These notions are not meant to be taken as distinct ideas neatly separated from each other. They are all ways of looking at the same multi-faceted, logic-bending entity: the astrological Moon.

THE REIGNING NEED

In his book *Holistic Astrology*, Noel Tyl describes the Moon as the "reigning need." This too is a helpful perspective. As human beings, we all have certain needs in common—food, shelter, and so forth. Survival is impossible if these needs are unmet. We naturally prioritize them. I have personally not eaten a fellow mammal since about 1974, but if I were starving to death, Betsy the Cow had better flee! I have a compelling need not to starve. Probably you do too.

Once we get down the list a bit, away from universal survival imperatives, individual variance enters the equations. That is where we enter the domain of the Moon. For example, everyone has a need for some kind of security in life. And everyone has a need for some adventure and some sparkle too. So, bottom line, will you quit your safe, boring job and go paddling up the Orinoco? Different people will answer that question differently.

For some, security is the *reigning need*—when push comes to shove, it has sovereignty over their need for adventure (Moon in Cancer?). Other people might say, "Give me a minute, I'll quit my job, grab my passport and meet you at the airport." (Moon in Sagittarius?)

In thinking about the Moon in terms of the reigning need, it is imperative to recognize that logic has almost nothing to do with it—but that *the feelings often masquerade as logic.* To the person who chooses to keep her safe job, she is just "making a reasonable adaptation to adult reality." Rational and realistic? Yes—to that individual. But to the one who flees to Amazonia, such caution is unrealistic. Such a person might say, "I am the ultimate realist—life is too short to waste on maintaining an illusion of some mythical safety that no one ever really possesses anyway." And that is another logically defensible position. Or more precisely, another reigning emotional need cloaking itself in reason.

These observations about reigning needs lead us to one of the most fundamental and helpful insights into lunar astrology. Meeting the needs of the Moon as represented in your chart is nothing less than the long-sought, uber-precious, ever-coveted . . .

SECRET OF HAPPINESS

With my students, one of my favorite aphorisms is, *The Sun is the Secret of Sanity and the Moon is the Secret of Happiness.* Like most insights that will fit on a greeting card, it is an oversimplification, of course. Sanity and happiness are closely related and hard to pry apart. But the world has no shortage of sane people who are not very happy, while one glance at the newspaper will usually demonstrate plenty of gleeful madness.

Listening to the Moon—which is to say, heeding our hearts—is what keeps life feeling soulful and worth living. And let's remind ourselves that the Moon has absolutely no affinity for the logic of the three-dimensional world. This is why materialist astrologers might call it "irrational." The actual reality, as we saw earlier, is that the Moon does make perfect sense—but only from the perspective of the laws that govern the inner world. Still, to listen well to the Moon, we must temporarily suspend our culturally-supported focus on outward reason. In practice, this often means temporarily ignoring a familiar list of soul-eating devils: *practicality, limits, productivity, realism, consequences, deadlines, efficiency, maturity, responsibility,* and *common sense.*

See? You feel happier already, just reading that sentence.

A soul is standing on the end of the cosmic diving board, about to incarnate. Her Guardian Angel has already explained the challenges of the life ahead. The Angel offers one final tip. "Sometimes you will surely feel exhausted and defeated, just ready to give up. When that happens, here's what to do: *Go play eighteen holes of golf.*" Seeing her unbelieving look, the Angel adds, "Trust me."

To cure existential nausea, we are supposed to chase a little white ball with a stick around a grassy field at great expense? "A good walk spoiled," as Mark Twain put it? This is obviously total nonsense—except that it actually works for some people. Lots of men and women enjoy playing golf and find that it resuscitates their spirits after a hard week at work. Is this rational behavior? Of course not. But again we do not expect "reason," as we conventionally define it, from the Moon.

In the golfing example, we might be looking at a woman with a competitive Aries Moon in her fifth house (fun and games). Playing golf is not the only possible manifestation of that astrological configuration, but it provides a good example. From a logical perspective, golf is an irrational waste of time—and yet the game enhances her happiness. Her Moon says "To recharge my emotional batteries, I would like to do something competitive, intense, and fun." If she listens, she will feel better.

A man has the Moon in Virgo conjunct Saturn in the sixth house. That suggests a serious mood and a person who takes pleasure in meticulous order. Perhaps we are contemplating someone who enjoys stamp-collecting or very precise handwork, such as weaving or stitching beads. He puts a few hours into such a project and he feels happier.

To benefit from this secret of happiness, to attune truly to the Moon, we need to stop thinking. We need to feel. We must cultivate the fine art of recognizing and succumbing to . . . whimsy.

WHIMSY

What do you feel like having for dinner tonight? Most of us are lucky enough to be familiar with that question. Want to stay home or eat out somewhere? Out? OK. What sounds good—Chinese or Italian? What about that new Ethiopian place we've been thinking of trying?

Prosaic lines. A protean scene all over the Western world. And it illustrates the *free-play of whimsical choice*. This too is the Moon's domain. One of the arts of living well is to recognize opportunities to indulge in such whimsy and to take advantage of them.

Let's say the couple having the foregoing conversation about dinner are a pair of busy professionals for whom food is basically fuel, not fun. They tend to take a package from a box and put it in a microwave oven. They probably eat it while they are reading something. If you asked them half an hour later what they had for dinner, they might miss a few beats before answering. These people are focused on the outer, solar world. It does not even cross their minds to ask their hearts what they feel like eating. They are estranged from whimsy.

So how can they ever be happy? Happiness is not easy to find, and these two aren't even looking for it! They would probably disagree with me about that. They would in all likelihood promise that they *will* indeed be happy when they "win the Jones account" or move into the McMansion that is part of their five-year plan.

But even then, they will still be in the same position: they are *going to be happy* . . . tomorrow.

The Moon is here and now. It tells you what to do immediately if you want to be happier. And it conveys that precious information to us in the form of whimsy. To be content in life, we must learn to read it, trust it, and at least occasionally give it free rein.

A woman with the Moon in Libra strolls past an art gallery. A painting catches her eye. The price tag is $999.99. She shakes her head ruefully and walks away. But the next week she goes in and buys it—on whimsy. She will wait another couple of months to replace her laptop computer, even though the hard drive is making funny noises and it would be a disaster if it died. In good lunar fashion, she says to herself, "What the hell, what the hell . . ." And that painting lights up her heart for the rest of her life.

THE HEALER

There is a short, hard passageway through which I invite you to follow me. You in all likelihood will not enjoy reading most of it any more than I enjoyed writing it. At the other end of the passageway, we will understand what is probably the single most elemental insight into the Moon's function in our psyches.

Fasten your seatbelts. Here we go.

Life batters us. Dreams don't often come true. Relationships end in bitterness or estrangement. Our bodies hurt. The news hurts. We bang our heads against the wall, then we die—but generally not before we have endured the deaths of many whom we love. We laugh or we cry.

Call me Mister Cheery, right? I would pity anyone for whom this lamentation was a complete cosmology. My litany of complaints must be balanced with the other half of the truth: love, magic, tenderness, beauty, mystical union, and so on. They are part of the truth too. But the nasty, hard half of the truth is real. In my experience, the ones who are most vehement in denying the awful aspects of life are often the ones who have been most wounded by them and are most afraid of them.

It gets worse.

This endless barrage of damage is cumulative. It tends to build up inside us. Someone marries and the marriage fails. Damage is sustained, yet we would often envision that person marrying again. But what if that second marriage also fails, and a third one after it? There is nothing rigid or certain here, but natural human empathy tells us that by the time we are facing the prospect of marriage number four, our heart carries some serious scar tissue. Three failed marriages is not just three times worse than one failed one. The quality of the damage is different. We have begun to *expect* disaster. We have lost some innocence and faith, or maybe lost them entirely.

And marriage is just an example here, just one part of life that can hurt us. It is a wonder that any person over thirty years of age can still love and trust and dream.

And yet, hallelujah, often we can! There are people a hundred years old who can still embrace life, despite everything that has hurt them and everything they have lost. How do they do it? How do we do it? What is the actual mechanism of this extraordinary quality of resilience of the human soul? The answer is one of those commonplace miracles to which familiarity blinds us: we humans are capable of *healing*.

This healing is the domain of the Moon and perhaps its most elemental function.

How does the Moon heal us? You might just reread this whole chapter in the light of that question. *We heal by trusting and honoring the laws of the inner world, by paying attention to our hearts and souls, by not compromising too much on our reigning needs, and by knowing that surrendering to the whimsy of the moment is one of the greatest secrets of happiness.* If we attend to these processes, we become resilient. We bounce back from life's harshness with our faith intact, looking forward to tomorrow.

A career-oriented man has been laid off from his job and thus has been stripped of a lot of his identity and dignity. He feels defeated, anonymous, and faceless. His Moon is in Leo, so one of his reigning needs is to earn positive attention through strong performance. He is in trouble. Wisely, he reaches out to some good friends who live in another state. They invite him to come for a visit. The night he arrives, they have a dinner party: six old pals, tried and true, sitting around a table. Conversation is flowing. Playful and forgetful of his troubles, our hero recounts the story of a youthful misadventure he shared with one of the guests many years before. He tells the tale well, with humor, theatrical sense, and a reasonable dollop of embellishment. His friends crack up. When he is finished with the tale they clap their hands with joy. He basks in their appreciative, wide-open attention.

This is simply the happiest moment this unemployed man has experienced in quite a while. Of course his practical problem—not having a job—has not been addressed at all. But the pain in his heart has been temporarily eased.

The next morning, the pain returns. But probably not quite as badly, at least for a while. There is some afterglow. His faith is stronger and his attitude is improved, as is his general sense of well-being. His Moon has been fed.

To me, it is not too much of a stretch to imagine his being more successful on his next job interview as a result. This change of mood radiates from him, lets him broadcast more of that regal Leo Moon air. To a personnel manager, the subliminal message might be that "this man has the soul of a king. Let's hire him."

A rationalist might object and say that a good giggle with friends is not much of a response to catastrophic job loss. And yet being mindful of the Moon's healing potential day by day is a powerful yoga. It erodes the stone of a hardening heart. Just look into the eyes of people a hundred years old who are still bright and engaged and open. This is their secret.

HEALING OTHERS

A good rule of thumb is that the way we treat other people is a reliable indicator of the way we are treating ourselves. To illustrate this notion, allow me to share a low thought with you. Perhaps you will get as much pleasure out of it as I do. Sometimes I am sitting in my car waiting for a red light to turn green. The joker in the car in front of me tosses a cigarette butt out onto the street. I experience a moment of pique; he is treating the world—my world—as his ashtray. Then I comfort myself with that promised low thought: *I realize that by smoking cigarettes he is also treating his physical body the same way.*

The principle is reversible too. Our capacity to be loving and gentle with other beings is ultimately rooted in our compassion toward ourselves. If we are forgiving and accepting toward ourselves, there is a much better chance we will see other people in a generous light. If we feel faith in ourselves, we are more likely to trust others. People who have responded well to the Moon display an attitude of caring and support toward others. (This is all quite independent of the technical sign or house or aspectual configuration of a person's Moon, by the way—they just tell you specifically how to succeed in doing it.) If we will not grant ourselves that blessing, we are not likely to offer it to others either. And if we actively care about ourselves, caring for others comes more easily. A person's style in expressing that caring will vary according to astrological technicalities, but the sweet essence of it is simply an outward expression of their open relationship to their own hearts.

A Scorpio Moon might express that healing energy through a nurturing kind of psychological confrontation—a sincere and heartfelt version of "I am only telling you this because I love you." A Pisces Moon might do it by offering someone the consolation of patience and unconditional love while that person acted out some drama. An Aries Moon or one in Capricorn might express that healing impulse by pressing another person toward the highest limits of her possibilities. This is what I mean when I say that the style in expressing that caring will vary according to the astrological technicalities.

When I see a strongly-placed Moon—the Moon on an Angle, for example, or in the sign Cancer, which it rules—one thought that enters my mind is that I am looking at the chart of a *natural healer*. Immediately I temper that positive thought with the kinds of perspectives we have just been exploring: if this person is making a suboptimal response to his or her Moon, then his or her potential as a healer of others does not yet have a foundation. It must be rooted in self care.

When I say "healer" in connection with the Moon, by the way, please look beyond the narrow confines of the physical body. Far more than the physical body can be broken or hurt. Many of us have been helped by a counselor. Is that person not a healer? Many of us have been helped through a dark night of the soul by a poet, a band or a novelist. Did they not help to heal us? Certainly a strong Moon supports the idea of physical healing—an outstandingly gifted acupuncturist, massage therapist or physician will very often show a strong natal Moon. But healing goes way beyond that. And the whole terrain belongs to the Moon.

THE VEXING QUESTION OF THE MOTHER

The time between two successive Full Moons is precisely 29.5305881 days. The time between the onsets of a woman's successive menstrual periods averages about 28 days. Our ancestors undoubtedly noticed the good fit between these two pressingly obvious realities. They began to draw a link between female fertility and the Moon. This eventually morphed into the too-broad notion that the Moon represents *the feminine*, which I believe is a serious error. For one thing, men have Moons! For another, "the feminine" is an exceedingly complex mystery—just take one glance at the pantheon of mythic and historical goddess-figures that have nothing at all to do with nurturing babies: Isis, Athena, Hel, Kali, and so on.

We could perhaps call the Moon *maternal* in that it does represent a caring, healing aspect of human consciousness. Trouble is, that word "maternal" subliminally sidelines the gentle, caring men. To my ear, the word "maternal" is archaic in this context—or at least very "1950s." It reminds me of the way everyone used to call humanity "mankind" when I was a kid, and just assumed that women would be content to include themselves under that banner. Personally I am more comfortable with the terms *parental* or simply *nurturing* to describe the Moon.

Still, tradition dies hard. There remains a tendency among some psychological astrologers to speak of the Moon as the Mother—and specifically, as indicative of your own mother. Worse, we often run into presumptions that anyone with a Moon-Pluto conjunction, for example, must have suffered grievous psychological damage from a fire-breathing mom who was modeled on the Wicked Witch of the West.

This destructive and unfair notion is easily refuted. While there are certainly people who have Moon-Pluto conjunctions and awful experiences with their mothers, there are also people with that configuration who experienced their mothers as intimate, nonjudgmental confidants, which is simply a higher expression of Pluto. Symbolism is not literalism. We can define its range of meanings, but we can never say exactly what anything will mean concretely in individual cases. People make choices within a range of possibilities. Archetypes are broad.

Let's add one more obvious problem and then just lay to rest this unproductive idea that the Moon describes your mother's character. Most of the time, kids with the same mother don't have the same Moons. This reality-check alone proves that there is really no way we could expect the Moon to say anything objective about anyone's mom.

Putting all this together, here is what experience has taught me about the Moon and the quality of our early childhood experience. The Moon does often give clues regarding our *subjective* experience of nurture when we were young—and note that I am saying "nurture" here, not "mothering." Along with the condition of the fourth house, the lunar configuration seems to give clues as to the childhood home situation in general.

The pivotal point is that, as always, the Moon fundamentally references an internal reality rather than an outward one. We would naturally expect it to tell us more about how we *felt* about our mother than about what color hair she had. Clearly, different children with the same mother often have divergent experiences of her—adult siblings talking about "what really happened when we were kids" are, more often than not, startled at how different their memories are. The poet Anne Sexton once wrote, "It doesn't matter who my father was; it matters who I remember he was." And of course the same could be said about mothers.

Speaking of which, let's also resist the gravitational field of traditional gender roles, which are increasingly irrelevant to many people. There are children in the world today being raised by "house-husbands," while their mothers are out in the world making the money that supports the family. When those kids grow up, I am confident that their Moons will tell us more about their experiences of their fathers than about their mothers. *Who was—or at least who was expected to be—the primary, nurturing caregiver?* I believe that is the right Moon question nowadays.

The Moon-parent is the one to whom you run when you are scared. Historically that was usually the mother. Nowadays we cannot be so certain.

BAD MOON RISING

The superb German poet Rainer Maria Rilke had an Aquarian Moon conjunct Saturn and opposed by Uranus. Shortly before he was born, his mother had lost a girl-child after only one week of life. When Rilke came along, she dressed him as a girl, forcing him to play the role of his deceased elder sister. Then abruptly, at age eleven, her mood changed and he was shipped off to military school.

Many a gloomy astrologer would feel vindicated by this awful story. Rilke had a "bad" Moon—and cooperated by having a "bad" mom. Fair enough it seems, at least on the "bad mom" point. But did his mother seem to him to be cold, distant, controlling and erratic? Given the facts, this is certainly a plausible conjecture. And it is quite consistent with a dark view of an Aquarian Moon conjunct Saturn and opposing Uranus.

But we should add two caveats. First, the only way we can really know Rilke's subjective experience is by asking him. Enigmatically, the poet once wrote, "And even if you were in some prison, the walls of which let none of the sounds of the world come to your senses—would you not then still have your childhood, that precious, kingly possession, that treasure house of memories?"

That he would express such a positive sentiment certainly suggests that we should tread lightly around any dogmatic assertions about his "miserable" experience of his early life.

Secondly, we must remember that many other human beings have been born under similar lunar configurations and have experienced their mothers quite differently—perhaps as delightfully zany and wise, open to experience, and supportive of their children's developing individuality. Those more encouraging qualities are also consistent with such a lunar configuration.

Let me prove it to you. Polar explorer Sir Ernest Shackleton had exactly the same lunar aspects and Moon sign as Rilke. Of his mother, the website www.antarcticconnection.com says, "she knew how to manage her husband and children, giving them a secure and happy home, wherever that might happen to be." But as Shackleton approached his teens, his mother became ill, and eventually an invalid. Thus, for the great arctic explorer, the lunar aspect was not played out lovelessly, but tragically. Again, symbolism is not literalism. How unfair we would have been to this woman to describe her as "cold, distant, controlling and erratic." Distance was imposed on her—and on her beloved son—by circumstance.

HOME, CLAN AND RADICAL COMMITMENT

Many of us are lucky enough to have at least a few people in life upon whom we can count utterly and totally. In these kinds of relationships, the bond is so deep and so independent of any outward conditions that one of us will almost surely go to the other one's funeral. That last line is a corker, but I cannot think of a better way to describe a lunar bond. The loyalty is that absolute. It is simply assumed that it will last a lifetime.

In the old days, all this basically translated into the word *family*. And here we use the term in its historical sense: marriage partners, parents, children, grandchildren, aunts, uncles, cousins—the whole *kinship group* from which we historically drew much of our primary identity. Nowadays, while that kinship bond remains a significant factor in most of our lives, its hold on us has weakened. Similarly, marriage was once assumed to be a lifelong commitment. That is not quite so true any longer, although most newlyweds still aim for it in principle. Such idealism—such serious, lifelong intentions, not to mention faith—seems to be a necessary ingredient for a truly lunar bond to gel. Relationships are difficult and it takes a certain steel to see them through. I heard about a fellow at a party in Manhattan a few years ago who introduced his fiancée as "my future ex-wife." I suspect his words proved prophetic.

Socially conservative people often lament the collapse of the traditional family. Indeed one of the crowning ironies in our overpopulated world is its epidemic of loneliness. But family, in the old sense, has not always brought people happiness, nor has it always cured loneliness. It has also often brought enmeshment, the suppression of individuality, rampant dishonesty, and worse.

I believe we are witnessing the birth of an entirely new paradigm of lunar bonding—a new paradigm of family. In a word, the institution is becoming voluntary, not so linked to sharing strands of DNA or having filed for a marriage license with the local authorities. Maybe in this new incarnation, family will have more breathing room.

One point is certain: So long as human beings have Moons in their charts, we will need these kinds of reliable, trusting, committed *roots* with each other. This is a truly elemental lunar need. It is the original Social Security—but what we pay into it is not money. It is *radical loyalty*.

If your Moon lies in Pisces, the members of your *natural family*—the one you actually need, not necessarily the one you were born into—all contribute to a feeling of mystical or spiritual connectedness. They may support this through channels of religion, but we do not need to be so narrow. They can also get there by being artists, visionaries, or dreamers. There is a feeling of surrendering to something bigger than yourselves. And there is also a pervasive sense of "the cosmic joke." That means a shared giggle at all the little monkeys in their uniforms imagining themselves to be serious and important players on the world stage. With the Moon in Pisces, this shared view, this humorously transcendent mood, is the fertile substratum in which the seeds of happy *familiarity* germinate and grow.

Maybe your Moon falls in Libra. Then your natural family may be composed of artists, or those precious jewels all artists value: a conscious, appreciative audience. There will also be a pattern of *courtesy* in such a Libran family. This does not mean stiff formality, but rather sensitivity toward each other's needs and sensibilities. There will be grace.

A couple years ago, I was walking down the street with a band-mate. He told me that he and his girlfriend were going to move in together. I loved them both and thought it was a great idea, so I congratulated him. He immediately assured me that their moving in together didn't really mean anything about any changes in their relationship—they were actually just doing it to save money. He was a real Moon-brother so I did the kind of thing men do when they have a lunar bond: I laughed merrily in his face. I had the impression I had annoyed him a little bit that way, but we kept walking. After a while he laughed too.

We both knew that "moving in together" was a big, archetypal step. When two people agree to live under one roof, arrangements vary. But it always means an increasing multidimensionality in the relationship. We go from the simple, delightful world of being lovers into the complex realities of shared friends, family, friends, and finance. In the past, among heterosexuals, living together usually led pretty directly to having children—and there we connect again with a primary lunar archetype—parenting and the virtually indissoluble psychological bond between parent and child.

What is the planet of love? Most astrologers, by reflex, would say Venus. My answer would be, show me a planet that is not the planet of love! Love takes everything we've got. The Moon's particular part in love is expressed most vividly when we "cross the threshold" together, literally, into a shared home. The Moon, when it is strong in the chart, represents a *reigning need* for such domestic commitments.

Immediately, we must remember that astrology is a celebration of human diversity—not everyone feels the need to share life with another human being, or human beings, so deeply. And not everyone has a strong or central lunar signature in their natures. But if the Moon is a major element in the logic of your chart, one of the treasures you took embodiment to seek is *roots*—a sense of place in the world. That sense of place is partly composed of walls and a roof. It may also have a component of *magical geography* to it—a physical land or city you love and where you feel at home—but it is primarily defined by the people with whom you have made your stand in this world.

THERE YOU HAVE IT

The laws of the inner world. Heart and soul. Our reigning needs. The mood of our life, averaged over a lifetime. The secret of happiness. How we heal ourselves and others. The role of whimsy in our lives. Our family of origin—and any family we might create. Those are the elemental ideas that underlie my astrological understanding of the Moon. They are all different facets of the same diamond.

In much of this book, we will explore these integral lunar concepts in the context of what for many of us is unfamiliar territory: the lunar phases. But lunar phase is just one factor in a complex mix. A New Moon in Gemini and in the twelfth house is a different beast than a New Moon in Leo in the fifth. Always, we must understand symbolism in its context. That is what takes astrology from Mickey Mouse to King Lear.

In Chapter Eighteen, we will look rigorously and methodically at how to link the Moon's phase to its sign and house, not to mention a few other factors that we will soon be exploring.

MOON TABLES

In the next four pages, we offer in tabular form some key concepts for the Moon in each house and each sign. These four pages could easily be four hundred pages, and a very different book! Still, I think they will provide a solid launching pad for your own speculations. The three factors—phase, sign, and house—are all of about equal psychic valence in my experience.

In reading through these four Tables, please also keep in mind the fundamental principle of Evolutionary Astrology: choice. Every astrological configuration represents a wide range of archetypal possibilities. Consciousness interacts unpredictably with these possibilities, creating actual biographical manifestations defined by the scope and limits of its own evolutionary level. In what follows, you will see high intentions described—and devils named. What happens in your life is something you create within that context of potentialities.

Table of Moon Signs

Sign	Evolutionary Goal	Mood	Reigning Need	Secret of Happiness & Healing	Shadow
Aries ♈	*Courage; Capacity to claim one's rights*	*Edgy; Competitive; Heroic*	*Victory*	*Regular adventures involving conquest of fear*	*Cruelty; Rage; Insensitivity*
Taurus ♉	*Grounding; Calming; Centering*	*Pragmatic; Down-to-earth; Realistic*	*Stability; Comfort*	*Attunement to the Inner Animal Wisdom*	*Rigidity; Boring one's self*
Gemini ♊	*A wide-open mind; Finding one's own voice*	*Curious; Restless; Outgoing*	*Stimulation; Novelty; Surprise*	*Fresh conversation & experience; Listening*	*Distraction; Living from the neck up*
Cancer ♋	*Healing Power, first inwardly then outwardly*	*Sensitive; Sweet Sorrow*	*Safety; quiet; home*	*Silent, soulful hours, alone and with dear ones*	*Fearful withdrawal; Hiding behind caregiving*
Leo ♌	*Spontaneous, confident self-expression*	*Quiet Dignity*	*Appreciation; Attention*	*Free-flowing Creativity before the right audience*	*Self-importance*
Virgo ♍	*Perfection of a skillful service; Self-improvement*	*Discontent with the status quo*	*To make something "just a little bit better"*	*Finding work that matters; balancing self-love with endless effort*	*Crippling criticism of self and others*

Table of Moon Signs

Sign	Evolutionary Goal	Mood	Reigning Need	Secret of Happiness & Healing	Shadow
Libra ♎	Serenity; Release of tension	Aesthetic; Affiliative; Graceful	Harmony with people, sounds, colors, and within the psyche	Relationship skills; Choosing the right partners; Valuing aesthetics	Too much compromise; dithering; codependency
Scorpio ♏	Honest connection with strong emotion	Intense; Probing; Suspicious	To get to the bottom of things; Intense Encounter	Facing inner and interpersonal fears	Moodiness; Isolation; Self-Absorption
Sagittarius ♐	Broad experience digested and turned into meaning	Expansive; Adventurous; Colorful; Philosophical	To divine the meaning of life from broad experience	To treat boredom and predictability as Cardinal Sins	Opinion; Dogmatism; Lack of a sense of responsibility
Capricorn ♑	Integrity and Great Works	Serious; Driven; Solitary	Achievement: Respect	Worthy work; The Discipline of Spontaneity	Time-serving despair
Aquarius ♒	Individuation; Gathering experience outside consensual reality	Questioning; Independent; Iconoclastic	Freedom of Thought and Action	Casting off the pitiful need for approval	Coldness; Dissociation
Pisces ♓	Transparency of ego; Surrender to Spirit	Sensitive; Attuned; Generous; Fanciful; Humorous	Contact with the world beyond material rationality	Meditative, trance-time; Anything that supports the visionary imagination	Dissipation of vital energies; Dreaming the life away.

Table of Moon Houses

House	Soul Intention	Mood is sensitive to	Reigning Need	Critical Whimsy	Soul-Cage
First	Learning to follow the heart	Everything; How the self is being seen	To give and receive care & attention	To make big decisions intuitively and quickly	Giving too much power to the fear of getting hurt
Second	Learning to feel worthy & legitimate via meaningful attainments	Dismissal; Humiliation; Perceived lack of resources	To prove one's self; to accomplish; To establish security	Supplying one's self with necessary tools and resources	Under-achievement; Mediocrity
Third	Learning; Teaching; Finding one's true voice	Rapid shifts in the ambient energy; nuances of speech	To be truly heard; To satisfy curiosity	Speaking up; Seizing chance	Becoming lost in a web of petty concerns
Fourth	To deepen one's soul within the context of long trusting relationships	The quality of the home life; Rejection; The Ambi-ence of Place	To create roots; Emotional safety	Trusting intuition about home and partners	Withdrawal into inner world
Fifth	To leave tangible evidence of one's inner life in the hands of the world	Audience reaction; Rebuff; Applause	The Joy of Being Appreciated	Confidently plunging ahead in self-expression	Giving too much power to the opinions of others
Sixth	Service; finding one's natural skill; Seeking mentors	Others' needs; The presence of true Teachers; Respect and Disrespect	To be competent and useful	Opening spontaneously to teachers and role models	Slavery; a life defined by meaningless duties

Table of Moon Houses

House	Soul Intention	Mood is sensitive to	Reigning Need	Critical Whimsy	Soul-Cage
Seventh	*Learning who to trust and how to trust*	*Other people's moods*	*A sense of connection*	*Taking the risk of initiating intimacy*	*Projecting one's own emotions onto others*
Eighth	*Deepening; Healing; Marrying passion and wisdom*	*Undercurrents of emotion; "chemistry" between people*	*A feeling of being deeply bonded*	*Overcoming inhibition and self-protection*	*Moody isolation*
Ninth	*Immersion in broad experience; Stepping outside one's cultural limits*	*Alternative paradigms; philosophical & moral issues*	*A meaningful life; fresh experience*	*A willingness to leap into the Unknown*	*Stultifying adherence to opinion & "religion"*
Tenth	*To bear fruit in the community; to leave a mark*	*The social ambience: Opportunity; Status*	*A sense of mission; Recognition*	*Stepping outside of a "job description"*	*Accepting external social definition*
Eleventh	*To cultivate commitment to long-term strategy; To establish strategic alliances*	*"Tribal" undercurrents; group dynamics*	*A sense of progress; meaningful membership*	*Letting the heart set the initial goals*	*Being consumed by the will and style of a tribal group*
Twelfth	*To behave as if spiritual growth were the main purpose of life*	*Psychic undercurrents; Energy; Subtle influences*	*Communion with deep psyche, God, soul—pick your term*	*Heeding the call to withdraw momentarily from the world*	*A state of being psychically overwhelmed; Escapism*

2

NUTS, BOLTS AND A FEW SURPRISES

The Moon's phases are not the only lunar feature that has been underutilized in modern astrological practice. There are many other curiosities connected with Earth's companion in space. Some of them are probably of small practical value in the astrological counseling room. But at least two of them have dramatic, easily recognized impacts—the speed of the Moon's motion and its extremes of declination. A third one, lunar parallax, shows the potential of becoming quite significant as well. Once you have worked with these techniques, I think you will share my surprise that they are not more widely known. There is nothing subtle about them. Their effects are powerful and obvious.

These and other lost pieces of the lunar puzzle are the subject of the next two chapters. To grasp them requires some technical understanding of the Moon's orbit and other motions outside the familiar context of signs, houses and aspects. I feel confident that learning about them will be worth your while as an astrologer, even though we will have to attend "science class" here for a while.

We will start with an easy piece, one you probably understand already.

PHASES

You are standing in the middle of a flat field in the middle of the night. A stone's throw away there is a five-thousand-watt spotlight aimed straight at you. Blinded, you turn your back to the light. In the distance you see a friend facing you—and facing the spotlight too, even though she is further away. You are midway between her and the spotlight, in other words. You can easily recognize her features; her face is brilliantly illuminated.

She walks in a circle around you toward the spotlight, so she is now standing between you and it. You turn your body to face her. She is still facing you, but now she is silhouetted against the dazzling light. What do you see? Just her profile. Against the glaring spotlight, she is black as coal. No way to see her face anymore.

In this analogy, the spotlight is the Sun. You are the Earth. And your friend is the Moon.

In the first situation, where you can see her face because the spotlight is behind you, we recognize the familiar geometry of the Full Moon. In the second situation where all you see is her dark body silhouetted against the light, that is the geometry of the New Moon.

Take it further.

Like the Moon orbiting the Earth, your friend walks in a big circle around you, always keeping more or less the same distance, and always facing you. When she is one quarter of the way around, she is side-lit— half her face is illuminated and half is in shadow. That is the familiar "half Moon," more correctly termed the First Quarter.

And so on around the circle.

TIDAL LOCKING

Let's take our analogy of the spotlight and your friend into less familiar territory. As she circles you, she is always facing you. Her nose is pointed straight at you no matter where she stands. The Moon does exactly the same thing. The same side of the Moon is always pointed at us no matter where it falls in its monthly orbit. That is why we can never see the far side of the Moon, at least not from the Earth.

A more technical way to say the same thing is that the Moon rotates once on its axis in precisely the length of time it takes to orbit the Earth a single time.

This synchronization is not a coincidence. It is because of something called *tidal locking*. Long ago the Earth's huge gravity distorted the Moon's shape a little bit. It pulled some of the Moon toward itself—just like your friend's nose. When that bulging part of the Moon tried to rotate away, the Earth's gravity slowed it down slightly. And every time the Moon rotated, the Earth's gravity "tugged its nose," slowing it down a little more. Incrementally, over millions of years, that bulging part of the Moon locked onto the Earth, just like a compass needle locking onto magnetic north. From the Earth's point of view, the Moon just stopped rotating. But if you could look down from above, you would see that the Moon's rotation did not stop at all—it just got in sync with the Earth so that the same bulging side of the Moon was always facing us.

GETTING A VISUAL

If you are better with visual thinking than verbal thinking, take a look at the following image, which illustrates the way the Moon's orbit around the Earth generates the familiar phases.

The side of the Moon that faces the Sun is always bathed in light. As the Moon orbits the Earth, sometimes its sunlit side faces us directly. That is the Full Moon, when Earth lies between the Sun and Moon. Sometimes, when the Moon is midway between Earth and Sun, the Moon's sunlit side faces away from us. That is the Dark of the Moon - the New Moon.

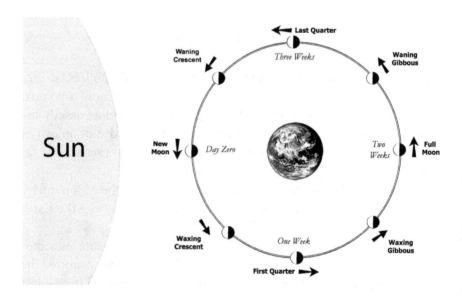

FIFTY-NINE PERCENT

From what we've learned above, it would follow that we could only see the half of the Moon that faces us. Actually, from the Earth we can see about 59 percent of the Moon if we are patient and make an effort. There are two reasons for that. One is called *libration*. The other is called *parallax*.

Libration boils down to a kind of wobble that lets us peek around first one side of the Moon and then the other. It comes from the fact that the Moon's orbit is not really circular. Like most orbits, it is a bit elliptical. That leads to the Moon speeding up and slowing down slightly in its orbit. It goes faster as it gets closer to Earth and slower as it gets farther away. The effect is to present us with slightly different perspectives over time. You can get a great visual image of libration on-line here: http://en.wikipedia.org/wiki/Libration.

Parallax is a familiar effect. The classic illustration is to simply hold a finger straight up at arm's length and then look at it first through one eye, then through the other. Of course the finger seems to jump back and forth against the background. But really study it and you will see that there is another, more subtle effect as well. Through your left eye, you see a little bit more of the left side of your finger. Through your right eye, the opposite. It works the same way with the Moon. People in different parts of the world can be looking at the same Moon in the same moment, but each will have a slightly different angle on it because of the distance between them. For example, a person might be looking at the rising Moon from New Zealand, while at the same moment someone in Spain is watching the Moon set. It can happen that way because those two countries are located at each other's antipodes—opposite sides of the Earth. Moonrise for one is approximately Moonset for the other. But each will see the Moon from a slightly different perspective. Another way to say this is that Spain and New Zealand have an 8,000 mile baseline between them running straight through the center of the Earth. And with the Moon only about 240,000 miles away, that baseline is long enough to produce a noticeable parallax view—back to looking at your fingertip through alternate eyes. Proportionally, it is as if you are looking at a globe that is thirty feet away from you. Then you slide over 12 inches to your left and look at it again. The view of the globe is basically the same, but if you look really carefully, you will notice that you are seeing that globe from a slightly different angle.

Parallax allows us to see about 1% farther around the Moon on each side. That is not much. You might be wondering why we bother to explore it in these pages. There is a very good reason. Read on.

THE PARALLAX MOON

Parallax also shifts the Moon's position against the starry background, just like the trick with your fingertip. This is a much bigger effect and one with serious, if little known, astrological consequences. What lunar parallax means is that if you think that your natal Moon lies in 14° Libra 35'. . . well, you might need to think again. That figure depends on your point of view. The positions of the Sun, Moon and planets as they are dished up in most modern astrological computer programs are actually the positions *as they would be seen from the center of the Earth!* The Sun and planets are far enough away that this mathematically-convenient illusion creates no real issues. But the Moon is relatively close to the Earth, so parallax generates a noticeable difference.

Here's why:

Maybe you are looking at the Moon rising against the backdrop of the starry sky from the top of the Mauna Kea volcano in Hawaii. Now imagine that you are suddenly shifted to the center of the Earth, looking up through a very long pipe directly at the Moon. The center of the Earth is about 4,000 miles away from Mauna Kea, enough to make that Moon jump as much as *about a degree* against the starry background. That is a lot—a degree is twice the Moon's own apparent diameter in the sky.

If this sounds obscure and technical, let me say it more directly. With parallax, we are talking about where the Moon *actually appeared to be* in the sky when you were born. Present day astrological software, with few exceptions, instead defaults to the convenient fiction that we were all born in the center of the Earth. Which approach makes more intuitive sense? To know where the Moon "really" was when you were born or to believe the computer?

Note that not everyone would see a shift of a degree. That is the extreme. If the Moon were directly *overhead* in Mauna Kea, being on top of the volcano or 4,000 miles straight down would not move the Moon at all. Remember how parallax works. If you had only one eye, it would not be an issue. There would be no parallax.

Thinking about parallax with the Moon is cutting-edge astrology. Because the biggest difference it can make—just a degree—does not sound extreme, it can seem like small potatoes. Even at maximum, that probably will not have much impact on a natal interpretation of the Moon—although do note that it could potentially shift the Moon into a different sign! Also, if you are using the Sabian degree symbols, the difference would often throw the Moon into the next or previous degree.

But there's more. In the extreme case, that degree does affect the timing of when aspects by transit or progression come into perfect alignment with the Moon. More critically, it throws off predictions based on the *solar arc* Moon by about a year. And it utterly and totally reframes the lunar return chart—these are charts based on the exact moment the Moon returns (each month) to the place it was when you were born. I have not personally found the technique of lunar returns to be very helpful or accurate. Maybe that is because my lunar returns have all been wrong by about an hour! That is the difference half a degree makes, and in my own chart the parallax happens to be that wide. Other astrologers I know swear by lunar returns. I suspect that, for them, the position of the parallax Moon and the "normal" one are not so far apart.

Perhaps the ultimate test for the parallax Moon lies in those situations where the Moon changes signs if we apply the parallax method. Say a person is born with the Moon in 0° Virgo 20'. Parallax could potentially shift that position by almost 60'. Forward or backward? You have to answer that question case by case. But if it is backwards, then that individual's Moon is not in Virgo at all—it is in 29° Leo 20'. And that is an entirely different situation.

Should we use the parallax Moon instead of the more conventional one? At this point, in all honesty, I am not convinced one way or the other. The distinction is subtle most of the time. My own personal experience is important to me, but the reality is that astrology advances best when hundreds of astrologers are sharing their collective experience—and it grows stagnant when the field agrees to ignore a question.

If you are interested in learning more about this parallax Moon topic, the best place I know to begin is the work of Alphee Lavoie, who has really been a major pioneer in the field. A click on www.Alphee.com will get you going. Hit Education>Astrology Reading Room and look for some articles he wrote based on his research. And, by the way, Alphee's *Millennium Star Trax* software allows you easily to calculate the parallax Moon, as does the popular *Solar Fire* program.

A COOL TRICK

I am sitting out on a patio during the first week of August with a group of my students. As the Sun sets, a perfect First Quarter Moon is revealed shining high in the sky. After a while, one of the students casually inquires, "What sign is the Moon in now?" That is often a tough question to answer off the top of your head since the Moon changes signs every couple of days or so.

That's my cue to adopt an all-knowing look. I glance up, meditate a moment, and say, "Feels like Scorpio to me, maybe about the middle degrees . . ."

Eyebrows are raised. Am I making this up? How can I know the Moon's sign just by looking—or feeling? The Sun has just set, and there are no stars out yet to give me constellation clues. How do I know that the Moon is in Scorpio? Easy. Here's how.

Since it is the first week of August, any baby born today will have the Sun in Leo, toward the middle degrees. That is basic astrology. The Moon is in the First Quarter phase, so the New Moon happened about a week ago and Full phase is a week ahead. That means the Moon is about one quarter of its monthly cycle ahead of the Sun, halfway between New and Full. Thus, 90° separate Sun and Moon—so the Moon must be in a waxing square aspect relative to the Sun's position in mid-Leo. What sign of the zodiac is 90° past Leo?

Voilà: Scorpio.

Given the early August date and the Moon's First Quarter phase, that Moon has to be in about the middle of Scorpio.

Once you understand the order of the zodiacal signs and approximately when the Sun enters each sign in its annual cycle, pulling off this trick is easy work. Off the tops of our heads, we generally know the calendar date, at least within a day or two. That gives you the Sun's position within two or three degrees. After that it comes down to understanding something truly elemental: *that the phase of the Moon is not just about the*

Moon alone. It is actually about the geometrical relationship between the Sun and the Moon.

A Full Moon on the Fourth of July? The Sun is in Cancer and the Moon is opposite the Sun—that Full Moon has to be in Capricorn.

A Last Quarter Moon on New Year's Day. Think ahead to 270°—three-quarters of the way around the Zodiac—from a point about a third of the way into the sign Capricorn, where the Sun would be on January first. That Last Quarter Moon must be in Libra.

Sometimes, of course, the date is nearing transition, when the Sun changes signs, and the Moon phase looks maybe a couple of days from Full. Under these fuzzier conditions, you cannot be totally sure about the Moon's sign. You have to make your best guess between two of them. But even saying, "hmm . . . feels to me like late Pisces or early Aries" is enough to give you an air of sagacity worthy of Dumbledore or Gandalf.

That this trick often actually startles astrologers says something about how little time we spend under the sky thinking about what we see, and how much time we spend in front of our computers.

HOW LONG IS A MONTH?

A tour guide outside Sedona, Arizona, got talking with us one day about dumb questions he had heard from tourists. His personal favorite came from a woman who asked after visiting the site of an ancient Native American settlement, "Why did the Indians build their village so far from town?" Right up there with this benighted inquiry is the observation, "Isn't it just *amazing* that Full Moons happen almost exactly once a month?" Of course to our ancestors, living so much closer to the Earth-rhythms than we do today, the Moon's phase cycle was a very obvious time-marker. The whole idea of "months" comes from the Moon cycle, as most of us know.

But just how long is a month? Obviously, our calendar months vary, so let's rephrase the question: how long is a Moon-month? The question is actually slippery. There are a variety of correct answers depending on exactly what we mean by one Moon-cycle.

Maybe you were born with the Moon in 14° Capricorn 42'. How long do you have to wait for it to return to that degree of the zodiac? The answer is 27.3216609 days. That's 27 days, 7 hours, 43 minutes, and 11.5

seconds. This cycle—one complete lunar circuit of the zodiac—is called the Moon's *sidereal* period. We might view this as the common-sense answer to our question about the length of the month. That's how long it takes the Moon to get around the circle once. End of story? Not exactly.

The return of the Moon to 14° Capricorn 42' does not have the visual or emotional impact of a Full Moon. It is not so obviously the beginning or end of a cycle. How long is the time between two successive Full Moons—or New Moons or any other specific phase? The answer here is a little different than the sidereal cycle, and the reason is simple: the Sun has moved onward through almost a whole sign of the zodiac while the Moon has gone through its complete cycle of waning and waxing again. When the Moon returns to where it was "a month" ago, it still has about 30 degrees to go before overtaking the Sun.

This cycle, New Moon to New Moon (or Full to Full), is called the *synodic* cycle and it is 29.5305881 days long. That works out to 29 days, 12 hours, 44 minutes, and 2.8 seconds. That is two days and five hours longer than the time it takes for the Moon to get back to where it started. The synodic cycle qualifies as a "month" too, and in some ways it makes a stronger argument for itself than does the sidereal, return-to-a-degree cycle.

While we are at it, let me add one more possible answer to the question of the length of a month. This one is the length of time it takes the Moon to return to the north or south lunar node, which is where the plane of the Moon's orbit intersects the ecliptic or zodiac. This version of "one month" might seem too picky, but it is actually a hugely significant cycle—it determines when eclipses occur. As with the synodic cycle, this lunar nodal cycle is made trickier because both the node and the Moon are moving points—except that with the nodes of the Moon, the motion is retrograde. That means that the node is rushing back to meet the Moon, so this one is actually the shortest of the three "months." It runs 27.2122178 days.

By the way, if you are not clear about what the nodes of the Moon are, you'll find a full explanation in Chapter Five of my book, *Yesterday's Sky: Astrology and Reincarnation*, "The Astronomy of the Lunar Nodes." Since this book is primarily about the phases of the Moon, we will not be paying much attention to the lunar nodes until we get to Chapter Twenty-One.

TWELVE AND THIRTEEN

Twelve signs in the zodiac and 12 months in the year—this pleasant symmetry puts smiles on the faces of astrologers. But people who enjoy taking the wind out of astrology's sails often like to point out that there are actually more like 13 lunar months in the year.

You have really got to read the fine print with this one! What kind of "lunar months" do they mean? When we consider the sidereal month—the cycle of the Moon through one complete turn of the zodiac—our critics are correct. That approximately 27-day cycle does repeat slightly more than 13 times in a year.

But as we pointed out earlier, the return of the Moon to 14° Capricorn 42' (or any other particular degree) does not have the visual or emotional impact of a Full Moon. Our ancestors were surely much more aware of the Moon's phase cycle than they were of the Moon returning to stand next to a certain star. Before electricity, before there was anything but firelight, a Full Moon was a big deal—we could see at night. We could dance. We could make love under it. "Returning to our senses," literally, always makes us better astrologers. And to our senses, it is the synodic cycle, not the sidereal one, that clobbers us.

There are indeed just about 12 twelve synodic—phase-to-phase—months in a year. The exact figure is 12.368746. Another way to say this is that there are about 12 Full Moons in a typical year. We can make a good argument that a 12-month year—and the idea of a 12-sign zodiac—all derive from this collective experience of the Moon's phases against the backdrop of the year.

Why are there 12 signs in the zodiac? The answer goes way beyond the Moon's cycle. The area is very rich and brings us into the interplay of astrology and physics. I explored it in detail in my 1993 book, *The Night Speaks: A Meditation on the Astrological Worldview*. But very probably the notion of a zodiac composed of 12 signs first arose in the minds of our ancestors when they contemplated the yearly cycle of four seasons embracing 12 Full Moons. It is obvious and it naturally divides the circle of the year into 12 smaller cycles. No one knows for sure because the answer lies in prehistory, but this lunar observation is probably the real cradle of astrology.

By the way, the standard elementary textbook explanation of why there are 12 signs is that the Sun, Moon and planets "pass through 12 constellations of stars" on their way around the ecliptic. This explanation collapses instantly when we realize that cross-culturally, the constellations are far from universal, and that the only limit on how that long band of stars has been divided is the human imagination. Astrology's sacred number 12 comes from the Moon, not from the stars!

FAST MOON/SLOW MOON

Swing a weight around your head at the end of a string. Gradually feed it more string, widening the circle. The weight naturally slows down. This observation is quite intuitive. We are looking at one of the fundamental laws of the universe. It works the same with any orbiting body, except that instead of a string we have gravity. Planets close to the Sun move forward in their orbits a lot faster than ones farther away. Note that we are not just talking about how planets farther from the Sun take longer to get around their orbit. That is true too, but it is not just because they have to go a longer distance. They are also moving a lot more slowly. Mercury, for example, is whipping along at almost 30 miles per second (47.89 km/sec), while Pluto trundles forward 10 times more slowly, at a stately three miles per second (4.74 km/sec). Here on Earth, we are logging about 18 miles per second.

Those speeds are all averages. The reality is complicated by the fact that planets vary in their distance from the Sun. None are in truly circular orbits. When their "strings get shorter," they speed up. When they get longer, the planets slow down.

As the Moon orbits the Earth, all this is true of it as well. In average terms, the Moon appears to move 1310' 35" forward through the zodiac each day, but the reality is that sometimes it slows down to the point that it only covers 11°06' in a day. Two weeks later, it is burning up the zodiac at a bristling 15°02' per day. That is about a 30 percent increase in its speed across the sky, like a car going from 45 mph to nearly 60. Quite a difference. (And note that these figures refer to the *daily* distance covered by the Moon. At a given moment, it might be going even faster or even more slowly.)

Astrologers have mostly ignored this variation in the Moon's speed as a factor in natal chart interpretation. They shouldn't! It is right up there with lunar phase in terms of its impact, at least at its extremes. Check it out yourself. If you look at a few charts of people you know well, I think you will be struck by the power of this simple technique.

First, how do you know the Moon's speed? Many software programs have an option for displaying it. That is the easiest way to find out. But you can also set up a chart for 12 hours before the birth and for 12 hours after the birth, and compare the Moon's positions. How many degrees and minutes has it covered in that 24-hour period? There is your answer. If you still have a paper ephemeris, finding out is even easier—just check the Moon's positions listed there in the 24-hour period in which you were born.

Before I describe the effect of the natal Moon's speed on the psyche, I need to throw in our eternal astrological caveat: your mileage may vary! Nothing in astrology operates outside the context of the whole. We may, for example, read that someone with Sagittarius rising will be socially extroverted. Fair enough, in general. But if that person has all his or her planets in the fourth house, you will see a much more indrawn kind of character despite that extroverted ascendant. It is the same with Moon speed: always see it in the larger framework.

A "fast Moon" is one moving at more than the average of 1310' 35" per day. A "slow Moon" is anything less than that. Obviously, if your Moon is moving only slightly slower than average at, say, 13°05' you are just about in the middle, and the effects I am about to describe will not be perceptible. They are more obvious as we get closer to the extremes of 11.6° and 14.8° per day. There are shades of gray here, as everywhere in astrology. Bottom line, people in the middle of the speed range—say, about half the population—will not find this technique relevant.

One way of getting to the root of the matter on Moon speed is simply to recognize that the Moon's velocity through the signs seems to resonate with the general *speed of the person's mind*. We have to be exceedingly careful, however, not to equate speed with intelligence. In the West, we place an inordinate value on speed. If we say, "Bellina is really quick," we seem to have praised her—even though in reality her snap judgments may often prove to be foolish ones! And of course, "Johnny is slow" has become a polite way of saying "Johnny is stupid," despite the fact that careful, deliberate thinking often leads to more reliable answers. Moon speed seems to have no bearing on intelligence *per se*, but it does say a lot about the style and the flow of mental processes.

If I were landing in gusty weather, I would like my airline pilot to have a fast Moon. If I were contemplating a dicey and perhaps unnecessary medical procedure, I would like my advisors to have slow Moons.

Fast vs. Slow Moon Speed

A Fast Moon suggests that a person is	A Slow Moon suggests that a person is
Quick to trust and connect interpersonally	*Slow to trust and connect interpersonally*
Initially revealing	*Initially more guarded*
Quick to process and digest information (and might therefore jump to conclusions)	*Careful in processing and digesting information (and might therefore be indecisive or plodding)*
Quick to adapt and adjust to new circumstances	*More resistant to new circumstances*
Inclined by reflex to say "yes" (manic?)	*Inclined by reflex to say "no" (depressive?)*
Alert and immediate	*Deliberate*
Good at seeing patterns	*Good at noticing details*

3

☾

THE TILTED LUNAR PLANE

S cience class continues for another chapter. We need to review some astronomical basics quickly to make sure we are all up to speed. Please bear with me for about 1,400 more words. If you follow them, you will understand a pivotal but little-used dimension of lunar theory. It is called the *Out of Bounds* Moon, and I can almost guarantee that learning about it will be an eye-popping astrological experience for you, as it was for me. Like lunar phase, the majority of astrologers have mostly missed it simply because *it hasn't been where they were looking.*

THE ECLIPTIC

Say that each morning you awaken before dawn and look toward the stars in the eastern sky. As sunrise approaches, the stars grow faint. By the time the Sun actually rises, you cannot see them any more—but maybe you can remember where they were. Do that every week for a year and you will see that *the field of stars into which the Sun is rising* cycles around in a regular fashion. By the time a year has passed, the Sun has traced out a circular path through the stars and is back to where it started. Repeat the experiment the following year and you will see that the path remains the same—on a certain date, the Sun is rising predictably into a certain star field, year after year, dimming the stars of Scorpio, then Sagittarius, then Capricorn and so on. Draw a line connecting all those sunrises against the constellations and you have the *ecliptic.* Or the zodiac.

(This correlation between the date and the constellation into which the Sun is rising actually does change, but so slowly we can ignore it for our purposes here. That is called the *Precession of the Equinoxes* and it takes 25,765 years to complete one revolution.)

Our ancestors noticed that all the planets also follow approximately the same path through the stars as the Sun does—and "approximately" is the key word here. Planets all actually ascend or descend above or below the ecliptic as they cycle around. Their distance above or below it is called *ecliptic latitude*. Some astrologers pay attention to it; most do not. It is not really our main subject here.

We can also project the Earth's equator out onto the starry background. It is important not to confuse this *celestial equator* with the ecliptic—they are different beasts because they are not "flat" relative to each other. (More about that later.) The Sun, Moon, and planets only rarely happen to be aligned with that celestial equator. For one thing, they stick roughly to the ecliptic, which is tilted relative to the equator—again, the ecliptic and the celestial equator are not the same. For another, they don't even really stick that closely to the ecliptic! Only the Sun does that.

How far above or below the celestial equator (not the ecliptic!) the Sun, Moon or a planet lies is called its *declination*. Declination is used fairly commonly in the astrological world. In a little while, we are going to use it too.

By the way, this imaginary "sphere of sky" with Earth at its center is called the *celestial sphere*. It is the basic fiction upon which astrology and much of astronomy rests. It is not a "real" truth, but it does reflect the truth of the way things look. From a simple point of view, as we look out into space, the earth appears to be at the center of a great sphere with stars planted on it and the Sun, Moon and planets moving against it.

The Moon orbits the Earth, of course. It is not a planet. But we can project the Moon's orbit onto the surrounding star fields as well. When we do that, we find that the Moon also shows a lot of variation in both declination and in ecliptic latitude. This is because the Moon's orbit is not "flat" either relative to the plane defined by the Earth's orbit around the Sun or to the equator. The Moon's orbital plane is tilted by five degrees eight minutes, relative to the ecliptic.

SEASONS, EQUINOXES, SOLSTICES

To get from here to understanding the Out of Bounds Moon, we need to put three more links in our chain of understanding.

Here is the first one. Back in school, most of us learned about why Earth has seasons. In summer, our planet is tilted *toward* the Sun. The visual effect is that the Sun rises higher in the sky and the days last longer. The opposite happens in winter—Earth is tilted away, so the Sun is lower and the daylight is briefer—and the weather cools down. Earth's angle of tilt varies over very long scales of time, but it is currently at about 23°28'.

Visualize it like this: say you are sitting in spaceship about a zillion miles above the Earth's equator—you are way off to the "side" of the Earth, so to speak. You are far enough out in space that you can see the Sun too, with Earth orbiting it. From your point of view, at one moment the top of the Earth seems to be tilted 23°28' to the left. Six months later, with Earth halfway around the Sun, it is *still* tilted 23°28' to the left. Its angle of tilt has not changed at all. So at first, with the top half of the Earth pointed sunward, the northern hemisphere would be getting most of the sunlight. Six months later, *with Earth still tilted the same way but on the other side of the Sun*, the top half of the Earth is now tilted away from the Sun. It is Australia's turn for a suntan.

That is the first critical link in our chain of understanding.

Here is the second one.

If you are in the northern hemisphere, you are always looking a bit "down" on the Sun. That is why "southern exposure" sells houses—in the north, the Sun always arcs across the southern sky. In the southern hemisphere, it is the opposite situation. There the Sun sticks to the northern sky.

In the noon-day heat of summer, we might be tempted to say that the Sun is right overhead. But it really is not. In the northern hemisphere, the Sun will always be just a little bit to the south, even at the summer solstice when the seasonal tilt is at maximum and the Sun is highest in the sky. Only close to the equator can the Sun ever be truly overhead. Another way to say it is that with the Sun truly overhead, a vertical stick would cast no shadow. To experience that sight, your timing has to be perfect, plus you have to be south of 23°28' North Latitude or north of 23°28' South Latitude—pretty close to the equator, in other words. Otherwise, the Sun will always be at least a small angle away from vertical.

This shadowless region of truly vertical sunlight is called the *tropics*, and they are defined precisely in this astronomical fashion. Only within the tropics—and even there only on certain days of the year—can the Sun physically be straight overhead. Outside the tropics, it can never rise that high. So "tropical" is not a vague reference to palm trees, margaritas, and hot weather. It is actually a rigorous astronomical term. That is the second link in our chain.

Ready for the third link?

Just as we have a celestial equator, we also have celestial tropics. Earlier, we saw that we can extend Earth's equator out into space and visualize it projected onto the imaginary "celestial sphere" that surrounds us. That is the celestial equator. Similarly, projected out onto starry space, the "celestial tropics" extend from 23°28' north of the celestial equator to 23°28' south of it—the same as on Earth.

The Sun in its annual cycle ranges between these tropical extremes, but it never goes beyond them. Thus, at the northern summer solstice, the Sun's *declination* is 23°28' North—that is how far it has risen above the celestial equator. That is also as high as it can get in the northern hemisphere. At the northern winter solstice, the Sun's declination is 23°28' South—even at high noon, it lies way down low near the southern horizon. Thus the *ecliptic weaves seasonally between the boundaries of the tropics*, crossing the celestial equator twice at the Equinoxes, but also reaching 23°28' above it and, six months later, 23°28' below it at the Solstices.

In the southern hemisphere, the timing is the same, except six months out of phase since summer and winter are reversed.

This maximum limit of 23°28' declination, south or north, applies rigidly to the Sun. But not to the Moon or to all of the planets. Most of them can go beyond it. Mercury and Mars can reach 27° and Venus can, occasionally, go a degree further. Using the filters in AstroDataBank and scanning many thousands of charts, I have learned that Jupiter and Uranus do cross the line, but not by very far, and quite rarely, especially in Jupiter's case. Neptune and Saturn never do. Pluto does so more often. This list varies over very long scales of time, by the way. When a planet's declination exceeds 23°28' North or South, it is described as being *Out of Bounds*. The term originated with the late astrologer Kt (say "Kay Tee") Boehrer in her now-rare book, *Declinations, The Other Dimension*. A decade ago, the NCGR's *Geocosmic* magazine published an entire edition strictly on declination (Spring, 1998). It was edited by the late, great Frances McEvoy, with whom I had many valuable discussions on the subject in her home near Boston. The issue contains articles by Charles Jayne, Leigh Westin, Karen Christino, Martha Ramsey, Ken Gillman, Barbara Koval, Richard Nelson, Valerie Vaughan, Bruce Scofield, Kris Brandt Riske, Charles and Lois Hannon, Edward Dearborn and Kt Boehrer herself. Still, despite that burst of fanfare, not many astrologers today employ this Out of Bounds technique. I suspect that a hundred years from now we all will, for reasons I am about to demonstrate.

This, by the way, is the end of science class. We are ready to mine some gold. As usual in astrology, we do that by heading for the English Department. Science simply provides the basis for the metaphors we interpret.

THE OUT OF BOUNDS MOON

What does it mean astrologically for the Moon to be Out of Bounds? Start with one merrily anarchic notion: when the Moon's declination exceeds 23°28' North or 23°28' South, it has escaped the physical space dominated by the gravitational "boss" of the solar system, the Sun.

Let that metaphor roll like a downhill snowball.

The Moon, when it is Out of Bounds, is then *out of the King's sight*. No longer *under Daddy's thumb*. We might say that has *moved beyond the Pale*. It has gone *out of control*. Gone wild. It has *broken the rules*. It has *shattered the boundaries, broken the mold, crossed the Rubicon*. Bravely or drunkenly, the Moon has said, "Roll the dice."

The Out of Bounds Moon is spontaneous, emancipated, liberated, released on its own recognizance, and utterly on its own. It has loudly proclaimed, "*You can take this job (. . . this marriage, church, obligation, moral principle, town, duty . . .) and shove it!*"

The Moon has claimed its genius, its passion, and its right to be itself. No need to obfuscate, to be diplomatic, or to lie to anyone anymore—unless you feel like it. No more coprophagous grin. No need to worry about staying in anyone's good graces. Out of Bounds, the Moon no longer plays the game. It rejects all rules that are not of its own making. "*Free at last, free at last! Thank God Almighty, we are finally free at last!*" said Martin Luther King, Jr.

The words stir the blood. But we need to let them stir the mind as well.

Structure, discipline, and a world in which our actions have consequences—these are not purely negative things. Society and its values can have a steadying effect upon us, even when we feel frustrated by them. The Out of Bounds Moon, like everything else in astrology, has an unpleasant, dangerous side as well as a divine purpose. Its dark side is sociopathic, even criminal—or merely selfish and insensitive to others. It can be cold, even inhuman.

You may detect some of the underlying spirit of the planet Uranus and the sign Aquarius in these words. That is quite accurate. In my experience, an Out of Bounds Moon has a distinctly Aquarian quality. We see the familiar Uranian "holy trinity" at work—the *Genius*, the *Revolutionary* and the *Criminal*. All three of them stand outside the normal structure of society, applying leverage to it—and meeting resistance, condemnation, and consequences for it.

Combining an Aquarian Moon with one that is Out of Bounds is obviously a supercharged situation. Cat Stevens, the 1960s pop star who turned his back on it all to become a Muslim, is a fine illustration of this "double-whammy" astrological configuration. Turning that around, we might consider Salman Rushdie, the novelist against whom a death-fatwa was directed for his writing. Rushdie's Moon is Out of Bounds and conjunct Uranus.

As with Aquarian or Uranian influences, the Out of Bounds Moon often thrusts alienating circumstances upon a person. This is of course the classic working of synchronicity—what we meet (or fail to face) in our inner world is encountered in the "random" realities of our outer lives. An example of this aspect of the Out of Bounds Moon is Olympic Gold medalist, Bruce Jenner. As a child he was dyslexic. The resulting mockery and ostracism triggered his extreme development as an athlete.

Inwardly, the Out of Bounds Moon often correlates with feelings of being an *outsider*, of *not fitting in*, of not having a place in this world. This can be painful—and it can also lead to an attitude of not giving a damn. Or to passivity. Or to resentment. And to radical forms of existential creativity. Gustave Courbet, the French realist painter who died in 1877, had the Moon Out of Bounds at declination 27°50' South. He was jailed. He was called a "terrible socialist" and a "savage." One of his paintings, called *The Origin of the World*, was simply a realistic representation of female genitalia. It was so controversial that its first public exhibition did not occur until 1988, or 111 years after his death. Courbet captured the spirit of the Out of Bounds Moon when he wrote, "I am fifty years old and I have always lived in freedom; let me end my life free; when I am dead let this be said of me: 'He belonged to no school, to no church, to no institution, to no academy, least of all to any régime except the régime of liberty.'"

DO I HAVE AN OUT OF BOUNDS MOON?

That question is easily answered, given modern astrological technology. Most astrological software allows you to calculate declinations. Just set up your birth chart and look for the Moon's declination. If it is greater than 23°28' north or south, it is Out of Bounds.

Most of the popular forms of software offer many different kinds of on-screen or printed charts. Typically, there are more technical versions, along with the simpler ones that an astrologer might give to a client. You will very likely find declination listed in the technical version. Similarly, many ephemerides also list declination.

More broadly, there are some years in which many babies are born with Out of Bounds Moons, and some years in which none at all are. This is related to the 18.6 year retrograde cycle of the Moon's orbital plane—the same phenomenon that creates the lunar nodes. Here's the bottom line: Every 18.6 years, the Moon reaches its maximum possible declination of 28°28', a full five degrees outside the tropics. In the years halfway between, we get a kind of "low tide" effect, with the Moon never getting more than 18°28' from the celestial equator. Under those latter conditions, the Out of Bounds Moon cannot exist at all. No one born in those years has one.

Thus, over a time-scale of 18.6 years, about half the people born *might* have an Out of Bounds Moon, and about half them could not possibly have one. Furthermore, some of the "good" years for Out of Bounds Moons are more productive than others. That is because at times when the Moon goes further Out of Bounds, it stays that way for longer as well. The odds improve. Even in "good" years, the Moon's monthly orbit brings it back "within bounds" as it passes through the neutral ground between maximum northern and maximum southern declinations. It may, in other words, be wildly Out of Bounds in one person's natal chart—but in the chart of a person born just a week later, the Moon is in 0° declination, as normal as vanilla ice cream. But then a week after that, it is wildly Out of Bounds again.

You really have to calculate it, is the bottom line.

Remembering all our caveats, here are the absolute peak years for Out of Bounds Moon births in living memory: 1913, 1931-32, 1950, 1969, 1987-88, 2006. We will have another one in 2024-25. Remember to give it perhaps a couple of years on either side—or, better yet, look it up. During those years a lot of kids were or will be born with Out of Bounds Moons. But they are mixed in with a large population of more steady, conventional types. Looking at those years, note how the correlations with periods of social unrest and social creativity are rather clear. And, as ever in astrology, what is in the air at a given moment lives on for decades longer in holographic form in the children.

NINE QUALITIES

I have identified nine qualities that are related to the Out of Bounds Moon. They are arbitrary and they overlap. Undoubtedly there are other categories waiting to be discovered. I will first briefly introduce these categories at a theoretical level, then follow with some well-known living examples that bring the theory into the practical realm.

These are my theoretical impressions of the Out of Bounds Moon, fleshed out by my experience in the astrological counseling room and in research. Following each quality, you will find a list of well-known people with Out of Bounds Moons in their natal charts. Some of the people appear more than once since they illustrate more than one feature of the Out of Bounds Moon.

CHOOSING TO LEAVE: Often people born under the Out of Bounds Moon display a tendency to walk away from situations which more conventional individuals might consider prestigious or desirable. Voluntarily, they exile themselves from success as it would be defined at the tribal level.

Examples: Henry David Thoreau giving up the normal comforts of life and society and choosing to live at Walden Pond. *Kurt Cobain*, a musician who committed suicide at the height of his fame. *Al Gore*, who left the American political world and choose instead to operate as an "outsider" environmental crusader. *Shirley Temple Black*, film star who left Hollywood to become a homemaker. *Queen Victoria*, who withdrew from the public for 40 years after her husband died. 1960s music star *Cat Stevens*, who left his stardom behind to follow his Muslim faith. *Grant Desme*, twenty-three year Oakland A's baseball power-hitter who quit to become a Catholic priest.

BOLD, GROUNDBREAKING GENIUS: The classic definition of genius is the ability to "think outside the box," and people born under the Out of Bounds Moon often display that quality abundantly. Of course they are not all necessarily geniuses who will be remembered in history. Far more often, they are more normal people who simply display unique talents and quirky interests. I believe that historical geniuses tend more than average to have Out of Bounds Moons, but it is also significant to note that many recognized geniuses do not have it.

Examples: Paradigm-shattering physicist *Albert Einstein*. *Sigmund Freud*, the great pioneer of psychoanalysis. The luminous Italian novelist, *Umberto Eco*. The endlessly brilliant British musician, *Peter Gabriel*. The avant-garde composer *John Cage*. The mind-twisting graphic artist, *M.C. Escher*. *Billie Holiday*, the blues singer who made being African-American sexy and relevant in white society. *Louis Pasteur*, who first understood bacterial infection. *Babe Ruth*, often considered the greatest baseball player who ever lived. *Duke Ellington*, who lifted jazz to the highest levels of art. *Gustave Courbet*, iconoclastic painter. *Anna Freud*, pioneer of child psychology. *Victor Hugo*, often called the greatest of the French poets. *Wilhelm Reich*, Austrian-American psychoanalyst and advocate of sexual liberation. *Sir Christopher Wren*, brilliant British architect. *Rodney Collin*, obscure but brilliant author of *The Theory of Celestial Influence*. *Henri Cartier-Bresson*, pioneer of photography as a legitimate art form.

BREAKING OUT OF SOCIAL CONSTRUCTS: We are all heavily programmed from childhood by the forces of sociology and demography. A soul born into the ghetto and a soul born into the country club set would naturally be expected to go down different roads in life. Yet with the Out of Bounds Moon, we often see a pattern of escaping these constraints of social training and expectation.

Examples: Oprah Winfrey, who transformed the face and purpose of television. *Jesse Ventura*, the pro wrestler who became a governor. *Arnold Schwarzeneggar*, the Austrian action movie star who became a governor. *Edgar Mitchell*, lunar astronaut turned psychic researcher. *Freddie Mercury*, openly-gay singer with the band, Queen, who was among the first to make being gay "cool." *Rosa Parks*, who famously refused to give up her seat to a white passenger on that fateful bus in Alabama in 1955. *Amelia Earhart*, who pioneered the female role in aviation. *Christopher Reeve*, actor who played Superman, and who became paraplegic. *Shirley Temple Black*, child star who became ambassador to Ghana and Czechoslovakia; she also was among the first to break the taboo about speaking out regarding breast cancer. *Bob Geldorf*, punk rocker knighted by the Queen. *Father Joseph Damien*, of Molokai, who broke the taboo against interacting with lepers. And again, *Billie Holiday*, who escaped some of the bounds of racist society. *Ross Perot*, a businessman who ran independently for president of the USA.

SOCIOPATHY AND CRIMINAL BEHAVIOR: On the dark side of the equation, the Out of Bounds Moon can indicate an indifference to consensual and universal laws of moral and ethical behavior. Cold-hearted destructiveness and amorality can arise—what we might call "criminal behavior" in an absolute sense rather than in a legalistic one.

Examples: Carlos the Jackal, the international assassin. *Peter Sutcliffe*, the Yorkshire Ripper. *Josef Dietrich*, head of the Nazi S.S. *Rudolph Hess*, Nazi leader fired for insanity. *Augusto Pinochet*, brutal Chilean dictator. *Roman Polanski*, film director and convicted pedophile. *Manuel Noriega*, corrupt Central American dictator. *Lucky Luciano*, early American Mafia figure. *Squeaky Fromme*, attempted assassin of U.S. President Gerald Ford. *John Wilkes Booth*, assassin of U.S. President Abraham Lincoln. *Paul Joseph Goebbels*, propaganda leader for the Nazi Party.

ALLEGED SOCIOPATHY AND CRIMINAL BEHAVIOR: Of course criminality is to some extent in the eye of the beholder. Those who simply follow their own path in accord with natural law might sometimes be accused of such deviations. Jesus was duly tried and convicted, for example. And then there are situations of crimes alleged but not proven, where the truth remains murky. Out of Bounds Moon people are often implicated in all of these kinds of circumstances.

Examples: Mary Queen of Scots, beheaded for allegedly plotting against the British Crown. *Salman Rushdie*, victim of a Fatwa for his irreverent writing. *Jimmy Hoffa*, murdered union organizer with alleged Mafia connections. Alleged tax-evader *Rupert Murdoch*, media mogul who has become a *bête noir* for the political left. *Edith Piaf*, French cabaret singer addicted to drugs. *Catherine the Great*, who allegedly had her husband murdered in order to become Empress of Russia. *Dorothy Parker*, humorist blacklisted during the McCarthy era.

"NICE" OUTLAWS: Where would we be without people who experiment with the boundaries of morality, normalcy, and risk? The naughty part of ourselves identifies with them and celebrates them. We might not be brave enough to follow in their footsteps, but part of us goes there vicariously and experiences an emotional lift. Out of Bounds Moon people often fit this description.

Examples: "Outlaw" musicians *Willie Nelson, Jimmy Buffet, and Tom Waits. Camilla Parker Bowles*, lover of Prince Charles. *Ken Kesey*, 1960s psychedelic iconoclast. *Ozzy Osbourne*, highly alternative family man. *Clint Eastwood*, iconic "good" (semi) bad guy. *River Phoenix*, "bad boy" actor. *Woody Guthrie*, social activist singer-songwriter.

THEOLOGICAL OUTLAWS: Every society has its religion in some sense of the word—a set of beliefs by which both reality and moral behavior are defined. The Out of Bounds Moon is often present in thinkers and spiritual teachers who stand outside that framework. They may illuminate us, or offend us, or simply encourage us to ask paradigm-challenging questions.

Examples: Spiritual teacher *Ram Dass*, Pagan visionary *Starhawk. Cat Stevens*, who espoused a religious faith unpopular in his own culture.

Stephen King, who has brought the occult into the mainstream. *Bhagwan Shree Rajneesh*, iconoclastic, controversial guru. Jeddu Krishnamurti, anti-guru guru. *Werner Erhard*, founder of Est training. *Pema Chodron*, American teacher ordained as a Buddhist nun. *Albert Einstein* bears mentioning here too, given the way his theory of relativity has re-shaped our collective view of reality itself.

ZANY CHARACTERS: Every town has its eccentrics. They may seem edgy and dangerous, entertaining, delightful, funny, or just weird. Each eccentric tends to be eccentric in his or her own way—that's really the point! In whatever style or fashion these eccentrics may go about stretching the limits of the expected, there is an elevated tendency to find the Out of Bounds Moon in their natal charts.

Examples: Russian president *Boris Yeltsin*. Activist and politician *Al Sharpton*. Amelia Earhart, who eschewed the "feminine" requirements of her time and thus looked zany in that social context. *John Belushi*, wild man comic genius. *Jesse Ventura*, the say-anything former pro wrestler turned governor of Minnesota. *Ozzy Osbourne*, rock star turned reality TV star. *Giovanni Casanova*, the "greatest lover in history." *Isadora Duncan*, Roaring Twenties iconoclast. *Yoko Ono*, artist and provocative wife of John Lennon. *"Dr. Ruth" Westheimer*, sex therapist. *Lucille Ball*, zany redhead of *I Love Lucy* fame. *Alice Cooper*, rock-as-theater pioneer. *Dan Quayle*, bumbling Vice President under George H.W. Bush.

LITERALLY, OUT OF THIS WORLD: Sometimes symbolism is very concrete. The Out of Bounds Moon is found in the charts of many who leave the boundaries of this world in more-or-less concrete ways.

Examples: Yuri Gagarin, the first man in space. *Neil Armstrong*, the first human to set foot on the Moon. *Edgar Mitchell*, who visited the Moon and later took up psychic research. *Leonard Nimoy*, as Mr. Spock, possibly the world's most familiar alien—the original *Star Trek* program aired under an Out of Bounds Moon as well. Again, *Amelia Earhart*, who disappeared from this world while trying to fly around it in 1937. *Alexei Leonov*, the first human to "spacewalk." *Judith Resnik*, second American woman in space, who died in the *Challenger* explosion on re-entry.

THE MOON "CLOSE TO" OUT OF BOUNDS

What if the moon is close to being Out of Bounds? That is, what if it is near the tropical limit of 23°28' north or south, but not quite there? There are elements in astrology that really seem to "click" when they cross a line, much the way electrons "click" from one orbital shell around the nucleus of an atom to another. Sign cusps operate that way. And there are elements in astrology that blur and blend—house cusps and aspects are good examples of that. In my experience, as the Moon approaches the tropical boundary—say, when it gets beyond about 19° from the celestial equator—we begin to see some of the Out of Bounds qualities in the character. Muddying the theoretical waters is the fact that a person might display many such qualities for other astrological reasons entirely—Uranus conjunct the Sun, for example. Still, I have come to believe that the Moon need not be 100 percent over the line before we begin to feel its zany, brilliant, or sociopathic dimensions.

Hitler's Moon was in 22°55'—half a degree short—but he clearly illustrates the darkest potentials of an Out of Bounds Moon. For zany characters, we have David Byrne of the Talking Heads (23°22') or Groucho Marx (19°09'). Carl Jung's Moon was in declination 19°24' North, and he perfectly reflects the quality of groundbreaking genius. Gender identity is an area fraught with social constructs. Here are two public figures who helped turn them on their heads in the last century: Liberace (21° 38') and the first transsexual, Christine Jorgensen (22°21'). The murderer Charles Manson's Moon was in 19°16'. Here is one of my favorite illustrations. It is someone of whom you have probably never heard: Valentina Tereshkova. Her Moon was at declination 22°52' South, just half a degree short of the tropic. She was the first woman to fly in space.

CONTEXT IS CRITICAL

Naturally, as always one must weave an Out of Bounds Moon into the warp and weft of a larger astrological framework. But it's clear that considering the Moon only in terms of conventional sign, house and aspects leaves out many potentially potent modifying factors. I look forward to the day when I ask about someone's Moon and hear, "Fourth house Libra, very fast, in Waning Gibbous phase, and Out of Bounds."

What might that mean, exactly, and how might it specifically deepen our understanding? *Libra*: her mood is characterized by a strong impulse toward intimacy and powerful aesthetic responses. But *Fourth House*: her intimate impulses are about long-haul commitments, and her creativity, while powerful, is something she might hide.

That's conventional modern astrology. But she's given us much more to go on. The *fast* Moon suggests that there might also be a certain impulsiveness in her nature. Since it's in Libra, this element of fast-Moon impulsiveness would probably manifest in intimate matters. Thus, that potentially injudicious quality would sometimes exist in tension with her urge for longer-lasting bonds. She may signal approach, and then withdraw, only to approach again. The *Out of Bounds* dimension of her Moon further suggests a tendency toward unconventional behaviors—and in this context, I would be thinking particularly about intimate or creative unconventionality. Deep, lasting commitments between people can exist in non-conventional frameworks—a stable bond among three people, for example. And art can shock.

Notice how much further we can take the interpretation just by adding the Moon's speed and Out of Bounds quality?

What about the *Waxing Gibbous* element? Of all the new pieces, I believe this one is the most significant. But we're not quite there yet.

PROGRESSED MOON OUT OF BOUNDS

The Moon can go Out of Bounds by secondary progression, with extraordinary effect. If we reflect for a moment on how secondary progressions are calculated, however, we soon realize that there are many people who will never experience this situation. The idea is simple: to know where your planets are by secondary progression on your thirtieth birthday, you count exactly 30 *days* forward in the ephemeris. Those planetary positions are your secondary progressions. Days become years, in other words. It follows that the transits of the first three months or so of infancy are the secondary progressions for the rest of your life.

But maybe you were born in one of the years in which the Moon's declination was never so extreme—say 1978, for example. The Moon did not begin to reach the critical 23°28' of declination until December

1982. If you were born in January 1978, you would have to reach the ripe old age of about 1,800 years before your Moon ever progressed Out of Bounds!

U2's singer, Bono, for example, was born in a quiet year. His Moon will not progress Out of Bounds in his lifetime. The same goes for the famously unflappable Barack Obama, born in 1961. Like Bono, he is immune to the Out of Bounds condition. But Kurt Cobain's life, although he was born just six years later, tells a different story. In summer 1991, his Moon progressed Out of Bounds—and he shot to superstardom with his band's major label debut album, *Nevermind*. His Moon reached its impressive maximum declination of 27° 48' toward the end of 1993. Four months later, locked in his expensive home, drugged, alienated, and in hiding, Cobain committed suicide with a shotgun.

As I write these words, the country is horribly captivated by the nightmarish mass murder which occurred on November 5, 2009 at Fort Hood, Texas. Military psychiatrist Maj. Nidal Malik Hasan killed 13 people and wounded 28 others in an insane explosion of frustration over the possibility of being deployed to Iraq or Afghanistan. The only birth data I have on him is that he was born on September 8, 1970, in Arlington, Virginia. Fortunately, for determining whether someone has an Out of Bounds Moon either in the natal chart or by progression, often knowing the date of birth is enough. At the beginning of the day of Hasan's birth, the Moon was at 26° 41'south declination. By the end of the day, it had reached 28° 07'. Thus, regardless of his actual time of birth that day, there is no doubt that he was born with the Moon Out of Bounds. When the killings happened, Hasan's Moon had just recently progressed Out of Bounds as well.

In Kurt Cobain's story we see tragedy, alienation—and a sad, but classic example of "choosing to leave." With Nidal Malik Hasan, "sociopathy and criminal behavior" are agonizingly apparent. In broader terms, we can apply the formulas we explored earlier regarding the natal Out of Bounds Moon to the progressed one. With progressions, instead of a fundamental, relatively stable condition of the psyche, we see the fingerprint of a more transitory one. By the way, with both Cobain and Hasan, their natal Moons were also Out of Bounds, and the interaction between the innate natal condition and the progression which exaggerates it is of course acute.

Arnold Schwarzeneggar was elected governor of California in October 2003. His Moon had progressed Out of Bounds in the spring of 2000 and remained in that condition until late 2004. In the improbable reality of a heavily-accented Austrian action film star turning into the governor of the most populous state in America, he nicely illustrates "breaking out of social constructs." He also offers a credible performance as a "zany character." Starting in the spring of 1960, with his progressed Moon also Out of Bounds, Schwarzeneggar literally broke into a closed gym on the weekends so he could train as a bodybuilder. I think we could fairly call that minor trespass "alleged sociopathy and criminal behavior." He was breaking the rules, but harming no one. Maybe he qualifies for "nice outlaw" too. The notorious "Satanist" rock star, Marilyn Manson, released his first album, *Portrait of an American Family*, with the Moon progressed Out of Bounds, thereby embodying "alleged sociopathy" and defining the outer limits of "zany character."

In 1517, Martin Luther published his famous *Ninety-Five Theses* disputing the Church doctrine that the forgiveness of sins could be purchased for money. The nailing of these theses to the door of the church at Wittenberg is widely seen as the critical moment of ignition in the Protestant Reformation. At that time, Luther's progressed Moon had just passed its peak, reaching a declination of 28°01' North—wildly Out of Bounds. Here we have perhaps our most historically momentous illustration of the "theological outlaw."

In September 1905, six months after his Moon had progressed Out of Bounds, Albert Einstein published the paradigm-shattering Special Theory of Relativity. He thus clinches our "bold, groundbreaking genius" award. Fourteen years later, his Moon again progressed Out of Bounds. Just as it was doing so, the Theory of Relativity was essentially proven when starlight was seen to be deflected by the Sun's gravity during a total solar eclipse. Instantly, Einstein was catapulted into the strange "Out of Bounds" world of fame, which his legendary name still occupies. Finally, with his progressed Moon Out of Bounds again between late 1946 and late 1950, Einstein espoused unpopular socialist beliefs and campaigned against nuclear proliferation. For that, let's give him a "nice outlaw" award. He deserves a mention for "zany character" too, given his wonderful hair and wise-bumbling affect, which was the inspiration for Yoda in the *Star Wars* films—which leads us, last but not least, to our "literally, out of this world" title. Since we do not have a chart for Yoda, who could be more deserving than the first man ever to orbit the earth? On April 12, 1961, Yuri Gagarin boldly went where no one had gone before—and his progressed Moon was at 27°26' South declination, every bit as Out of Bounds as he was.

As with the declination of the natal Moon, we often find that periods of a person's life when the progressed Moon *approaches* its extremes of declination are colorful, groundbreaking times—or fairly crazy ones. That remains true even if the Moon does not actually cross the 23°28' line. In October 1925, Josephine Baker opened in Paris at the Théâtre des Champs-Élysées, beginning a triumphant run as a dancer and paving the way for African-American performers to find a respect, dignity and success in Europe which were precluded by racist conditions in America at the time. Her Moon had progressed to a modest peak declination of 20°21' three months before—and seven years earlier, she had been a homeless 12-year-old eating out of garbage cans and living in a cardboard box in the alleys of St. Louis.

For a very different illustration, consider Johannes Kepler. In September 1616, his Moon progressed to a maximum declination of about 21°09' South—over two degrees short of being technically Out of Bounds, but marking an extreme in the context of his own life. In 1615, Kepler finished the first volume of his most influential work, *Epitome Astronomia Copernicanae*, which detailed the "three laws of planetary motion" and insured his place in the pantheon of scientific geniuses. And during this same period, when his mother was accused of witchcraft,

Kepler had to devote much time and energy to her defense—illustrating the "exile" aspect of extreme lunar declinations.

We modern astrologers have been bombarded by an avalanche of new techniques. Life is too short to learn them all, let alone to use them in any practical context of astrological counsel with the clock ticking and another client due in an hour. All of us must pick and choose among these riches. I hope I have made the case to you that the Out of Bounds Moon, while often overlooked, is a major piece of the astrological puzzle.

THREE GLASS DISKS

Picture a piece of modern sculpture: three stacked disks of glass impaled through their centers on a single column. At their centers they are fused together, but they are tilted relative to each other. One is flat relative to the ground—horizontal, in other words. The second one is tilted 23°28'. The third one is tilted another 5°8'—so it is tilted 28°36' relative to the horizontal disk.

The Three Glass Disks

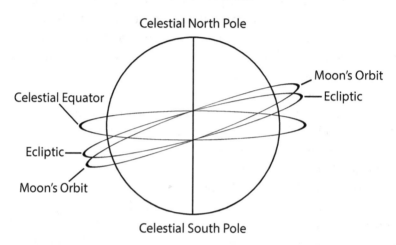

Once you have that image visualized, you are in a good position to understand a lot of astronomy. The first disk, the horizontal one, is the celestial equator—Earth's own equator projected outward onto the celestial sphere. The second, tilted disk is the ecliptic—the yearly path of the Sun through the constellations. The third, more extremely tilted disk is the Moon's orbital plane. Make the sculpture mobile and ethereal rather than actually solid. The lunar disk is slowly rotating backwards, actually moving through the glass of the other two disks as it does so. It takes this lunar disk 18.6 years to make one revolution. (That is the cycle of the lunar nodes—the north node being where the lunar disk crosses the ecliptic heading up or north, and the south node the opposite.) The lunar disk is riding on the ecliptic disk. Earth is on that ecliptic disk too, taking a year to revolve all the way around. Therefore, in the course of a year, we are sometimes watching everything from the most highly-tilted parts of the ecliptic. Those are the Solstices. Other times, at the Equinoxes, we are on the part of the ecliptic-disk where it crosses the equator-disk. Since the Moon is orbiting Earth, we have brought the Moon with us, so it is lower at the Equinoxes too.

Remember that the Moon's disk is the most tilted of the three glass panes. Its highest edge and its lowest edge are higher and lower, respectively, than any point on the other two disks. But the parts of the Moon's disk that are *not* highest and lowest are "within the bounds" of the disk representing the ecliptic. The Moon itself can be anywhere on the Moon-disc, just like a painted pony can be anywhere on the merry-go-round. From all this, you can see why the Moon is only Out of Bounds occasionally—to be so, it must be more than 23°28' above or below the flat disk of the equator. Most of the time the Moon is closer than that and not Out of Bounds at all.

There are times when the Moon is *very* much Out of Bounds. That happens when the tilt of its slowly-rotating orbital plane is at its maximum possible 5° above the maximum possible 23°28' tilt of the ecliptic, all relative to the flat plane of the celestial equator. Remember that the Moon's plane is "riding" the disk of the ecliptic—and remember that the Sun only reaches its extremes of declination at the solstices. For the Moon to reach its *maximum* Out of Bounds condition, it requires this "perfect storm." Because it takes the Moon's plane 18.6 years to complete its rotation around, it follows that this extreme condition can occur only once every 18.6 years.

All this may sound obscure and technical, but the visual effect is dramatic. Around that time of maximum lunar extension, the Moon gets as high in the sky as it possibly can reach. It climbs and climbs, night after night, until it has reached that maximum of about 28.5° above the celestial equator. This moment was a big deal to our ancestors. One theory about the purpose of Stonehenge is that it was designed to calculate and predict these *Major Lunar Standstills*. That term was coined by archaeologist Alexander Thom in his book *Megalithic Lunar Observatories* (Oxford University Press, 1971). The Moon does not, of course, really stand still—it just stops getting higher and higher in the sky night after night, and begins to get lower and lower.

By the way, half a nodal cycle later—a little over nine years down the road—the Moon would reach another peak, but a lower one. This occurs when its plane is 5° *below* the 23°28' tilt of the ecliptic, or just about 18.5°. That is quite a lot lower. It is called the *Minor Lunar Standstill*.

We described the Major Lunar Standstill as the time when the

Moon is maximally high in the sky. That is correct, but we can take it further. It is also when the Moon reaches its *lowest* point. Here's why. Since the Moon gets around its orbital plane in just one month, it hits both extremes. Over a period of just two weeks, it will go from about 28.5° North declination to about 28.5° South declination—from that far above the celestial equator to that far below it. So it is riding way overhead, higher than you have ever seen it. Then, just two weeks later, it is just skimming the horizon.

It is easy to see why our ancestors noticed these aspects of lunar behavior. If we are paying attention to the Moon, these are dramatic visual effects. Almost undoubtedly, you have noticed them yourself without really registering what was going on. "Gee, look at the Moon shining through that high window. I've never noticed it doing that before." Our forebears felt it was important enough to build Stonehenge to help them measure and predict these patterns of lunar motion—which meant schlepping 80 stones, weighing about four tons each, 240 miles from the Prescelly Hills at the southwestern border of Wales all the way to the Salisbury plain. That's motivation!

Those megalithic astrologers understood the Moon in ways that we do not. But perhaps we are now remembering, as I hope to demonstrate more deeply in later chapters.

THE ROLE OF THE LUNAR NODES

Remember that the Moon's nodes tell us where the Moon's orbit crosses the ecliptic. From all of this you can see how closely they are related to the Out of Bounds Moon and its extreme expression in the Lunar Standstills. It works out in practice to a simple formula. For your natal Moon *possibly* to be Out of Bounds, your north node of the Moon must be in one of these signs: Capricorn, Aquarius, Pisces, Aries, Taurus or Gemini—with an occasional spill-over into the last degree of Sagittarius or the first degree of Cancer. The Major Lunar Standstills will only occur right in the middle of this period as the Moon's nodes retrograde out of Pisces and into Aries. This would represent the most extreme expression of the Out of Bounds quality we have been exploring. Note that having your north node in these signs does not mean you have an Out of Bounds Moon. It only means that you *might*.

Here are the dates in the relatively recent past and relatively near future in which the **north node of the Moon transits into Pisces**. These would be very close to the **Major Lunar Standstills**, although to learn the exact dates of maximum lunar declination, you would need to check the Moon's daily changes in declination within the lunar month that contains these dates.

○ December 14, 1914

○ July 25, 1933

○ March 6, 1952

○ October 6, 1970

○ May 27, 1989

○ January 7, 2008

○ August 18, 2026

○ March 29, 2045

Our bottom line is that the Major Lunar Standstill, although fairly rare, represents the most extreme expression of the Out of Bounds Moon.

THE METONIC CYCLE

One more lunar curiosity remains. It is called the Metonic cycle, and it is one of the most fundamental rhythms in astronomy. As astrologers sharpen their lunar vision, it will likely take on increasing importance in astrology as well.

Start by remembering something I discussed a few pages back when I was attempting to define the word "month." There we learned that we might think of a month as the return of the Moon to some arbitrary starting point in its cycle—0 Aries would be the conventional marker. That, as we saw, is called the *sidereal month*. Or, we might think of the month as the length of time between successive New or Full Moons—the *synodic month*, which is a couple of days longer. Let's add a third Earth-cycle to our considerations: the *year*, which we could here define as the length of time between two successive Spring Equinoxes.

These three natural cycles are locked together. This is the *Metonic cycle*. Here is the formula:

235 synodic months = 254 sidereal months = 19 years.

This formula is accurate to within less than 18 hours. These three cycles repeat this pattern of synchronization reliably and faithfully, millennium after millennium. *Thus, within a single day of your nineteenth birthday, all three of these cycles are back where they started.* Something in you hits reset. And the same is true around your thirty-eighth birthday, your fifty-seventh, your seventy-sixth, and your ninety-fifth.

These birthdays are turning points in the soul's journey, times when the solar system seems to encourage us to remember who we really are and what our lives are really about. If we have gotten too distracted or caught up in other people's scripts, these are times of spiritual crisis—of either reclaiming ourselves or slipping into cynicism and defeat. In a wiser world, they would be marked and honored as times of sacred reflection.

This Metonic cycle is close to the more familiar nodal cycle of 18.5997 years, which marks a kind of karmic reaffirmation or evolutionary new start. The study of the interaction between the Metonic cycle and the nodal one is yet another lunar frontier.

CONCLUSION

Here is what I hope you have gotten out of these last two rather long and technical chapters.

- ○ A sense that there is still much for astrologers to learn about the Moon at the basic level, and that accomplishing that goal depends upon our breaking out of the ghetto of thinking only in terms of the Moon's sign, house and aspects.

- ○ The knowledge that the speed of the natal Moon is a hugely significant factor, easily verified by anyone who contemplates it.

- ○ The knowledge that the Out of Bounds Moon is also a hugely significant factor, again easily verified by anyone who contemplates it.

- ○ The realization that, because of parallax, our natal Moons might actually not be in exactly the part of the sky that our standard calculations claim, and that if we are at the maximum one-degree shift, it can have some serious practical implications.

- ○ An appreciation of the possible importance of the nineteen- year Metonic cycle in human psycho-spiritual development.

Since these are all frontier areas in astrological culture, I made the decision in writing these two chapters to be rather unmerciful in terms of presenting the technical underpinnings of the thinking. That was so that you, patient reader, might be empowered to reflect deeply on these matters and maybe see some of the things that I have undoubtedly missed.

We are now almost ready to move forward into softer territory and the heart of the matter of this book—the phases of the Moon. But before we do that, there is one more wrinkle to understanding the practical uses of Moon-consciousness. Little by little, in totally practical ways, the following technique could change what we might call your "luck." It is sufficiently powerful and complex to warrant its own chapter. And, among its many virtues, it could even make you money! It is time to meet the Void of Course Moon.

4

THE VOID OF COURSE MOON

The more slowly something moves, the more momentous it is. That is a reliable rule of thumb in all developmental forms of astrology. And by "developmental" I mean transits, progressions, solar arcs, and other "predictive" methods. The reason is simple: slower events *have longer to interact with your consciousness.* They have time to develop depth and complexity of meaning. It is easy to test this principle. Ask any astrologer which of these events is a bigger deal: Pluto transiting through the conjunction to your Venus, or Mercury transiting through that same conjunction? They will pick Pluto every time, and for good reason.

Pluto hitting Venus is a fateful event. Since the planet takes nearly two and a half centuries to get around the Sun, some people never experience it. For those who do, the transit dominates three or four years of their lives. During that period, Plutonian themes press on their relationships. They adapt, they maladapt, they fall into despair, they make breakthroughs. Most of us check "All of the Above," and we are wiser for it. We probably have scars to prove it.

Mercury transiting through the conjunction to your Venus, by comparison, is a commonplace, dime-a-dozen event. It happens to everyone many times unless they die in infancy. It only lasts for a few days and then it is gone. My father lived almost to his eighty-third birthday. Transiting Mercury conjuncted his Venus 107 times in the course of his lifetime. But he never experienced Pluto crossing his Venus. For that to have happened, he would have had to have reached the age of 97.

Pluto is slow. Anytime it arrives anywhere, your astrologer is going to talk about it.

All the foregoing sweeps one reality under the carpet. *During the few days that Mercury is crossing your Venus, it is every bit as powerful and pressing as Pluto.* You will be communicating (Mercury) like crazy regarding the Venusian part of your life. You will be talking with your partner or friends. You will be getting lots of email and phone calls. You will be negotiating deals, compromises and truces. And in a few days, all of that will be history. None of it was "important" in the sense of being something that changed your life—as Pluto transiting your Venus surely would be. But Mercury's effects were quite obvious and real, and *for the short duration of that transit,* every bit as powerful as those of Pluto.

There is a tendency among deeper, more psychologically-oriented astrologers to discount the rapid transits of the inner planets. I do it myself. When I sit with a client, most of the time I am looking for the big picture. I want to talk about existential strategy, not tomorrow's luncheon plans. But in the context of short time frames, those rapid transits are pressing.

Of all these rapid-fire transits, those of the Moon are by far the fastest. Every couple of hours, the Moon moves about one degree. That is over *3,000 times faster than Pluto.* This sheer speed creates what is perhaps the most fundamental paradox of the Moon in modern astrological practice. The natal Moon—the one in the birth chart—is one of the most weighty elements in all astrology. No astrologer would look at anyone's chart for 30 seconds without turning his or her attention to the Moon. But, with two huge exceptions, the transiting Moon is almost completely ignored.

HORARY AND ELECTIONAL ASTROLOGY

Horary astrology answers questions such as, "Where did I leave my credit card?" It might say something along the lines of "It is to the southeast, down low and under something, and will be hard but not impossible to find."

Electional astrology tells you *when* to do things, such as getting married or opening a business. It picks the "lucky moment." Essentially, you use Horary to determine *whether* you should take some action, while you use Electional to determine *when* you should do it.

These two techniques have the patina of ancient times about them.

In many ways, they are more suited to a bygone era, even though they are still potentially helpful today. I personally have a love-hate relationship with both Electional and Horary. I use them; they work pretty well. Where I get into trouble with them is at the philosophical level—I have great faith in the power of freedom, choice, and imagination. All my serious astrological work is predicated on the assumption that we create our own lives through choices we make—and that a human birth is a precious opportunity for growth through good choices. So I have no patience for determinism, believing that it is not only inaccurate, but also that it tends to harm the human spirit. But I admit that most of the time Horary and Electional astrology, in their utterly deterministic ways, do seem to produce rather accurate results concerning practical questions.

In the spirit of the Moon, I shrug my shoulders and try to give life permission to be complicated.

I bring up these two traditional techniques here because in both of them, the transiting Moon, which we nearly dismissed a few paragraphs ago, plays a huge role. It is arguably the most important element of both techniques. *In day-to-day, minute-to-minute life, the Moon rules everything.* I rarely make any important decisions without considering the condition of the transiting Moon. There are a few wrinkles to doing this, but the heart of the matter is a lunar technique that goes back to astrology's long-ago roots: the Void of Course Moon.

The Moon requires an average of two days, six hours, to pass through a sign. During that passage, it will probably make some aspects to other planets. If, for example, the Moon is passing through Capricorn while Venus is in Cancer, at some point the Moon must oppose Venus. It must do that because anything that passes through Capricorn is bound to be opposite anything in Cancer sooner or later. Similarly, the Moon will likely contact many other planets as it crosses through Capricorn—many, but not all. If, for example, Mercury is in Gemini at the time, the Moon will make no aspect to it while it is in Capricorn.

And here of course there arises a chorus of "Buts . . ."

The Moon will indeed *quincunx* that Mercury. That is true—but for these purposes we only consider the so-called major, or Ptolemaic, aspects: the conjunction, sextile, square, trine, and opposition. By the standards of these major aspects, as the Moon passes through any sign, it will generally aspect some planets and miss others.

But at some point the Moon will have made the last Ptolemaic aspect it could possibly make while still in that sign. From that moment until it crosses into the next sign, it is said to be Void of Course.

Right now, for example, as I sit here writing on a Sunday morning in September 2009, the Moon is in Libra. It crossed into that sign on Friday evening, so it is now nearing the end of its passage through that sign. While in Libra, the Moon has already made a square to Pluto, a square to Mars, and a trine to Jupiter. In about three hours, it will trine Neptune, which is near the end of Aquarius. Then it will make no more aspects before it crosses over into Scorpio at 9:52 local time this evening. So starting in about three hours, after it makes that last aspect to Neptune, I see that the Moon will be Void of Course. I would be very hesitant to commit to anything of significance during that time. And that is the basic idea—that *something started under a Void Moon will go nowhere.*

The Void of Course Moon, often ignored in modern psychological astrology, is an incredibly powerful and vivid manifestation of the energy of the Moon. Ignore it to your peril! But first, understand it. Often, among astrologers who know only a little bit about it, the Void of Course Moon is simply considered to be bad or unfortunate. That attitude is crudely helpful, but we can look at it in a far more sophisticated way. In some situations, a Void Moon is your friend.

A LITTLE LUNAR THEOLOGY

The Moon is the Great Mother. One of Her tasks is to bring Her children into the world. Her "children" in this case refer to all of manifest reality—the success of your business proposal or romantic proposition are on Her list too. To accomplish this birthing, She works through Her fellow gods and goddesses—the Sun and the rest of the planets. She needs them, as they need Her. They must receive Her wish and bring it into material manifestation.

Remember—the Moon deals mostly with the inner realms. To make something "happen" in the practical sense of the word, She needs a helping hand In astrological terms, that means that the Moon has to make an aspect to *some* planet before it leaves the sign it is in—before it "changes the subject," so to speak—if the intention is going to come to pass in the physical realm.

So in the traditions of Horary astrology, when an action is undertaken under the Void of Course Moon, the presumption is that "nothing will come of the matter." There will be no material manifestation. The Moon had no assistance. The core idea is that there are *no further implications* of the choice or intention. It is what it is—only a notion. The matter ends there.

Here's another traditional phrase about the Void Moon: *There is nothing to worry about.* That's very different from saying that the Void of Course Moon is unlucky. Contradictory? Not really, if you think about it carefully. Sometimes "nothing" is the happiest outcome of all. If, for example, a doctor gave me a scary diagnosis, I would take comfort if I knew the Moon were Void at the time I first heard it.

Confusion about this point is why many astrologers have marbles in their mouths about the Void of Course Moon. Behind the confusion is one simple, coherent idea, neither intrinsically good nor bad: *Nothing will come of the matter.* Sometimes that's good news, other times not.

MAKING THE VOID MOON WORK FOR YOU

Let's say you have bet your life savings on a health food restaurant you are opening. You have to choose a day to open the doors and seat your first customers. Naturally, that is a big moment. Do you want *nothing to come of it?* Of course not—you want a zillion more happy customers, word-of-mouth buzz, prosperity, and so forth.

Never start a business under a Void of Course Moon!

Let's say you were caught speeding. You can pay your fine by mail. Beyond that unpleasantness, would you like there to be "further developments?" No, you want this annoying drama to be concluded. Drop your fine in the mail under the Void Moon—then there will be "nothing to worry about." Sign routine papers concluding things where you have no further desires under a Void Moon.

Whenever you are ready to let go and be done with something—ready to forget about it—use the Void Moon. It is your friend. But when you *want something to happen*, when things are dicey and you have desires and intentions and are hoping for a good result, avoid the Void Moon like you avoid icky bugs. At times such as those, that is when you want . . .

THE MOON ON YOUR SIDE

Understanding the Void of Course Moon and ducking it when you have desires in an environment of uncertainty is enough to shift the odds in your direction. But there is another big piece to this Moon-puzzle.

The last aspect the Moon makes before it leaves the sign it is in bears heavily on the final outcome of the matter.

So let's go back to that health food restaurant you are opening. For sure, you want something to come of opening your doors for business. As we have seen, you avoid the Void of Course Moon. But what *do* you want? In this case, prosperity and happiness might come to mind. Therefore you want the *final aspect the Moon makes before it leaves the sign through which it is currently passing* to suggest prosperity and happiness!

It is as simple as that.

Knowing that the Moon is not Void means that *something* will come of the action. Exactly *what* will come of it is reflected in the final aspect the Moon makes before it passes into Void mode.

What might you choose for your restaurant? A trine to Jupiter? A sextile to Venus? Those planets come to mind right away. Days when either of those aspects are the last thing the Moon is going to do would be great times to open your business. Bottom line, you want the Moon to make a *soft aspect* to some planet as the last thing it does before leaving its current sign. In corollary fashion, you do not want the Moon to make a hard aspect to any planet as the last thing it does before leaving its current sign.

What about conjunctions? Classically, the conjunction is a "yes," but I have learned to be a bit skeptical of that. I want to see the fine print. A conjunction to Jupiter or Venus sounds encouraging to me. But what about a conjunction to Saturn or Mars? I would not reject them right away—Saturn and Mars can be good allies. But, for example, in electing a wedding chart, I would shy away from Saturn or Mars representing the final outcome. For a sporting event, I might like the conjunction with Mars a lot more. That feels like victory. For a long-sought business deal, a conjunction with Saturn to seal the bargain would feel good to me.

By the way, several paragraphs back, I noted that as I write these words the Moon happens to be in Libra and heading for a final trine to Neptune before going Void. After it goes Void I will be cautious, but if, for example, my email pinged right now and it was someone of whom I had never heard inviting me to offer a lecture in London, I would feel encouraged and willing to open negotiations immediately. Were that email to come just a little bit later, after the Moon had gone Void, I would sense a significant probability that nothing would come of the invitation. In that case, I certainly would not respond until the Moon was in a more open-ended place.

HORARY VERSUS ELECTIONAL

Often in Horary astrology, we are looking for yes or no answers—will I get the job? Will Tyler agree to marry me? Horary is complicated, full of rules and procedures. I do not want to oversimplify it here. Suffice it to say that a significant element of horary astrology lies in simply seeing what the Moon's final disposition is before it leaves the sign it is in—the very thing we have been exploring. Generally, Void Moons and hard final aspects suggest a "no" answer, while final easy aspects or comfortable conjunctions suggest a "yes."

As I say, Horary is more complicated than that by far. If you would like to learn about that branch of astrology, I would recommend the three books that have been most helpful to me. Ivy Goldstein-Jacobson's *Simplified Horary Astrology*, Alphee Lavoie's *Lose This Book and Find It With Horary*, and Anthony Louis's monumental work, *Horary Astrology*.

As with most areas of astrology, Horary is a contentious field with many different traditions. These three books, especially the first two, have resonated best with my own experience. Anthony Louis's book is superb too, but he attempts to deal more evenhandedly with the various branches of the field. The result, a fabulous, full-spectrum introduction, leaves you better educated than either of the other two books—but with less of a sense of what to actually do. Louis now has a more streamlined edition titled *Horary Astrology Plain and Simple*.

Horary is always based on the *moment* the question arises—you set up the chart for that time and place. The minute a question arises in your mind, or the minute your client contacts you—that is the time you use. Unlike Electional astrology, you have no choice about the time. You take potluck on what the Moon is doing, along with everything else. Your answer is woven into the symbolism of that moment. You simply read the answer—and smile or weep. You have no power over it.

With Electional Astrology, you are in an entirely different situation. You have a span of days or even years ahead of you in which you can take your chosen action. You are trying to pick the "best chart" in that time frame in order to maximize the probability of getting what you want. Once again, the technical details are beyond the scope of this particular book. But they are essentially the same as those of Horary, except that your task is to choose an optimal chart rather than interpreting an existing one. If you have learned Horary, in other words, you are 90% of the way to mastering Electional, and *vice versa*.

Our cardinal point here is that in both Horary and Electional astrology, the often-ignored transiting Moon rules the roost. When it comes to the ever-shifting daily realities of life, the Moon is the hub of the wheel. The quality that makes the Moon's transits insignificant in long-term developmental astrology—their sheer speed—is what hands them the scepter as we analyze the shifting anatomy of minutes and hours. No book about the Moon could be considered complete without celebrating this extraordinarily efficacious and helpful element of lunar theory and practice.

PROOF IN THE PUDDING

When the first airplane hit the first of the Twin Towers in New York on September 11, 2001, I looked at the chart of that tragic event and quickly noticed that the Moon was Void of Course. It was in the last couple of degrees of Gemini. Its last aspect, a trine to Uranus, had been made many hours before.

The event was spectacular, horrendous, monstrous—choose your adjectives. But ask yourself one coldly critical question: Did the people who created this appalling incident actually realize their intended goals? Did it turn out the way they wanted? *Did it work for them?* In the short term, obviously the answer is yes: buildings and lives were destroyed. But many analysts, including Michael Scott Doran, professor of Near Eastern Studies at Princeton University and Senior Fellow at the Council on Foreign Relations, suggests that bin Ladin's actual aim was to turn the moderate elements of the Islamic world against the West, sparking pan-Islamic revolutions throughout the Middle East. But did war arise between all Islam and the Judeo-Christian cultures, as the perpetrators hoped? What actually came of the attacks? Is the Muslim world now unified against the West? Reading the news, it sometimes seems that way. But the reality is that only a minority of Muslims—and of Islamic nations—are radicalized. The Pew Global Attitudes Project survey of 2007 actually revealed a *decline* in Muslim support for terrorist violence. According to the report, "Overall, majorities in 15 of 16 Muslim publics surveyed say that suicide bombings can be rarely or never justified."

September 11th is a good illustration of the Void of Course Moon, *once you place yourself in the position of the people initiating the action.* And that is what must always be our focus. The buildings came down, but the intended results were not achieved. On a merrier note, a couple of generations ago, on the evening of February 9, 1964, the Beatles came over from England and played live on the Ed Sullivan show. This is commonly viewed as the beginning of "Beatlemania" in the United States We can presume that John, Paul, George and Ringo held intentions of success for their performance and their future in America. Presumably Ed Sullivan wanted big ratings. The Moon was in Capricorn that night, heading for a final sextile to Neptune in Scorpio—an easy aspect, suggesting that the Moon supported their intentions. And of course, as they say, "the rest is history."

By the way, when the band hit the stage that night, Venus was in the last degree of Pisces. A quick look at the chart might suggest that the Moon's last aspect would have been a sextile to Venus. The reality is that Venus crossed into Aries before the Moon could catch up with it. The Moon/Venus sextile did form—but only two days later with the Moon in Aquarius and Venus in Aries. In working with the Moon in this way, be wary of those kinds of situations. When the apparent last aspect is to a fast planet near the end of a sign, make sure it will still be there before the Moon moves into its next sign.

The Teflon President

Ronald Reagan was often described as the "Teflon President" because nothing would "stick" to him. The media was struck by his run of inexplicably good luck, but the best explanation they could come up with to explain it was to assert that he was coated in Teflon—a fine metaphor, but it really doesn't cast any light on the reality of the matter. When it came out in 1988 that Reagan was consulting astrologers, the media pilloried him for it—and ultimately decided to deflect blame onto his poor wife, Nancy. To my knowledge, no one outside the astrological world ever commented publically on the possibility that there might be a connection between Ronald Reagan's "Teflon coating" and his use of astrology.

I heard one of Reagan's astrologers, Joan Quigley, speak at a conference in San Francisco many years ago. She struck me as a decent person and a competent technical astrologer, albeit of a more predictive disposition than my own. A large chunk of what she did for Reagan is what I have been writing about in the last few pages.

Whatever you think of Ronald Reagan, it obviously worked for him.

Apollo 11

Let me complicate the picture a little further with a fourth illustration. The Apollo 11 mission, which allowed humans to set foot on another world for the first time, was launched from Cape Canaveral, Florida, on July 16, 1969 at 9:32 in the morning. The chart shows the Moon in mid-Leo, heading for a final square to Neptune—a hard aspect, suggesting a negative element in the picture.

Obviously, they made it! A simple look at the chart might have suggested the opposite—that they might, for example, have wound up "lost in space," Neptune-fashion. Did our techniques fail here? Let's dig a little deeper.

Please do recall that the Moon needs help from a planet to bring something into manifestation. That condition was indeed met here—the Moon was not Void of Course. When Apollo 11 launched, Neptune served that midwife purpose, albeit via a square. The intention might still be realized, but some problem would be encountered, some price exacted.

Had I seen that chart on the morning of the launch, I would have been nervous for those men. I would not have chosen such a chart for the mission. Catastrophic outcomes were certainly possible, but years of experience have taught me to consider less dramatic possibilities as well. All I would have known for certain was that *something of an afflictive Neptunian nature* was almost certain to make itself felt in the unfolding storyline.

The intention was obviously to land on the surface of the Moon and then get home again in one piece. That aim was realized successfully. But the details of Apollo 11's lunar landing are instructive. See if you can detect Neptune's woozy signature in what follows.

As the two astronauts began their descent to the surface of the Moon, they quickly saw that they were passing over the prescribed lunar landmarks four seconds ahead of schedule. At those speeds, that four second error was a big deal. It meant that they would land *miles* west of where they intended—on uncertain, dangerous, boulder-strewn terrain, far beyond the smooth plain for which they were aiming.

On top of that problem, while descending and still over a mile above the lunar surface, the navigation and guidance computers started sending out alarms. Remember, these computers were on about the level of the earliest 1980s consumer computers, barely functional by today's standards. The alarms meant that the machines were overloading and that certain critical calculations had to be postponed.

Postponed?

They were *one mile* above the surface of the Moon, and already running low on fuel!

Later, it was discovered that part of this problem stemmed from how the astronauts had been trained. Oops.

The lunar lander was still heading down, riding a column of flame. With the computers gone crazy and a frighteningly rocky landing zone looming ahead, Neil Armstrong improvised. He took over from the computers and just *flew* that fragile machine down by the seat of his pants. With his partner, Buzz Aldrin, calling out numbers—their speed and their altitude—and their fuel running out, Armstrong brought the *Eagle* safely to rest on the surface of the Moon.

When he shut down the engine, they were miles from their targeted landing place and they had *25 seconds* of fuel left.

They made it! But do you feel the fingerprint of the Moon squaring Neptune in that story? Without the cool heroism of those two courageous men, Apollo 11 would have come to a tragic end.

As we saw earlier, there is more to Horary and Electional astrology than simply learning to pay attention to the Moon's position. Apollo 11 was launched under a "bad" chart and the mission succeeded anyway. That is both astrological and historical reality. And yet in the light of how the story unfolded, who could doubt the eloquent relevance of that final lunar square to Neptune?

I like this Apollo 11 story very much. Beyond the obvious reasons for appreciating the way it turned out, there is one critical, concrete point I would like to underscore—it was the *quality of consciousness* in Armstrong and Aldrin that tipped the scales away from tragedy. There is, in my opinion, too much passive fatalism in astrology. That is especially true of older forms of the art, such as Horary and Electional. But we humans are not so powerless. As these two heroes demonstrate, the magical power of will interacts vigorously with every astrological configuration. In lesser human beings than Armstrong and Aldrin, the more fatalistic interpretation could very easily have come true. They could have gone down like deer in the Neptunian headlights. That they avoided such a tragedy is not a triumph of will over the planets. It is a demonstration of how the wild cards of human self-awareness, courage, and innovation interact unpredictably with the multidimensional archetypal fields of astrological possibility.

THE BONES OF THE MATTER

If I buy a lottery ticket under a favorable Moon, I am still probably not going to win. But if I ever won a lottery, I would be very surprised if it did not turn out that I had indeed bought the ticket at a "lucky" Moon moment.

The common sense in those two sentences is really the essence of the matter. You cannot control the future with astrology—or anything else. But by living in harmony with the natural cycles of the Moon, you can tilt the table in your direction.

In so doing, are you messing with your karma? Dabbling at the edges of the Dark Side of the Force? Or are you simply opening up spiritually and psychically to a larger world, one dominated by Mother Moon, who just loves it when you are happy and feeling good?

I am betting my karma on the second possibility.

PART TWO:

LUNAR PHASE

5

HOW MANY PHASES?

In a never-ending circle, the Moon cycles continuously through its phases. Like any circle, it has no natural divisions, no beginning or end. Arbitrarily, we usually choose to think of the New Moon as the start of the cycle. That is the darkness out which the visible phases emerge and grow, so calling it the point of initiation makes intuitive sense. But the Moon is dark for about three nights. Should we start the cycle when the Moon first disappears, or do we wait another day and a half for the more precise (and more abstract) moment of the true Sun-Moon conjunction? Or should we start the cycle when we get our first peek at the "new" waxing crescent Moon? Any one of those three answers could make sense, even though they are very different.

What is a "lunar phase," anyway? Where does one stop and another start? In its organic reality, the Moon's cycle is just a seamless circle. All our systems of phase division are human inventions. In a very real sense, the Moon is in a different phase every millisecond.

If you have ever had the joy of gazing at the Moon at a high magnification with a good astronomical telescope, you will know that if you are patient, you can actually watch Earth's shadow, called the *terminator*, moving across the lunar landscape, slowly revealing more mountains, plains and craters. That, of course, is what creates the phases however we define them. Physically, at the Moon's equator the terminator advances at about 9.6 miles per hour—about the pace of an enthusiastic jogger. In a couple of weeks, it reveals the whole disk of the Moon, and in a couple more, it erases the Moon from the sky. Bottom line, it is one continuous sweep, and again any human attempt to divide the process into "phases" is simply a projection of the human mind.

In this book, we will be exploring a system of dividing the lunar cycle into eight phases. Other systems exist, and we will consider them briefly in the next few pages. If someone presented a system of 1,728 phases, I would be nervous about how cumbersome it would have to be, but I would have no reason to doubt that it could work. The key here is to realize that phases have at least as much to do with human consciousness as they have to do with anything objectively intrinsic to the Moon itself.

When I began the thinking and research that led me to write this book, I was not able to find an existing system of phase division that resonated consistently with my heart and my mind. Dane Rudhyar's eight-phase system came the closest, and I am building my system on his chassis. But as you will see, my understanding of it is substantially different from his. Before I got there, I explored a number of . . .

BLIND ALLEYS

A few lines ago, I brought up a system of 1,728 phases. The number is not random. It is 12 times 12 times 12. Given the centrality of the number 12 in astrology, such a system would have a certain inherent credibility. Ditto for a system of 144 phases (12 squared). Or very simply, why not a system of 12 phases corresponding to the signs of the zodiac?

That is where I started. In my despair at not being able to find an existing system of phase division that grabbed me, I experimented. A twelve-phase system seemed plausible. Why not imagine an "Aries phase," followed by a "Taurus phase," and so on?

But where to begin? What sign of the zodiac would correspond to the New Moon?

The New Moon starts the lunar cycle, and conventionally we think of Aries as the first sign of the zodiac. But making Aries the sign of the New Moon did not feel right at all. The New Moon is subtle and invisible, while Aries is fiery and in your face. So Cancer, maybe, since it is quiet and internal and the Moon rules it? Or Capricorn, since it relates to the dark of winter, which might resonate naturally with the Dark of the Moon? Those two seemed like good ideas—better, at least, than trying to make Aries correspond to the New Moon.

I tried them both. They failed. While you can make almost anything "work" in astrology if you want it badly enough, that kind of wishful thinking and the resulting self-deception have been the bane of the craft for centuries. Long ago I learned that whenever something begins to feel forced, I should trust my guts and abandon it. That is what happened with my attempts to start a cycle of 12 phases with Capricorn or Cancer.

Busteed, Tiffany, and Wergin, about whom you will soon learn more, in their book, *Phases of the Moon*, chose 0° Pisces to correspond to the New Moon. They had their reasons, but that idea felt uncomfortable to me. The "four corners" of astrology have generally been taken to be the Cardinal signs—Aries, Cancer, Libra, and Capricorn—and it seemed to me they should line up with the obvious four corners of the lunar cycle: the New Moon, the Full and the two Quarters. But I wasn't having any luck, so I tried their Pisces-based system too. More about that below, but again, the bottom line is that it just did not work well for me either.

Eventually, I tried lining up the twelve-sign roulette wheel in, literally, a dozen different ways. No matter what I did, I just could not make it fly. I had lunar notes on about a hundred people I knew well and personally, as well as AstroDataBank and its countless charts of famous people. I would come up with a hypothesis for what a certain sign-to-phase correspondence should mean. And it would crash and burn in the face of the human realities.

Thus for me, the appealing idea that there are 12 lunar phases corresponding to the12 signs turned out to be a blind alley. I followed it, got lost, and eventually gave it up. Such a system may work for someone else—a system of 17 phases may work for someone else, for that matter. But I was looking for that loud, unmistakable click in my heart, and it just was not happening with a 12-phase system.

RETURNING TO THE SENSES

I took another blind alley, one that my own biases made it very difficult to escape. To the eye, the Moon appears to be Full for about three nights. Similarly, it vanishes from the sky for about three nights. Those are not rigid principles, just mainstream visual experiences. Most of the existing systems of phase division started the cycle at the instant of the New Moon, which is to say when both Sun and Moon were aligned in the same degree, minute and second of a sign. The result is that half of the actual period of the Dark of the Moon would be in one phase, leading up to the conjunction. The other half would be in another phase. I didn't like that. I believe that astrologers don't spend enough time looking at the sky. I believe we should return to our natural, sensory relationship with the heavens, and that our eyes and hearts will never lie to us.

Feel the pulpit materializing around me?

I was totally wrong. I spent a long time trying to make the New Moon into the literal Dark of the Moon, the time when we genuinely cannot see the Moon. And, by the same logic, I tried viewing the Full Moon as the period of time when it looked Full—the three days or so centered on the moment of the technical Sun-Moon opposition.

And I got nowhere.

My list of a hundred friends kept making a liar out of me. Paraphrasing the Talking Heads, the facts didn't do what I wanted them to. I am now convinced that the lunar phases start at the true Sun-Moon conjunction and that the period just before that actual alignment represents a very different energy than the time just after it, even though visually they are indistinguishable.

On my way to formulating the system that I present later in this book, I had one more cherished attachment to release . . .

WILLIAM BUTLER YEATS

Ask me about my favorite poet and, after I roll my eyes at the impossibility of the question, my reflex for 40 years has been to say William Butler Yeats. Most of us have heard of him and read some of his work in school. How many people know that he wrote an astrology book? Called *A Vision*, it is a dense, profoundly weird piece of work about the phases of the Moon. Because I love Yeats, I really wanted to make his theories work for me.

The poet married Georgie Hyde-Lees in the autumn of 1917. "On the afternoon of October 24th 1917, four days after my marriage, my wife surprised me by attempting automatic writing. What came in disjointed sentences, in almost illegible writing, was so exciting, sometimes so profound, that I persuaded her to give an hour or two day after day to the unknown writer . . ."

What emerged over the next several years was an exceedingly elaborate system of lunar phase interpretation. It was based on a division of the lunar cycle into 28 phases. *A Vision* was published in 1926 and received no reviews and sold very few copies. By then, Yeats was a respected figure on the world literary stage. His foray into occultism was politely ignored.

To give you a taste of the work, I have opened my copy of *A Vision* at random. I quote: "Because his Creative Mind is at Phase 7, where instinctive life, all but reaching utmost complexity, suffers an external abstract synthesis, his Body of Fate, which drives him to intellectual life, at Phase 21; his Will at a phase of revolt from every intellectual summary, from all intellectual abstraction, this delight is not mere delight, he would construct a whole, but that whole must seem all event, all picture."

This is not beach reading.

I do not mean to make fun of it. As feat of cerebral acrobatics, *A Vision* ranks with the crystalline spheres of the pre-Copernican astronomers. There is an astonishingly consistent array of internal cross-references within the system it presents. And it is laced with truly profound insights into human personality types.

The exceedingly dense literary style was obviously an obstacle to its wider acceptance. I doubt Yeats gave a damn about that. He was an active occultist of the old school, with much affinity for secrecy and degrees of initiation and doctrines only made available to people who had demonstrated certain attainments. He was not interested in popularizing this material.

There was another problem. Even though the system in *A Vision* is clearly about the phases of the Moon, the book never actually defines them rigorously. What, exactly, does Yeats mean by the New Moon? Does it start with the conjunction or with the Moon's disappearance into darkness? Yeats never tells us. Vexingly, he gives living examples of people who illustrate each of the phases. For Phase 19, for example, he lists, "Gabriele d'Annunzio (perhaps), Oscar Wilde, Byron, a certain actress." Trouble is, these illustrations have nothing to do with the actual lunar phase under which these people were born! They just seem to have struck the right illustrative note in Yeats's mind.

Then there is the problem with the number 28. It is obviously a wonderful number for this kind of thing: 4 times 7. It divides each quarter of the Moon's cycle neatly into a week. It gives 14 days between New Moon and Full. The problem is that the actual cycle of the Moon's phases is 29 days, 12 hours, 44 minutes, and 2.8 seconds. Twenty-eight days is nothing more than a convenient fiction. Dividing the actual length of the lunar phase cycle into 28 equal parts makes each one about an hour and 19 minutes longer than a day. Each phase would then be 12.86° wide. Is that what Yeats intended us to do? And, again, where do we start the wheel turning? Is *A Vision* even fairly considered to be work of astrology? If so, it is a very incomplete one. Astrology, in essence, is a system of correspondences between celestial conditions and human ones. If the exact celestial conditions are not defined, we have not fully entered the astrological realm. We are left instead with some tantalizingly elegant lines of Yeats's poetry, alluding to an astrology that we can feel but not understand . . .

> *Hunchback and Saint and Fool are the last crescents.*
> *The burning bow that once could shoot an arrow*
> *Out of the up and down, the wagon-wheel*
> *Of beauty's cruelty and wisdom's chatter—*
> *Out of that raving tide—is drawn betwixt*
> *Deformity of body and of mind.*

Yeats himself seemed to sense that his book might take a while to find an understanding audience. He wrote, "*A Vision* reminds me of the stones I used to drop as a child into a certain very deep well. The splash is very far off and very faint."

It took 48 years for that first echo to arrive.

BUSTEED, TIFFANY AND WERGIN

In 1974, Shambhala published *Phases of the Moon* by Marilyn Busteed, Richard Tiffany, and Dorothy Wergin. Their work is solidly and avowedly based on Yeats. But they made two critical contributions. First, they clarified the intellectual system behind *A Vision*. Without dumbing it down (or oversimplifying it), they expressed it in far less opaque language. Second, they came up with a system for defining Yeats's lunar phases in terms that are precise enough for practical astrological use. What these three authors did was to make a bold and somewhat counterintuitive move. Instead of dividing the lunar cycle into 28 equal phases, they created a system of four big phases of 30 degrees width and 24 smaller phases of 10 degrees. The four big phases fall at the New Moon, the First Quarter, the Full Moon, and the Last Quarter, beginning with the 0° conjunction of Sun and Moon. Similarly, their other big phases begin at 90, 180°, and 270° of separation between Sun and Moon.

As I mentioned earlier, Busteed, Tiffany and Wergin make Pisces correspond to the New Moon-all 30° of it. Aries, which comes next, embraces three of their smaller 10° phases, as does Taurus. Coming to Gemini, we are at First Quarter and so another full 30° phase. And so on around the circle. Thus, it is the Mutable signs—Pisces, Gemini, Virgo, and Sagittarius—which frame this system. They are the signs that "turn the wheel," so to speak.

All systems of lunar phase division agree on the salient importance of the Moon's four main, obvious faces: New, Full, and the two Quarters. It makes a kind of sense to give these major phases extra scope. And the system that Busteed, Tiffany and Wergin created does allow us to relate Yeats's lunar cosmology directly and comfortably to the heavens, without dealing with "days" that are 25 hours 19 minutes long. And thus we can at least actually test it and see if it speaks to us. Let me introduce you to a man who did that.

MARTIN GOLDSMITH

In 1988, Whitford Press published Martin Goldsmith's *Moon Phases: A Symbolic Key*. In this relatively little-known work, Goldsmith builds on the Busteed, Tiffany and Wergin system. One of his great strengths is research. He and his brother Ken have amassed a data base of 10,000 charts, and they test their hypotheses systematically against them. If a theory does not pass the reality test, they dump it. Goldsmith corroborated much of the Busteed, Tiffany and Wergin system, and where it did not seem to be working, he let the data and his own intuitive abilities as an astrologer correct the perceived errors.

Furthermore, Martin Goldsmith writes lucidly and with a human touch. He is scholarly, but not fussy. For each of the 28 phases, he created an evocative image: The Trickster, The Warrior Princess, the Wise Serpent. He provides two or three dozen living examples for each phase—people who actually have it in their charts. He proves, to me at least, that Mr. and Mrs. Yeats had connected with something very real in their otherworldly way. If you find this system attractive, hunt for Martin Goldsmith's book. It is a gem.

But this book I am writing is not about the system in *A Vision*. That system is the real deal, but I found myself uncomfortable with the arbitrary use of 30° and 10° phases. It felt forced. And while I could relate to the interpretations, especially the ones in the Goldsmith book, I was not bowled over by them.

A BRIEF REFLECTION

The Moon's reality is the reality of dreams. In the dream reality, you can fly. You can be two places at once. And even when you awaken and remember your dream state, that dream might be susceptible to half a dozen different interpretations, all of which are true. Similarly, we can divide the mysterious cycle of the Moon's phases in many different ways, all of which can be meaningful.

But some are more meaningful than others. I got closer to what I felt to be the heart of the matter when I returned to the work of . . .

DANE RUDHYAR

Toward the end of World War II, the great Dane Rudhyar published a book he had entitled *The Lunation Birthday*. Due to a misunderstanding with his publisher, it was released under a title of which Rudhyar heartily disapproved, *The Moon: The Cycles and Fortunes of Life*. It sold a thousand copies and disappeared. In 1967, he published a greatly expanded and reconsidered version of similar material under the title *The Lunation Cycle*. It is a luminous, seminal piece of work, still blessedly in print two generations later.

A point that Rudhyar pounds home wisely and relentlessly is that the "phases of the moon tell us nothing about the moon herself, or the position of the moon in the sky. They refer only to the state of relationship between the sun and the moon . . . what changes is the solar-lunar relationship, rather than the moon. The moon only reflects in her appearance to us the changes in the relationship."

Writing when he did and being a product of the times in which he lived, Dane Rudhyar unabashedly connects the Moon with women and the Sun with men—a gross oversimplification from today's point of view. He writes words with which I personally disagree (and which could get him tarred and feathered nowadays) such as, "Likewise woman, when closely identified with a man, normally reflects the spiritual-mental character . . . of him who fecundates her body and her psyche."

Yikes.

Two generations pass, and the world is a very different place. Still, Dane Rudhyar's *The Lunation Cycle* is a magnificent piece of astrological thinking. Much of my understanding of the phases of the Moon stands on the foundation he built. I will be quoting him at times in the following pages. To me, Rudhyar's great gift was the idea of there being eight lunar phases, each one 45° wide. That resonated with me. When I divided my list of a hundred friends up in that fashion, something felt right— at last these eight groups had a certain emotional, affective cohesion. I had given up on 28 phases. I had given up on 12. I found a home with eight—and, as you will soon see, with the numbers two and four which lead up to it.

Still, despite my gratitude for and enthusiasm about Rudhyar's approach, his actual descriptions of the eight phases were brief at best. They left me hungry. There was clearly something right about them—and equally clearly, something was missing. I began to wonder if there might be some other tradition of eight phases somewhere, something which that might cast a different light on the questions, and add a richness to the mix beyond what one person could be expected to provide.

It turned out to be right under my nose.

THE PAGAN CALENDAR

I have been immersed in Celtic and Nordic mythology for many years. Jodie's Nordic-Celtic historical fantasy trilogy, whose first book is *The Rhymer and the Ravens*, inspired me to write a couple of rock operas based on the trilogy's storyline. We sprouted a band, dancers, another band—really, a community around the projects, which went on for fifteen years or so. See this MySpace site if you are interested in them: http://www.myspace.com/dragonshipmusic. The real point is that these mythic and pagan traditions supplied the perspective I had been seeking.

I knew them and I knew astrology. I just needed to make the connection. Like most traditional cultures, the pre-Christian northern Europeans, Britons, and Irish celebrated the Solstices and the Equinoxes, which mark the four seasons. They also celebrated four "cross-quarter days," midway between each Solstice and Equinox. Thus, the traditional pagan calendar was built around an endlessly-repeating cycle of eight holidays spread evenly throughout the year. We still celebrate many of them in various disguises—Halloween and May Day are two obvious examples. Each holiday had its own unique flavor and meaning. And for millennia my own ancestors—and maybe yours as well—were immersed in creating the very thing for which I was searching: a progressive cycle composed of eight phases and based on the natural astronomical rhythms of the Earth.

Merrily, a compelling and obvious way to connect the yearly cycle of pagan holidays with the monthly lunation cycle practically leapt out. No more wondering what sign might connect with the New Moon. The Dark of the Moon would relate naturally to the darkest, longest night of the year: the Winter Solstice, known to our Celtic forebears as Yule. How could it be otherwise? That key insight was utterly obvious. All I had to realize was that an eight-phase *yearly* cycle might resonate naturally with an eight-phase *monthly* one.

Merging Dane Rudhyar's eight-phase system with the pagan holidays, and reflecting on, experimenting with and tweaking it in the light of my list of a hundred friends and a similar list of famous or notorious people triggered most of the understandings that I will present in the next several chapters.

6

☽

THE MYSTERY OF ONE

At the risk of sounding as obscure as William Butler Yeats in his book *A Vision*, our journey toward an understanding of the eight lunar phases begins with an immersion in the Mystery of One, proceeds through a contemplation of two interlacing Mysteries of Two, leads from there to a meditation on the Mystery of Four, before finally arriving at the Mystery of Eight.

Translation:

We must begin with an appreciation of the underlying unity and inseparability of the entire cycle of lunar phases. That is the "Mystery of One." This will entail facing some of the blinding cultural biases which, in my estimation, have prevented lunar phase from being integrated effectively into modern astrological practice. That is the subject of this present chapter.

Chapter Seven, called "Two Mysteries of Two," is a consideration of two separate *dualistic* perspectives on the lunar cycle. The first is the critical distinction between a waxing and a waning Moon in the natal chart. The second, equally telling, is the distinction between the darker and brighter halves of the lunar cycle—the one dominated by the Dark of the Moon and the one illuminated by the Full Moon.

Blending those two dualities leads us to Chapter Eight, "The Mystery of Four." There, we study the four quadrants of lunar phase created when we superimpose waxing and waning upon dark and bright. These are: New waxing to First Quarter; First Quarter waxing to Full; the waning of the Full phase down to the Last Quarter; and Last Quarter being re-absorbed down into the Dark of the Moon. The effect on the human psyche of lunar placement in any of these four quadrants is dramatic, useful in practical astrology, and easily verified. The quarters exist in relationship to the eight lunar phases in the same way that the four Elements of classical astrology relate to the twelve zodiacal signs. As Fire, Earth, Air and Water are the foundation of the zodiac, the four quadrants are the foundation of lunar phase theory.

Finally in Chapter Nine, "The Mystery of Eight," we come to the practical heart of the system: a detailed consideration of our eight-phase system. It is there that we will fully explore the yearly pagan cycle before launching into eight more chapters detailing each one of the phases.

A natural temptation might arise just to get to the heart of the matter by cutting ahead to the chapter about your personal phase. If your interest in astrology is casual, that would not be the end of the world. But I encourage you to watch the story develop through the mysteries of one and two and four. I suggest doing that partly because it will vastly enrich your understanding of the eight phases. I also encourage it because, as I believe you will soon see, there is much material of utterly practical astrological relevance in the earlier chapters. Knowledge of the four quadrants is every bit as profound as phase information—in practice, I often find myself paying more attention to quadrant than to phase. Even knowing simply whether a person was born under the waxing Moon or the waning one reveals a great deal of information about him or her. That kind of material will be implicit in the material about the eight phases, but I believe you will find reading about it explicitly to be helpful.

UNITY

Two philosophers are discussing cause and effect and how it might relate to fate and free will. A third person interrupts the conversation saying, "Yes, but if Time itself does not exist, none of those questions matter anyway."

Comments like that are show-stoppers. What can you say? Maybe at some ultimate level, time really is an illusion. And then almost everything we think and believe about how life works collapses. There is something deep inside us all—something distinctly *lunar*—which can sense the possibility of a timeless "Eternity." That means an Eternity that has more in common with the word "now" than with the notion of "a very, very, very long time." But how do we wrap our minds around such an idea? How do we think deeply about our human experience without including the common sense notions of cause-and-effect, consequences, development—the passage of time?

Those two philosophers discussing cause and effect were engaged and alive. Their conversation was contributing to the growth of their wisdom. Their friend might have made a valid point, but it stopped their discussion. And maybe their friend was not so much wise as intellectually lazy, just wanting them to stop stressing her with big, complicated thoughts. She knew how to shut them up.

Or, just possibly, she was a Bodhisattva.

Buddhism is full of references to *ultimate truths* and *relative truths*. It is a helpful distinction. Ultimate truths cannot be perceived by the intellect. They can only be witnessed—although even that word is wrong—by the advanced mystical mind. Relative truths are what allow the rest of us to talk. They let us put a conceptual handle on the world. Time is a relative truth. The separate "I" is a relative truth. So are Right and Wrong. Subject and Object. Evolved and Unevolved. Body and Mind. Me and You.

But it is the Moon in us all—what we might call the *intuition*—that naturally resonates with the ultimate truths of life. In the first chapter, we saw how Tuesday might be the day after Wednesday in a dream, and in the dream state, that does not bother us. It is only morning's waking light that leaves us scratching our heads. The Moon is not burdened by the need to think or to understand in linear fashion. It can simply *feel* these ultimate truths and be content.

A fundamental perspective in Buddhism is that nothing is ultimately separate from anything else—you and me, yesterday and tomorrow, mind and reality. Everything arises out of other things and disappears into other things, and therefore nothing has any separate or inherent reality. Oneness—or a primal zero-ness—is the ultimate truth of the universe. Who can understand this, at least in the solid, comprehensible way that we understand that two plus two equals four? Yet the Moon in us all sits easily with it. Could anything be more precious? Or mysterious?

In my zeal to create a system of lunar understanding with two parts—or four or eight or 28—I want to be careful not to sacrifice this fundamental lunar unity.

ENTER THE PAGANS

Not only Buddhists feel the underlying unity of all things. It is a very common belief among most so-called primitive people. Since in this book I will be borrowing from the early cultures of Europe, I will use them as an illustration. Ralph Metzner, in his 1994 Shambhala book, *The Well of Remembrance: Rediscovering the Earth Wisdom Myths of Northern Europe*, writes:

> "The gods and goddesses of the pre-Christian European pantheon were conceived as great spiritual and powerful beings, associated with the primordial forces of nature, including earth, sky, sea, mountains, sun, moon, winds, and thunder, with whom human beings could and did communicate and interact through prayer, ritual, and sacrifice . . . One could characterize this worldview as animistic, pantheistic, and shamanistic. *Animism* is the term used by anthropologists to describe a view in which all forms of life and all natural phenomena are seen as animated by vital force and sentience . . . In such a world view, the distinction we now make between animate and inanimate matter is meaningless. Everything is alive and sentient, and human beings occupy no privileged or uniquely superior position."

One can of course easily discover similar attitudes in other societies. Native Americans, for one obvious example, were completely nonplused by the utilitarian European attitude toward the land and the animals. The white man seemed to have no sense of unity. Incomprehensibly, he seemed to believe he could *buy or sell the land!* He seemed to have lost touch with his Moon.

Astrologers are always conditioned by the underlying views and attitudes of their cultures. It must be that way or we couldn't help anyone, simply because we would not speak the same language. In the last chapter, we encountered gender attitudes in Dane Rudhyar, writing just two generations ago, that would today brand him old-fashioned at best and sexist at worst. No one is immune—I smile to think of someone reading this present book 50 years from now, thinking how quaint some of Steven Forrest's attitudes are!

One thesis in this work is that our collective inability as astrologers to integrate lunar phase into our practice derives from a blindness to its real meaning—a blindness created by cultural biases. It is time for me to be specific about those biases. To my mind, there are two confusions that have created this problem, now dissipating as a result of cultural evolution.

The first bias is the culturally-pervasive tendency to equate darkness with evil and danger, while equating light with goodness and safety.

The second is a bias suggesting that disembodied heaven is better than fleshly manifestation—which is to say, that the world and the body are bad, and that transcendence is good. Another way to frame this second bias is to claim that Hell is right here beneath our feet in the body of the Earth—and Heaven is elsewhere.

The first bias has prevented us from understanding the light-dark cycle of the Moon's phases. The second has blocked our understanding of the waxing and waning phases. We will dismantle them one at a time.

LIGHT AND DARK

"The latest economic forecast is dark. Investors are in a black mood. Many blame benighted governmental policies and expect a long, cold winter before we see any the light at the end of the tunnel."

As members of Western civilization, none of us would have any difficulty divining the sense and intention of that statement. In our underlying storehouse of poetic metaphor, we all know what darkness connotes. It is *bad*.

"Things are looking a lot sunnier lately for Larry. He stopped seeing what's-her-name, that gloomy woman. He's with Jane again—and it was a dark day when he left her in the first place. He's been under a black cloud ever since. I've always thought that Jane was just such a luminous person, the way she brightens up a room. That other one could leach the light out of a sunny day. Larry says that prospects are glowing in his business too—definitely a new day there. It just makes me want to beam—I love Larry and it's good to see him getting past his dark night of the soul and finally seeing some light at the end of the tunnel." Ditto. Any trouble translating?

This linguistic bias pervades our culture. Inevitably, it adds a subliminal message whenever words such as "light" and "dark" come up. In the gospel of John, Jesus declares, "I am the *Light* of the World." In the Old Testament Book of Daniel, we read "The Ancient of Days did sit, whose garment was *white as snow* . . ." Today, a lot of the emails I receive are signed with variations on "Love and Light." The Vajrayana Buddhists encourage us to embrace the Clear *Light*. We have Black Magic versus White Magic. The darkest hour. The darkness before the dawn. The Dark Side of the Force.

It goes on and on. The usual patterns of Caucasian and Asian racial prejudice are an obvious correlate—not to mention their success at marketing some of those poisonous attitudes in darker-skinned third world economies.

Our pan-human *love of light* is natural: in the light, we can *see*. That is a great comfort to us! Darkness can be scary. The point here is not that we should abandon thinking of light as good. The point is that to understand the phases of the Moon, we must lose our bias against darkness. We need to love it, too. And please note that when I say "darkness" here, I do not mean evil. I simply mean the absence of light.

Which do you actually prefer, night or day? Many of us would view the choice as so forced and silly as to be beneath our contempt. Night is lovely. So is day. Who would want a world with only one of them? .Many of us are ambivalent about getting up in the morning, but almost everyone looks forward to turning out the lights and going to bed at night. Stress dissipates; the dream-world calls. We can relax. Few of us have, in other words, lost our natural appreciation for the dark. We just trip over cultural biases when we speak of it. It was not always that way. Quoting Ralph Metzner again:

"A striking reversal of symbolic value occurs in the meanings associated with the colors white and black. In the Goddess-worshiping farming communities of Old Europe and the Mediterranean, black is the color of the richly fertile earth, which brings forth new vegetative growth and nourishment. Residues of the black Earth-goddess appear in the imagery of the Black Madonna, or Black Virgin, of which over five hundred examples can be found in Christian churches all over Europe, testifying to her persistence."

Sacred blackness! This is not some exotic, politically-correct concept. Close your eyes. It is dark in there. And yet many of us close our eyes to meditate or to pray. We *seek* that deep blackness. Blackness, in some ways, is our most direct experience of the Divine. When we have a big decision to make, we often "sleep on it." Lying in bed, eyes closed, but insomniac with hyperactive thoughts about our decision, we actually often work through things—in fact, our cultural tendency to pathologize "insomnia" is one more manifestation of the bias we are considering. We have demonized the dark and the night, but spending some time lying there consciously in both inner and outer darkness is a primary support for human *sanity*. Perhaps we descend into sleep, only to emerge in the morning with an answer to whatever question was plaguing us. How can we explain that gift, except through a reference to the grace of the nurturing, fertile dark?

For two weeks out of each month, the Moon is less than half illuminated. That means that the Moon is closer to the Sun too—it has not yet swung out to 90° from the Sun or it has swung back through the Last Quarter phase to within 90° of the Sun again. All that is true in the sky as well as in the astrological chart, which means the Moon is pretty close to the Sun. In those darker phases, the Moon is not only smaller and less bright. It is also simply below the horizon for more of the time. Another way to say it is that it is not only right around the New Moon that we see no Moon in the sky. Even when the Moon is in "half" phase, it is only visible in the sky for half the night, rising (Last Quarter) or setting (First Quarter) around midnight. That is because it is staying close to the Sun, so when the Sun is below the horizon, there is a good chance the Moon might be there too—invisible, in other words.

We will explore the specific human meaning of these darker phases—and the brighter ones—in the next chapter. Suffice it here to say that only by embracing "the Dark" with the same enthusiasm we naturally feel for "the Light," can we understand the Moon's natural cycle of dark and light. Everything is born out of darkness, then moves into the light of physical manifestation, then back into darkness again. This is a basic principle of reality, light years beyond anyone's philosophy. We are literally born into light, emerging from the darkness of the womb. The delightful Spanish phrase for giving birth is *dar a luz*—literally, to give to light. And is the mother giving the child to the light of day, or giving light to the child?

But the life-cycle has another turn: all of us are called back into the sweet darkness at the ends of our lives. And of course black is color of funerals and of mourning.

Do we need to demonize death and project terror onto it? Certainly that is exactly what we do in our darkness-fearing society. But maybe we can be like Van Morrison, and sing, "When that fog horn blows I will be coming home. And when that fog horn blows, I want to hear it. I don't have to fear it."

These are vast subjects. We will explore their practical applications in the next chapter. Just to put it very simply, *the cultural poison we have absorbed is the idea that darkness is bad and light is good. The remedy is the understanding that the inward, invisible realms must naturally come into manifestation, then all things must return home.* There is no "darkness" in the sense of evil and dread; there is only the sweet darkness in the sense of the birth-womb from which we all emerge and the death-womb to which we all return.

The system may be fierce, but it is one precious, integrated whole.

WAXING AND WANING

To our Paleolithic forebears living close to nature thousands of years ago, the Dark of the Moon would have been a pressing fact of life. A human being, for example, might feel a need to step outside the cave in the middle of the night. Scary! Venturing into pitch black darkness lit only by the feeble light of the stars, into a world inhabited by large and stealthy predators, would be an entirely different experience than stepping into the comforting moonlight. With the Moon in the sky, at least *one could see.* It is a matter of record that the Aurignacian culture in the Dordogne region of what is now France had a lunar calendar showing the Moon's phases—cycles of 29 scratches etched in bone. Humans have felt engaged with the Moon cycle since the beginning of our history.

Feel this ancient time with me again. It is not difficult. All of this primordial ancestral experience has sunk like a stone into the collective unconscious—the realm of eternal archetypes. Close your eyes and you are there . . .

. . . *out of the sheer blackness of the Dark of the Moon, there appears a brilliant crescent of light. It does not last long; the Sun sets, and the crescent Moon quickly follows it down. We are plunged again into pitch darkness. But there was a ray of hope, at least. And the next evening, the Moon is a little bigger, a little brighter, and a little higher in the night sky. It illuminates the landscape almost an hour longer. And on the third night all those pleasant qualities further increase. You can almost feel the exuberance mounting as the Moon waxes toward the brilliant, all-night comfort of the Full Moon.*

But then the process reverses.

That Full Moon, still brilliant and long-lasting, is a little diminished. And more so the next night. We can feel where this process is heading. Each night will be incrementally darker until we plunge again into the absolute blackness of Moonless night . . .

Don't think about the geometry of aspects. Forget astronomy. Put no solar wall of intellect and cognition between yourself and this monthly phenomenon. Just feel it. If you succeed in that, every cell in your body will understand the distinction between the exuberance and hope of the waxing part of the lunar cycle and the more reflective, mature, poignant spirit of the waning cycle.

In the next chapter, we will explore the particularities of the personal and psychological significance of being born under the waxing or the waning Moon. Here we reflect upon it more philosophically and broadly. Doing so, we quickly run into a wall of cultural blindness every bit as thick as the one we encountered with light and dark.

HOW WE LOST THE WAXING MOON

"In the beginning God created the heavens and the earth. The earth was without form and void . . . and God said, let there be light!" These familiar words from Genesis are echoed, before and after, in a multitude of spiritual and metaphysical traditions. They reflect the almost universal theological notion that the world we see arises from a pre-existing condition of emptiness. The religious formulas vary, but they all say virtually the same thing. Out of the darkness, light. Out of the mental plane, the world of manifestation. Out of *nirmanakaya, sambhogakaya.* Out of energy, matter. Out of the dimensionless singularity of the Big Bang bursts the universe of atoms and galaxies. The building was once a dream in the architect's head.

Many of these mythic constructs also assume a reversal of the process. The elaborate Hindu system of long Ages, or *Yugas*, is followed by the "night of Brahma." Or consider the Christian notion of the Apocalypse and the End of Days—unlike the Hindu version, that Judeo-Christian one does not come packaged with a rebirth. As we mentioned earlier, the jury of modern physicists and cosmologists is still out—some postulate an eternally-expanding universe, post Big Bang. Others assume it reaches a point of maximum expansion, then recedes back into a singularity, only to explode again. The latter view is remarkably like the ancient Hindu version—and of course echoes the Moon cycle *con brio*.

It is easy to imagine that our foremothers and forefathers came to this primary metaphysical formula inspired by the Moon's cycle of phases. Every month the Moon disappears. And then, like a miracle, the Crescent Moon emerges from the darkness, renewed. And it grows into the fullness of manifestation, then wanes down back into the darkness. Out of darkness, light. Out of light, darkness. Literally. There is the basic cosmological template, built right into the lunar rhythm.

A strong and obvious parallel can be drawn with a woman becoming pregnant. At first, like the Dark of the Moon, there is no evidence of her condition. But then she begins to "wax." After a while comes the critical moment of birth, when the infant emerges from the darkness into the light of the world, just like the Moon emerging from the womb of night into its first visible phase. And then, of course, that little Moon—the child—continues to "wax," visibly gaining in size and capability. Midlife—often seen as the height of our powers—can easily be made to correspond symbolically to the Full Moon. And then we begin to wane, at least physically. We often literally get smaller. And eventually we disappear.

THE QUINTESSENTIAL QUESTION

So how do we as a culture actually feel about "becoming flesh?" What metaphors and beliefs do we inherit? How do we feel about the material world? How do we feel about our bodies? These issues are profoundly connected to the meaning of the Moon's waxing cycle in particular.

The waxing cycle is about three-dimensional manifestation—and thus about engagement with life, and thus inevitably about *entanglement* with life too. It is about sex and community and compromise and joint efforts. It is about risking failure in order to achieve success. It is about *wanting things*. It is about *imperfection*, and how we must let go of utter idealism in order to manifest any ideals at all. All of this is encapsulated in a line one of my computer-savvy friends taught me: *Sometimes perfect is the enemy of good enough*.

Our global cultural inheritance is ambivalent in its messages about this process of embracing the world of manifestation. Hinduism is full of references to this world as *Maya*, mere illusion. Buddhism and Islam warn us of the snares of fleshly, worldly temptation. The Bible, especially the New Testament, has some particularly harsh perspectives. Consider these lines from Galatians 5:16-21:

> *"But I say, walk by the Spirit and do not gratify the desires of the flesh. For the desires of the flesh are against the Spirit, and the desires of the Spirit are against the flesh . . ."*

Or these from Romans 8:5-6:

> *"For those who live according the flesh set their minds on the things of the flesh, but those who according to the Spirit set their minds on the things of the Spirit. To set the mind on the flesh is death, but to set the mind on the spirit is life and peace."*

Emphatically, this black-and-white opposition of spirit and flesh does *not* pervade the Bible! That is a prejudicial attitude based a very selective reading of Scripture. One need only read the sexy Song of Solomon to prove that point. Putting aside both conservative Fundamentalist zealots and "liberal" Bible-bashers, anyone who actually *reads* the Bible with an open mind quickly discovers that it is a very diverse book containing a wealth of contradictory viewpoints. Like the Moon itself, the Bible reflects the idea that irony and ambiguity are part of reality.

But there is a pattern in the prejudices here. The Song of Solomon is an Old Testament book, held in common by both Jews and Christians, while Galatians and Romans are in the New Testament and purely Christian work. Quoting the wonderfully lucid scholar Elaine Pagels in her book, *Adam, Eve and the Serpent* (Random House; 1988), speaking of the suspicion of "the flesh" which is so widespread in the New Testament:

> ". . . the sexual attitudes we associate with the Christian tra-
> dition evolved in Western culture at a specific time—during
> the first four centuries of the common era, when the Chris-
> tian movement, which had begin as a defiant sect, eventually
> transformed itself into the religion of the Roman Empire. I
> saw, too, that these attitudes had not previously existed in their
> eventual Christian form; and that they represented a departure
> from both pagan practices and Jewish tradition."

Before we get immersed in the looming red state/blue state quag-
mires here, let us introduce a note of common sense: only a minority of
people in the Western world view themselves as Christian Fundamental-
ists. Our mainstream culture is secular. Increasingly and obviously over
the past three or four generations, there has been a loosening up of the
tight reins on "the flesh." To describe Western culture as puritanical is
today far from accurate. Instead there is a tension between extreme Puritanism and an existentialist, amoral, materialistic hedonism. And they
feed off each other. Could pornography exist without a puritanical background? If we were genuinely comfortable with the realities of the human body, pornography would seem incomprehensibly silly! How many
"dirty jokes" would collapse unless supported by a culture of shame and
repression? There is a dark symbiosis here. *It is not Puritanism, but rather
that dark symbiosis of Puritanism and pornography that has blinded us to this
waxing dimension of the Moon's cycle of light.*

The Moon's waxing corresponds to a process of embodiment and
manifestation. It is the erotic longing of life for life itself —and the word
"erotic" here is not simply sexual. It is about unabashed, unembarrassed
animal vitality.

Our culture distorts our understanding of the waxing lunar cycle in
complex ways. We react to it both from the puritanical and the pornographic perspectives. When we are sitting in our pious "spiritual" selves,
we thrust shame, suspicion, and dismissal upon the material world. On
the other hand, when we relax, we often become totally lost in the world
of *stuff*—hypnotized consumers, gazing at the "pornographic" shelves of
the world market.

Either way, whether we are looking through the *puritanical eyes of aversion* or the *pornographic eyes of attachment*, we cannot see clearly.

Think of how you first perceive a new lover—total idealization. Then think how you feel about him or her after a serious betrayal or failure—rejection, judgment and "transcendence." First desire, then the antithesis of desire. Are either of these perceptions grounded in reality? Aversive Puritanism and hungry, insatiable pornography distort them utterly. The same ambivalence, the same oscillation between two false views, has obscured the meaning of the waxing lunar cycle. For the same reasons, we have not been able to see it clearly either. In these bodies, we are not sure if we should be in a hyper-eroticized state of appetite, or simply ashamed of ourselves. Both messages are pressed upon us from the cradle to the grave.

HOW WE LOST THE WANING MOON

The waning lunar cycle has been similarly twisted. It is about endings and the second half of life, which culminates in death. What are our cultural feelings about the process of "returning home?" Getting old is something we are taught to dread. Death is widely viewed as the "worst case scenario," as if it were not an essential and natural part of life, even possibly a relief. It is feared and denied, made into a taboo topic.

Wrestling with the metaphors of old age, dying and death is inseparable from the process of understanding the Moon's return to darkness and the unmanifested realm. Think of the attitudes that the world has tried to thrust upon you relative to the aging of your own body. When you get into your early forties, you have, in a sense, entered the Full Moon phase of your life—and you are taught that, apart possibly from more encouraging financial prospects, "it is all downhill from here."

As is typical of the way we deal socially with collective fears, most of this judgment is shrouded in jokes and humor. We giggle about "senior moments." We laugh about Botox and Viagra. But jokes are only a buffer. We all know what really lies ahead. Eat, drink, and be merry, for tomorrow you may die. And on the way to that mortal moment, you will become funny-looking, ridiculous, anachronistic, boring, tragically unhip, and profoundly undesirable sexually—or so goes the cultural assumption.

What is the remedy for this madness? What, very simply, is the actual truth of life? *That it is good to be born and that it is good to die.* The *journey* is good. Unity! The whole trip is a blessing. Would you really like to be immortal in this body? Would you like to wake up looking at the same face in the same mirror, worried about the same psychological trivialities 877 years from now? Death, after a good, meaningful life, can feel sweet, right and welcome.

That is one liberating, taboo secret of the waning Moon.

From an evolutionary perspective, soul enters the world of fleshly manifestation in order to gather necessary experience. We engage co-creatively with the world of community, friendship, and sexuality. We share our wisdom. We give concrete form to our issues and our blockages, *so we can see them better.* We project everything that exists in our inward "Dark of the Moon" psyches onto the "Full Moon" canvas of physical life. We see it there, in a form that is hard to deny. We have a chance to work with it.

We also experience its consequences.

As we move into the second half of life, we are increasingly enmeshed in those consequences. The waning Moon feels like that—mature and complicated. Think of the delightful cliché, "As you get older, you have the face you deserve." A pretty young thing scowls in dissatisfaction and pique for 40 years. How does she look after the Full Moon of her life? Sweet justice—or is it really just the actual workings of the immutable Laws of Spirit?

The second half of life can be bitter or it can be sweet. Much depends upon the choices we made in the first half of life. There is rightness and fairness in this. It is simply the law of consequences—of *karma,* if you prefer. In the second half of life—corresponding to the waning cycle of the Moon—we are immersed in the *results of our actions*, free to reflect upon them and to learn from them.

Even if we have not done well in the first half of our lives, we are free in life's second half to release our attachment to the dramas and the judgments. We are free to forgive others and ourselves. The error *humbly digested and turned to hard-won wisdom* may, from the waning Moon perspective, ultimately be more valuable to the soul than glorious victories, shiny possessions, and the *People* magazine frou-frou of a "successful" material life.

These reflective, grown-up perspectives arise far more naturally under the waning Moon than they do under the waxing one.

But so do feelings of sorrow and defeat.

All this logic reaches an inevitable culmination at the close of life. It is a truism that we often die the way we have lived. Those who have lived bravely and lovingly, experiencing life as an adventure, will often face death the same way. And those who have been so afraid of life that they spent it cringing in front of a television face the prospect of death similarly: cringing before their various diagnoses.

TODAY

Our culture is evolving. Doors of perception are opening. The body-shaming religions, while still powerful, have lost their stranglehold on us. Secular psychology has presented a view of happiness *in this life, in this world*, as a reasonable human goal. The metaphors of Goddess worship, Neo-paganism, and nature-mysticism are everywhere, even among people who would never use such terms. Men and women in their fifties are dating. Sex is a vastly less taboo topic. Kids know what condoms are. The "right-to-die" movement is beginning to spawn a more honest dialogue about life's ending. Hospices have proliferated, de-medicalizing the dying process. For good or for ill, almost everyone now has some manner of diagnosed medical condition—and increasingly genetic analysis will present healthy 14-year-olds with probable scenarios for their own deaths long before they get near them. These developments are complex, and they have distinct dark sides. But they are all part of a major cultural shift.

One effect of the shift is that the curtain is rising on the meaning of the Moon's cycle of phases. Collectively, we are ready to see them clearly for the first time in two or three millennia.

Let's look.

7

☾

TWO MYSTERIES OF TWO

Could we understand up without down? Or light without dark? The list of such mutually-defining polarities is endless: good and evil, wet and dry, hot and cold, male and female, past and future, me and you, object and background. This dualistic principle is so fundamental to our experience of consciousness that we hardly notice it. Yet duality pervades our perceptual field and our innermost thoughts.

Mystics teach us that there is a state beyond duality. Start today and you might arrive there in a hundred lifetimes or so! Somewhere below the profound and ineffable mysteries of unity, we enter realms of which we can actually speak. This is where we live. And these familiar realms begin with polarities.

In practical astrology, polarity is symbolized by the opposition aspect—a 180° separation between planets. In the simplest forms of conventional astrology, the opposition aspect is viewed as difficult or unfortunate. In that context, a person with Saturn opposite Venus would be expected, for example, to experience endless frustration in relationships. But this sad situation actually occurs only when the two planets *polarize*. They then create a damned-if-you-do, damned-if-you-don't situation. In simple terms, this individual's need for solitude and self-sufficiency (Saturn) undercuts his Venusian need for the exchange of love, and *vice versa*.

With opposition aspects, there is potentially higher ground. Instead of polarization we can find *complementarity*. The opposites balance each other, and each benefits. The individual with the Saturn-Venus opposition finds a committed relationship with someone who is fully available—but not needy or high-maintenance. Boundaries and time apart are integrated into the bond. The cake is thus both kept and eaten. Oppositions can be beautiful.

In the previous chapter, we emphasized the underlying *unity* of the Moon's cycle. We began to understand the possible *complementarity* of the waxing-waning elements, as well as the bright and dark halves of the lunar cycle. We began to see how they fit together, completed each other, needed each other. We saw how cultural blind spots have confused us about this potential complementarity, driving us collectively downward toward polarization. In this chapter we explore these "two mysteries of two" in a more practical, astropsychological way.

THE FIRST MYSTERY OF TWO: WAXING AND WANING

Years ago, when I acquired my first primitive computer, I was delighted to find that the program—an early offering from Matrix software, called Blue Star—had a research module. I could scan my client files for everyone with, say, Mercury in the first house. I would sit there for hours comparing my theories with reality—and mostly, I hope, letting reality win. It was a great learning tool. It was also my first inkling that computers were going to do more for astrology than speed up the chart calculations.

One day I decided to check out the waxing and waning Moon. Obviously that divided my whole database into just two groups. I started clicking through the names of friends and clients and quickly realized there was something quite powerful happening. The people with waxing natal Moons felt more "forward" somehow—that was the word that crystallized in my mind.

I switched the rules on myself and began guessing, person by person, between waxing and waning *before* I saw the answer. I startled myself. I was correct about 80% of the time, simply based on my personal impressions of these people. The determination probably took about five seconds in each case.

Usually, no single factor in astrology works quite that well. Once you become experienced with it, you quickly realize a good rule of thumb is that nothing astrological means *anything* out of its context. A Capricorn with a Sagittarian Moon is a whole different beast than one with a Virgo Moon. The symbols marinate in human consciousness; everything flavors everything else. That said, the waxing-waning Moon distinction was practically hitting me over the head. It was unusually obvious, in other words. Context still mattered, but not much. I was only wrong about 20 percent of the time in my guesses—a triple Sagittarian born under a waning Moon could fool me into thinking her Moon was waxing. The "forward" quality of Sagittarius could overwhelm the quieter and more reserved spirit of the waning Moon. But it took an extreme astrological situation like that to mask this single variable.

Strangely, the honest truth is that I did not do anything with this experience. I did not reflect on its connection with the Rudhyar material, which includes similar observations, nor did I link it to the old notion of planting seeds under a waxing Moon for more reliable germination. To this day, that avoidance of making practical use of the waxing/waning distinction is one of my greatest career befuddlements. I have broken enough other rules in the AstroWorld, but somehow the unspoken rule to downplay lunar phase swept me along. It was not until about 10 years ago that I began to pay it attention again.

Let's look at the waxing and waning Moon from a personality-profile perspective. Initially, we will catalog the obvious principles. Mostly I will rely on simple key words to give you a sense of each half of the cycle. Then we will ask some harder questions and penetrate the mystery more deeply.

Please realize that not everyone with a waxing Moon will identify with every one of these words and phrases. The waxing and waning Moons divide all humanity into two boxes. The boxes are large. As with every other branch of astrology, each individual will make choices within the context of the broad archetypal field. Also, the specific reality of each person's complex of natal factors will interact with the condition of the Moon, enhancing or weakening certain of its possible expressions.

THE WAXING MOON

The Theory: A psychic impulse is rushing out into manifestation. The abstract and the ideal are struggling to become the concrete and the actual. The correspondence is with the first half of human life, birth to midlife.

The Orientation: To "doing."

The Mood: Forward. Eager. Enthusiastic. Keen. Ardent. Optimistic. Youthful. Positive. Active. Impatient. Trusting. Hopeful. Driving. Vigorous. Lively. Fascinated with the alien "other." Concerned with the future. Vital. Healthy.
The Virtues: Faith and Energy.

The Shadow: Naive. Self-Possessed. Aggressive. Gullible. Offensive. Insensitive. Blundering. Loud. Foolish. Exploitive. Artless. Presumptuous. Clueless. Intrusive. Inappropriate. Barbarian.

THE WANING MOON

The Theory: A psychic impulse is recognizing limits, its mortality, and the brevity of life. There is a humbling sense of enmeshment in previously-created circumstance. The correspondence is with the second half of life, midlife to dying and death.

The Orientation: To "being."

The Mood: Reflective. Mature. Aloof. Cautious. Experienced. Withdrawn. Tempered. Pensive. Seasoned. Guarded. Concerned with the past. Detached. Reserved. Thoughtful. Contemplative. Compassionate. Humble. Patient.

The Virtues: Wisdom, humility, and forgiveness.

The Shadow: Depressive. Resigned. Flat. Passive. Spiritless. Apologetic. Acquiescent. Fatalistic. Defeated. Self-absorbed. Self-pitying. Uninspired. Vulnerability to illness. Hypochondria.

WAXING MOON: THE FEELING

A pleasant aspect of my astrological practice is that I see people of all ages, from old folks down to the late-teenage years. I like sitting with young people. Today, many of them are concerned with the fate of the Earth. Often they have a plan for saving it, too. I get the impression many of them feel that if we could just put them in charge of everything for a year or two, the Garden of Eden could be restored. We would have peace, love, and understanding among the nations, and an environmental utopia—tastier salads, too. I am not making fun of them; this faith and energy are invaluable. It is a contemptible elder who would nickel-and-dime their idealism. These young people will learn some hard lessons. Some of them will be defeated, broken in spirit. But if there is any hope for the world, it resides in these precious, enthusiastic, naive vessels of hope whom we call the young.

If you can truly feel what I am saying, you understand the spirit of the waxing Moon.

WANING MOON: THE FEELING

I remember long ago, back when age 40 seemed geriatric, a friend of mine crossed that line a few years ahead of me. Someone gave her a sweatshirt emblazoned with the words, "Youth And Enthusiasm Are No Match For Old Age And Treachery." She wore it a lot. We all laughed. But of course there is truth in those words. Life teaches us a few tricks, often the hard way. We get good at staying alive—or life weeds us out. We naturally expect young people to make more mistakes than older people. In fact, if we are wise, we welcome the mistakes of the young because we know that wisdom is often forged in cauldrons of error. By the time we get toward midlife, we have usually been "forged" pretty well. We have had failures. We have done shameful things. We have learned that everything we do has consequences. And, in the words of William Butler Yeats, we have rarely seen "a finish worthy of the start."

To a young person, these might seem like bitter words. And yet there is a richness in this humility, in this sense of life's brevity, this appreciation of our flawed natures. As time passes, goals for which we were desperate lose their luster. Quiet peace in the here-and-now becomes easier to find. The monstrous burden of an insecure ego is somewhat lifted. We have time for other people and, to paraphrase some familiar words, we "forgive them their sins as we have forgiven ourselves our own."

If you can truly feel what I am saying, you understand the spirit of the waning Moon.

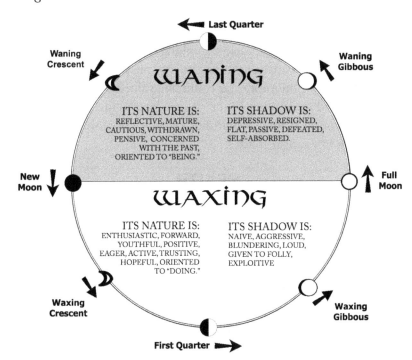

WAXING AND WANING IN RELATIONSHIP TO THE LIFE CYCLE

In these last two sequences, I have built heavily on the correlation between chronological age and the Moon's waxing or waning condition. The symbolism is compelling, and it provides the best route I know into the emotional heart of the matter. But I cannot emphasize strongly enough that one need not be over 40 to understand the waning Moon. Simply *having* a waning Moon in your birthchart is sufficient! The psychological differences between the first and the second halves of life provide us with a powerful, evocative metaphor, that's all.

Happiness is complicated, and probably derives more from our choices than from any other single factor. But I believe we can make a case that it's easier for a person born under the waning Moon to be happier in the second half of life. As the natural effects of the aging process on one's psyche interact with cultural training and expectations, a better fit with one's innate nature arises. And of course, the natural exuberance and forward quality of the waxing Moon blends more easily with the realities of life's first half.

With all that said, there's also something to say for the opposite point. Waning Moon people, in youth, may be cast meaningfully among their peers in the role of philosopher or counselor, valued for their thoughtful perspectives. And the waxing Moon person, later in life, might be valued for vitality, enthusiasm and a "youthful" attitude, remaining popular with and accessible to younger folks.

HEALTH

The enthusiasm for incarnation that is characteristic of the waxing Moon sends a positive psychosomatic message to the physical body. Broadly, there is a pattern of health, strong recuperative powers and a generally robust quality about people born between the New Moon and the Full Moon. Conversely, those born under the waning Moon are in some fundamental way already aware of a world beyond this one, already heading home. It is as if their vital force has begun to orient itself to the spirit world. This orientation can often be seen to correlate with increased vulnerability to illness. Balancing that, these individuals' deepened awareness of the transitoriness and inevitable disintegration of the physical body also enhances their alertness toward disease. The good news can simply be better self-care and sensitivity to early signs of bodily maladies. A piece of potentially bad news is a heightened risk of hypochondria.

In any case, these are some psychological and practical insights into these two lunar types' differences. What about the deeper, spiritual meaning of the waxing and waning of the Moon?

THE SPIRITUAL SIGNIFICANCE OF THE WAXING AND WANING MOONS

When we are frustrated with a friend who refuses to take our good advice, we often say "Well, if you want to learn it the hard way . . ." The implication, of course, is that only a fool would prefer learning anything the hard way, and that the friend ought to hew to our suggestions. Yet often when we learn something through error, the experience sinks far deeper into our bones than if we avoided the lesson through blind obedience of the rules.

Consider this example. In separate situations, two people refuse to steal despite an opportunity to filch some easy, untraceable money. The first one refuses because "Thou Shalt Not Steal" is the eighth commandment, and he does not want to burn in hell despite the sweetness of the temptation. The second one refuses to steal because she actually *did* steal once and got away with it. But she found that the guilt and the paranoia were agonizing, and she squandered the stolen money just to be rid of it. She has no desire to repeat the experience.

Of these two people, which one learned the more profound lesson? And, pointedly, which one would you prefer to have join you for dinner this evening?

Born under a **waxing Moon**, a person's soul intention is to leap boldly into life, to trust impulses, and to take chances. Down this road, there will be existential shipwrecks and catastrophes for sure. And that's all right. There are sufficient faith and exuberance implicit in a waxing Moon to survive most of them. The soul is committed to embodied experience. The essential evolutionary strategy is to lay the karmic cards on the table. *The intention is to project the realities of one's inner evolutionary state onto the fabric of the three-dimensional world and to work with them there.*

With the **waning Moon**, the intention is more subtle. Much can be worked out in the imagination, without having to manifest it so concretely. We contemplate an opportunity to steal. We take mental possession of the object of desire. We taste the experience in the inner world of reflection without having actually to manifest it. How does that stolen money feel in the moment? Tomorrow? A year down the road? And perhaps we pass up the chance at larceny, having learned the lesson on the inner plane without actually living it out.

A soul born under a waning Moon is committed to an examined, reflective life. More is held back. Much can happen inside without much occurring in terms of visible worldly drama. The soul intention is the digestion of old experience and the cultivation of more of an *observer's point of view.*

The waxing Moon is heading outward into the world of physical reality, while the waning Moon is withdrawing into the deeper realms of consciousness—realms the wise ones tell us survive the death of the body. My intuitive impression, despite how some of this might sound, is *not* that waning Moon people are more spiritually evolved than waxing Moon people! Rather, it is that a waning Moon person is probably nearing the end of a cycle of incarnations that had a common theme. There has already been enough physical, outward experience of those themes. At this point in the evolutionary process, *contemplation* and *digestion* are the soul intentions. Conversely, I believe that waxing Moon people are typically beginning new cycles of experience. They do not really know yet what they are doing, and so they dive in and see what happens.

Both are sacred, honorable paths, and I suspect that all souls oscillate between the two evolutionary methods about evenly over many lifetimes.

THE SECOND MYSTERY OF TWO: DARK AND BRIGHT

Some nights are dominated by bright moonlight. Even without a flashlight, you can find your way around. Shadows are cast. Stars are mostly washed out. In the eerie luminosity, the world takes on the cast of magic. Other nights, the Moon is visible only for a short while, if at all. Deep darkness reigns. You step carefully. The stars are in glory. The Milky Way is bright as a neon ghost. With the Moon gone, night itself is the Presence.

Were we living as close to the natural cycles of the world as our ancestors, the difference between these two kinds of night—moonlit and dark—would be an unmistakable, practical reality. Because simply *being able to see* is so important to us, these two conditions would be even more pressingly obvious than the distinction between the waning and the waxing cycles. But unlike waxing and waning, there is no sharp line of demarcation between the bright and dark faces of the monthly lunar cycle. The visible Moon eases and flows from dark to bright, from a minor role to a major one.

The bright-dark distinction is real and vivid, even if the timing of it is not always crisp. Arbitrarily, for our purposes here, we will define the Moon's bright hemicycle as the period between the First and Last Quarters, centered on the Full Moon. The dark hemicycle begins at the Last Quarter, diminishes down to nothing at the New Moon, and continues as the baby Moon gradually gathers itself up to the First Quarter.

In practical lunar astrology, this bright-dark distinction is as pivotal as the distinction between waxing and waning. It provides equal insights into the human psyche in its own way. And once we ally an understanding of it with the waxing and waning Moon, we will have a basis for understanding the four quadrants of the Moon's cycle—the subject of the next chapter.

The elemental mythic foundation of all the Moon's cycles lies in the notion of soul-impulse emerging out of the realm of abstract potential *(the astral worlds, the mental plane, the Mind of God . . .* choose your term) and coming into concrete physical manifestation in this three-dimensional world. And then, with experience gathered, soul-impulse begins the process of extricating itself and eventually returning to that realm of abstract potential, to be born again. Thus, the dark hemicycle of the Moon corresponds to a more inward, abstract orientation of consciousness, while the bright hemicycle refers to one that is more outwardly engaged. There is, as you are probably already thinking, a vast difference between the waxing and waning halves of the bright and dark hemicycles. That four-part distinction is what we will explore in the next chapter. Before we get there, we need to grasp bright and dark.

As we did with the waxing and waning Moon, let us start by considering this dark/bright distinction from a personality-profile perspective. As before, we will initially sketch the basic outlines of the theory using simple key words and phrases. Then we will ask some deeper questions. Once more, please remember that the language here is meant to cover a wide range of possibilities. The specifics of your birthchart and your evolutionary state will underscore some of them and soften others.

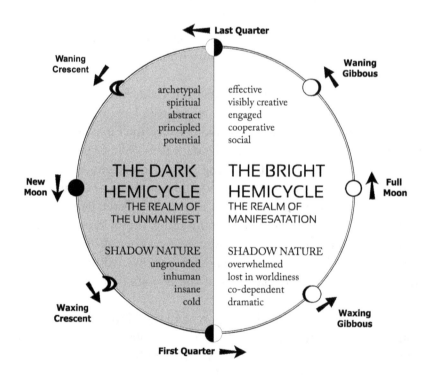

THE DARK HALF OF THE MOON'S CYCLE

The Theory: The soul-impulse is inwardly absorbed and contained. A radiant potential is gathering force. The attention is focused on principles, archetypes and transcendent perspectives.

The Orientation: Inward, toward consciousness. Toward the realm of the unmanifest. The subjective reality of the Moon penetrates the ego-mind reality of the Sun, impacting it strongly, blurring the distinction between facts and emotions, reality and its interpretation.

The Mood: Transcendental. Expectant. Abstract. Mysterious. Self-contained. Archetypal. Spiritual. Principled. Idealistic. Interiorized. Theoretical. Hypothetical. Introverted. Visionary. Independent. Isolated. Numinous. Charismatic. Otherworldly. Utopian. Quixotic.

The Virtue: Self-awareness.

The Shadow: Ungrounded. Insensitive. Insane. Inhuman. Cold. Disengaged. Fanatical. Unloving. Uncompromising.

THE BRIGHT HALF OF THE MOON'S CYCLE

The Theory: The soul-impulse arrives in the world of external reality, projecting detailed outward expressions of its inner nature onto the stage of the world. It is hungry to engage co-creatively and to experience relationship in all senses of the word.

The Orientation: Toward cosmos. Toward the realm of manifestation. The subjective reality of the Moon is further from the ego-mind reality of the Sun, impacting it less strongly.

The Mood: Pagan. Engaged. Interested. Caring. Creative. Open. Cooperative. Nurturing. Social. Busy. Curious. Experimental. Concerned. Fascinated. Extroverted. Romantic. Investigative. Inquisitive. Hungry. Sensual. Adaptable.

The Virtues: Openness to Engagement. Attention to others.

The Shadow: Enmeshed. Overextended. Self-dramatizing. Overwhelmed. Clueless. Stuck. Lost in worldliness. Engulfed. Overpowered. "The deer in the headlights."

We all live in two worlds, as we saw in Chapter One. There is nothing inherently mystical about this statement; it is easily verified by anyone, even a nihilist. There is the outer world of more-or-less shared experience—what we are conditioned to call "reality." And there is the inner world of thought, dream, reflection, and more exotic states. In a nutshell, the Moon's dark hemicycle refers to our attention to the inner world and the bright hemicycle to our attention to the outer one. A person born under the dark half of the lunation cycle has a natural orientation to the inner world, and someone born under the bright phase, to the outer world. Immediately, please be wary of those cultural distortions we explored in the previous chapter. Neither of these orientations is inherently good or bad. A person born under the dark part of the cycle might be sensitive, spiritual, and visionary—or so utterly self-absorbed as to be sociopathically disengaged from other people's needs, pains, or their full reality as human beings. Similarly, a person born under the bright parts of the Moon's cycle might be loving, creative and alive—or materialistic, consumed by desire, and enmeshed in endless, irresolvable personal dramas. As always, it is consciousness that determines the actual nature of the expression of an astrological configuration. In common with everything else in astrology, these structures are only tools in the hands of the soul, nothing more.

DARK HEMICYCLE: THE FEELING

Let me bring this down to earth. Maybe you have a friend who is politically liberal. If you refer in his presence to someone who is politically conservative, he immediately disparages that person—assumes she is selfish, materialistic, militaristic, and so forth . . . environmentally insensitive, against a woman's right to choose, homophobic, enthusiastic about the death penalty, snotty with her "inferiors." Perhaps none of this is fair. The world is full of politically conservative people who are thoughtful and kind, and to whom many of those attitudes do not apply. But your liberal friend does not see *people*. Because he sees *ideas* and *principles*, the incredible subtlety and diversity of the real world is somewhat lost on him. His attention naturally rests in the realm of archetypes and abstract potentials—cartoon characters, in essence.

If you know such a person, you have grasped the Shadow-dimension of the dark hemisphere of the Moon's cycle.

What about its positive expression? I'm reminded of broadcast journalist Dan Rather's words after interviewing Nelson Mandela. He said that the man's power "is the power of the idea and the ideal. Nelson Mandela knows in what he believes. He knows what he's literally willing to die for, and that carries with it tremendous power, and it radiates from him . . ." Nelson Mandela's natal Moon was actually waxing toward brightness, but these words so perfectly capture the spirit of the Moon's dark cycle that I quote them anyway. The point is that there can be something deeply impressive about the conviction, charisma, and faith of a person born in the darker phases. He or she seems to have one foot in the next world—a quality of divine inspiration or daemonic overshadowing.

BRIGHT HEMICYCLE: THE FEELING

Jane would really love to leave Frank. The marriage, in truth, ended long ago, although they still share a bedroom and have sex sometimes. But the twins are in high school—and anyway, paying for their college just couldn't happen if she and Frank divorced. There is all that—plus when Frank's parents die, there will be this fantastic inheritance, and Jane doesn't really have any career skills, so that inherited money might equal survival. Of course, those parents are healthy as horses now, but you never know. And besides, Jane's boyfriend Ralph can't get out of his marriage either—he's Catholic, and he has a kid with Down's Syndrome, and he lives in Delaware and has to stay there because of his kid and anyway, if Jane left Frank, he'd undoubtedly try for full custody and so Jane's moving to Delaware couldn't happen for a few more years no matter what . . .

Know someone who has managed to weave his or her life into such a tangled web? *If you do, you have a good understanding of the Shadow-dimension of the bright phases of the Moon's cycle.*

What about the good news? I mentioned Nelson Mandela a moment ago. He was actually born in the bright hemicycle, and he illustrates the best of what it can mean: a total engagement in the world. A willingness to *negotiate* one's ideals, to achieve *advantageous compromise*, to deal with the real world. When Mandela was in jail, he made an effort to learn to speak Afrikaans so he could communicate with the men who were jailing him. The abstract principles of love, negotiation, and respect were brought to bear upon the real world, with its warts and all.

It takes a certain kind of person to be open to connecting with people very different from one's self. We often see this quality in bright-Moon people—they are fascinated with the *alien other*. Willing to learn, to adapt, to listen. These virtues represent the soul of the positive expression of a bright Moon. Above all, it is *engaged*.

TWO MYSTERIES OF TWO

These are our "two mysteries of two." When we let them overlap, four quadrants emerge. The dark hemicycle has a different face when it is waxing than when it is waning. Similarly, no one would mistake the waxing part of the bright hemicycle for the waning part of it. Thinking this way, the granularity of our understanding is doubled. That is the doorway through which we enter the subject of the next chapter, the mystery of the four quadrants.

8

THE MYSTERY OF FOUR

The Moon's monthly cycle presents two natural divisions: the waxing and waning periods, and the equally dramatic split between bright nights dominated by Moonlight and darker nights when the Moon is mostly or completely absent. The exploration of this pair of dualities was the subject of the previous chapter.

What happens when we overlap the two divisions? That produces a pattern of four quadrants, each with its own composite signature. What about the one quarter of the Moon's cycle that is both waxing and dark—that is, the week or so from the moment of the New Moon to the First Quarter? And what about the other three quarters—waxing up to Full, waning down to the Last Quarter, and finally disappearing into darkness again? The Moon's presence in any one of these four quadrants is, as you will see, unmistakable in its impact upon the character and the evolutionary agenda of the soul. In considering them, we move into a more precise and nuanced system than we could achieve with the two-fold systems we have investigated so far. In the eternal trade-off, we lose some breadth and gain some depth and specificity.

The quadrants are analogous to the four elements, Fire, Earth, Air and Water. As the elements underlie the zodiac, the quadrants are the foundation of the system of eight lunar phases, which we will begin exploring in the next chapter. In practice, most astrologers speak more frequently of the twelve signs than of the four elements, yet few could imagine understanding the signs without the underlying logic of Fire, Earth, Air and Water. In exactly the same way, the four lunar quadrants empower us to grasp the eight "pagan" lunar phases.

Waxing out of the Dark. When the abstract, otherworldly quality of the dark phases allies with the outrushing enthusiasm of the waxing Moon, an *active expression of idealism* arises. Its Shadow is both naive and also insensitive to the needs and individuality of others. The first quadrant is of the nature of *Fire.*

Waxing into the Light. When the engaged, social, and concrete quality of the bright phases allies with the outrushing enthusiasm of the waxing Moon, a spirit of *partnering and co-creation* arises. It seeks expression in crusade, service, and sexual union. Its Shadow is destructive conflict and the loss of one's philosophical and moral bearings. The second quadrant is of the nature of *Earth.*

Waning out of the Light. When the engaged and relationship-oriented quality of the bright phases allies with the reflective and withdrawing qualities of the waning Moon, a *generous, caring, mature,* and often *selfless* spirit arises. Its Shadow is hopeless, seemingly inescapable enmeshment. The third quadrant is of the nature of *Air.*

Waning into the Dark. When the subjective, otherworldly and transcendent qualities of the dark phases ally with the reflective and withdrawing qualities of the waning Moon, both *a poignant sense of endings* and *a mystical sense of the transparency of this world* arise. Its Shadow is madness and despair. The fourth quadrant is of the nature of *Water.*

Underneath these brief thumbnail sketches, you will recognize many of the notions we explored in the last chapter. The Moon's rush toward Fullness corresponds to the soul's need for fleshly, voluptuous engagement in outward experience. This is one way that we learn and evolve. But in entering the world, we perhaps lose all perspective and become ensnared in drama, hunger, and confusion. In the Moon's return to darkness, we see reflected the soul's impulse to digest its worldly experience and bring it back into the archetypal realm—heaven, the Bardos, the astral planes, core consciousness. We also recognize here conditions of dissociation, shell shock, defeat and despair.

Let's analyze each of these four quadrants in detail.

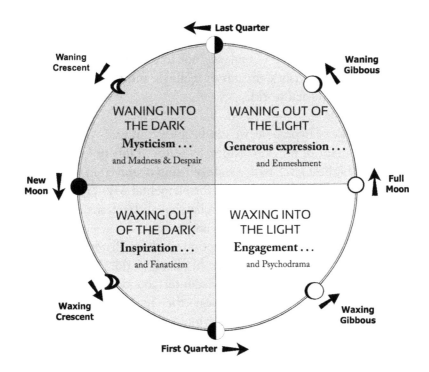

WAXING OUT OF THE DARK

Between the two moments when the Sun and the Moon arrive at a precise conjunction (the New Moon), and when the Moon reaches ninety degrees ahead of the Sun (the First Quarter), a period averaging a bit over seven days and nine hours elapses. The Moon moves then from a state of dark invisibility to one of half-illumination. A heady mix arises as the sheer animal energy of the waxing Moon integrates with the transcendent archetypal abstraction of the dark phases. It's a little like driving 100 miles an hour with no headlights—a dangerous pastime. But also a bracing one.

Dane Rudhyar, in his book *The Lunation Cycle*, is hard on this first quarter of the lunation cycle. What he says about it defines its Shadow dimensions quite precisely, but I believe he was blinded to the higher dimensions of the first quarter by a cultural blind spot we discussed earlier—a negative attitude toward darkness.

Here are his words:

This is a period of instinctive, youthful, essentially unconscious and irrepressible activity. What consciousness there is, is essentially subjective, with a tendency not to distinguish accurately between inner wishes, dreams or feelings, and the actual realities of the external world.

At the risk of hyperbole, we can balance Rudhyar's view by considering the moment of the New Moon to be the "Holy of Holies." It correlates, at its highest level, with a state of being dissolved in the Divine, in impeccable union and oneness with the elemental Mystery. In this condition, consciousness is attuned to archetypal abstractions: perfect Love, perfect Wisdom, perfect Generosity, and so on.

Most of us can relate to the notion of these Platonic ideals—but few of us have actually seen them in this crazy world! As ideals attempt to come into manifestation, they encounter countervailing conditions. They compromise; they sustain damage; they make deals. That humanizing process is the domain of the Moon's bright phases. But here, in the First Quadrant, we see the pure essence of this idealism. Rudhyar is correct in emphasizing its subjective and internal bias. What I believe he misses is the sheer power and glory of undiluted aspiration and principle, never compromised and fervently held. William Butler Yeats, in his 1919 poem, *The Phases of the Moon*, puts it this way:

> *From the first crescent to the half, the dream*
> *But summons to adventure and the man*
> *Is always happy, like a bird or a beast.*

While we are at it, we should note that there is also a set of "ideals" on the Dark Side of the Force: perfect Cruelty, perfect Cluelessness, perfect Amorality, and so forth. The first quadrant Moon can also embody these bleaker abstractions—witness gangster Al Capone or the serial killer John Wayne Gacy. Consider the paranoia of J. Edgar Hoover or the amorality of the notorious "Hollywood Madam," Heidi Fleiss.

The point is that people born while the Moon is waxing out of the dark tend to embody ideals across the spectrum. Positively or negatively, they easily become *emblematic* in the minds of other people, as if they were "figures" rather than multidimensional human beings. Often they possess a quality of *charisma*, or at least of a great natural authority. This quality can be colorful, or serious, or sexy, or austere—that all depends on the particularities of the birthchart. The key is that there is an underlying sense that this individual *represents* something of a transcendent nature. He or she is overshadowed by an archetype, much as a Voodoo practitioner might be overshadowed by a *loa* or a medium taken over by a spirit.

We spoke of perfect Love, perfect Wisdom, perfect Generosity. For the first two, consider the Dalai Lama, who was born with the Moon in this first quadrant. For the third quality, perfect Generosity, consider Florence Nightingale, also born in this first quadrant. For iconic charisma, consider Elvis Presley, Bruce Springsteen, or Frank Sinatra. One of my favorite illustrations is the brilliant, blind musical genius, Ray Charles, who literally lived sightlessly in "the dark of the Moon" and brought something up out of those private depths that riveted almost anyone who listened to him.

A conservative Christian might honor another example of a person born with in this first lunar quadrant—Billy Graham. Such a person naturally would be predisposed toward belief in Christian charity and devotion to Jesus. But after hearing Billy Graham preach, that individual's faith would be enlivened and recharged. In fact, the cultural term for such an event is a *revival.* The world can be understood in many contradictory ways. A lot of them are compelling and convincing. Yet exposure to Billy Graham and his *embodiment of an archetype* has the effect of enormously reinforcing the particularly Christian interpretation of life.

I like this example of the Reverend Graham because of the way it supplies a kind of ink blot test. Some astrologers might be ill-disposed toward conservative Christianity, taking a jaundiced view of Billy Graham. Others, more warmly disposed, will see him in a more positive light. This is the nature of the first quadrant—the archetypes and ideals embodied by such an individual may or may not be to your taste. You may experience appreciation, even devotion. Or you may experience a negative, even judgmental reaction. What you will not experience is neutrality.

Born with the Moon in this quadrant, people might lose sight of human diversity. They may not easily honor other people as independent centers of thought, action, and the creation of values. They may interpret the world as a battleground. Compromise—peacemaking, diplomacy, the middle ground—might not enter their minds. And yet they carry something of the Higher Worlds in them. They may exasperate us, and yet we would be lost without their inspiration.

WAXING INTO THE LIGHT

The Sun sets and the brilliant half-Moon is revealed high in the sky—and in this quadrant, it generally has to be well above the horizon, since it is 90° from the setting Sun. This combination of altitude and sheer "wattage" casts an eerie glow across the landscape. Nighttime falls, but you can still see well enough to move around. And it is going to remain that way until around midnight when the Moon finally sets.

Let your ancient DNA speak. Moonlight was a big deal to our ancestors. Your Paleolithic grandmother might have been engendered because of a moonlit night! Before the age of electricity, before the age of efficient lamps, the Moon's First Quarter signaled that we were entering a two-week period of far greater nocturnal freedom. Socially, sexually, artistically, ritually, it was a time of *engagement*. Darkness calls us inward, into our own minds. And light calls out us out into the world.

Although absent in American speech, in British English the term *fortnight* is still in common usage. Just to be sure it wasn't becoming quaint and antiquated there, I emailed an English friend and asked him if people in his country still actively used the word. He responded, "Verily, we do."

Etymologically, fortnight is a modernization of the Old English *feowertyne niht*, a term dating from before the twelfth century. Obviously enough, it simply means "14 nights." It is interesting to note that "fortnight" is absent from American English, which is a more modern variant. Back when Old English was spoken, a period of two weeks was a very natural measure of time, as evident as a day or a year. Thus it needed a name. It referred to the waxing or waning periods of the Moon—or, more obviously, to the bright two weeks of the month, or the two weeks of dark. Fortnight is an organic, experiential word, easily lost in a world in which electricity alienates us from the natural rhythms of the night.

Passing the First Quarter Moon and heading up to the Full Moon, the exuberance and forward quality of the waxing phases interacts intoxicatingly with the spirit of social engagement and creative manifestation that characterizes the bright phases. Suddenly, it is like the difference between a 15-year-old without a driver's license and a 16-year-old with one: the stakes are abruptly much higher. In the First Quadrant, we are still dealing somewhat safely in the realm of ideas, ideals, and potentials. In the second quarter of the Moon's cycle, we actually roll the dice with money on the table. It is no longer a dress rehearsal.

Dane Rudhyar is easier on this second quarter of the lunation cycle than he was on the first. He speaks of how "as we come closer to the full moon the indications of personal maturity and enlightenment become stronger. With such a lunation birthday, the individual should reach some kind of fulfillment, objective understanding or illumination." Despite Rudhyar's enthusiasm, it is easy to demonstrate that there is no shortage of people born under this quadrant who get themselves into all sorts of interesting trouble! Rudhyar acknowledges this dimension too when he writes, "The period following the first quarter phase is one in which obstacles must be overcome, the enmity of the old world must be met." He refers to "confrontation, the shock of which is sharp and at times devastating for the unprepared organism."

Maybe you get excited about politics. Say that you are drawn to the progressive side of the political spectrum. You become actively involved, volunteering to work locally for your party. Your special passion is the rights of women. But once you have rolled up your sleeves and actually entered into relationship with your party machine, you discover that the chairperson is much more focused on environmental concerns. He does not oppose women's rights, nor do you oppose a clean environment. But your passions are not aligned.

What happens?

Let your imagination range over the possibilities. In so doing, you are internalizing the spirit of the Moon's second quadrant. Idealism is colliding with the real world—people, society, limits, co-creative possibilities. Maybe you clash with the chairperson. Maybe that leads to your becoming a pariah, defined as a "troublemaker." Or maybe that clash leads to your starting your own splinter party. Or possibly there is no clash; you accept that the chair is the leader and you focus on supporting that agenda. Maybe inside of a year, you are a passionate environmental crusader and no longer so concerned with feminist issues. How do you feel about that? Compromised? Or is that too strong a word? Maybe we should only say "changed." Both are possibilities.

Go further. After a long, bitter battle, the local chemical company agrees to cut the pollution it generates by 40%. That means that instead of there being a hundred new cancer diagnoses in your county this year, the projection is down to 30. You have helped to save 70 lives—and agreed to the deaths of 30 people. How do you feel about that? Was this a victory or a terrible loss?

A charismatic woman is running for office. You are blown away by her style and vision. Before you know it, you have become her press secretary. That was never your intention, but now it is your reality. She is successful. You serve her faithfully until your retirement. As John Lennon said, "Life is what happens to you while you're busy making other plans." In one sense, you did not follow your own star in life: you went into orbit around another person, serving her vision. But her vision was meaningful to you, and you helped make the world a better place. An error? Self-betrayal? Don't those judgments seem harsh?

In your life as a party *apparatchik*, you of course have many significant social encounters. Friends and enemies are made. You date. You experience a few emotional train wrecks. Maybe you marry. Strangers have entered your consciousness, in other words. They have changed you and presumably you have changed some of them. The convenient terms *self* and *other*, while still part of your vocabulary, have actually gotten blurry. Is that blur just you being a spineless wimp—or have you attuned to one of the universe's deeper mysteries?

With your Moon phase in this second quadrant, between First Quarter and Full, you are invited to live in this *engaged* way. You are invited to let yourself be changed. Messed with. You are invited to live passionately, even if that involves making some mistakes. Think of the romantic poet Lord Byron or the beat novelist Jack Kerouac, both born in this second quadrant. They hurled themselves into life, took their blows, and delivered wisdom and beauty into the collective conversation.

You may find yourself vaulted into positions you could not have foreseen as a result of cooperating creatively with other people. Witness Bill Gates, who could never have developed the personal computer alone, or the first man on the Moon, Neil Armstrong. Could he have gotten there by himself? You may be swept forward by the historical currents of principles that seem to call you—consider U2's singer, Bono, and his work for African debt relief. Or Nelson Mandela.

And, with the Moon in this second quadrant, you may run afoul of historical forces as you try to stand up against them, right or wrong. Likely the results would not be as dramatic for you, but some good examples are assassinated Pakistani Prime Minister Benazir Bhutto, right-to-die crusader Jack Kevorkian, or exiled Soviet dissident Aleksandr Solzhenitsyn.

In *Phases of the Moon,* Yeats says of the person born in this quadrant, "He follows whatever whim's most difficult, *among whims not impossible.*" The italics are mine. Here in this second quadrant, we have entered the real world. We roll up our sleeves and we negotiate.

WANING OUT OF THE LIGHT

A fortnight—plus 18 hours and 22 minutes—has elapsed since the moment of the Dark of the Moon. We are now at Full phase. In terms of light, we have continuous coverage—the brilliant Moon rises in the east, white as a bone, just as the Sun sets in the west. At midnight, it will reach its maximum height in the sky, bathing the world in shadows and phantasmal luminosity. And it remains in the sky all night, round as an apple, until the Sun rises on a new day. One can almost feel the ancestral ecstasy. No wonder so many Pagan rituals were tied to the Full Moon. Dancing, drumming, and making love in the ghostly meadows—who could ask for more?

And yet, this moment of maximum illumination is also the beginning of the end. From now on the Moon will shrink night by night. It will also rise later and later until, at the Last Quarter, it remains completely absent until around midnight. Darkness is eating the light, bite by bite. Here is the underlying principle: *When things are "as good as they can get," we know that it is "all downhill from here."* Everything changes. Peaks are thus poignant. Nothing lasts. All born things die.

If you can feel in your heart the spirit of the last paragraph, you are feeling the essence of the third quadrant, the Moon's waning out of the light.

Formally, in this third part of the four-fold lunar cycle, we witness the co-incidence of the logic of the bright hemisphere and the logic of the waning Moon. The bright hemisphere is social, communal, and oriented toward manifestation. The waning cycle is reflective, mature, oriented to endings and leave-takings. Put them together and a certain *generosity* arises—a desire to leave something of ourselves in the hands of others. It is not about us anymore. We have hurled ourselves into the world. We have made mistakes. We have tempered our idealism in the cauldrons of experience. Now we begin to sense the call of the homeward journey. And wisdom, unlike money, has the wondrous property of growing wider and wilder as we give it away. Here is how Dane Rudhyar expresses it:

> The waning period of the lunation is thus a period of growth for the active power of consciousness. Consciousness, once it is formulated, can be shared with others, and thus can actively affect and transform others. As a result, the vision of purpose of the cycle-as-a-whole can become incorporated in the substance of human society.

Earlier, we recognized that there is a distinct parallel between the human life-cycle, cradle to grave, and the lunation cycle. The sheer animal exuberance of the waxing Moon corresponds to the period from birth to midlife. The Full Moon would then indicate something of a "midlife crisis." Acquisition, empowerment, rising glory, erotic possibility—these engines drive us through the first half of life. But at midlife, we stop and wonder, is this all there is? What does it all *mean?* We start to feel how short life is, and how empty it can be if all we do is chase after "stuff," then die. One of my favorite curses is, "May you have a job that pays only money." Diabolical, eh? It stings at age 30, but not like it stings at age 45. As we get older—or past the midpoint of the lunation cycle—the simple, primeval life-force is not enough to sustain us anymore. In his poem, *Phases of the Moon,* William Butler Yeats takes only seven riveting words to say it: "The soul begins to tremble into stillness." We need something beyond biological and ego-driven motivations now. Paradoxically, it comes more from giving than from receiving. Rudhyar describes the quadrant beginning at the Full Moon as a time in which our energy:

> . . . becomes gradually exhausted. It can however be replaced, to some extent, by the new type of power made possible by the sharing of purpose and will with an organized group of human

beings ... *Social power* thus energizes the consciousness and the mind, which in turn hold together the organism whose *biological power* is waning.

The arc of a marriage provides a classic example of third quadrant psychology. Two people fall in love. Famously, colors are brighter, jokes are funnier, and the future beckons them with blithe promises. Push the hands of time ahead 15 years, into the symbolic terrain of the third quadrant. They may still love each other, but they have also failed and disappointed each other—who doesn't? They have a mortgage, a house to keep up, and a family dog. They have three children, each one presenting the usual array of joys, difficulties, and needs. In low moments, they wonder how all this could have befallen them. What happened to their freedom? Their dreams? In their darkest hours, they probably dare to glimpse a fantasy of escape—but of course, how could they possibly act on it? They are totally enmeshed in the life they have created. They can only ride out its consequences. In *Phases of the Moon*, of people born in the third quadrant, Yeats writes:

> *... body and soul*
> *Estranged amid the strangeness of themselves,*
> *Caught up in contemplation, the mind's eye*
> *Fixed upon images that once were thought ...*

Depressing? Of course. As naiveté is the curse of the waxing lunar cycle, despair is the curse of the waning one. In the words of Zorba the Greek, our couple is caught up in "Wife, children, house, everything. The full catastrophe." They created it; they now behold their creation, which they cannot escape and from which they feel alienated. Their minds are now "fixed on images that once were thought"—thought has become concretized as fact; the New Moon impulse is now fully incarnate. Intentions and desires have materialized into physical "images." Could they have actually created all this? They might very well feel "estranged amid the strangeness of themselves."

But despair is optional. There is higher ground. We might imagine two people in the same material situation: marriage, family, mortgage. And they are happy! What is their secret? *Generosity*, in a word. They support each other. They love their kids and celebrate their blossoming. They draw energy from each other's spiritual prosperity. In serving the little society of their family, they find a freedom from identification with their own issues and problems. They radiate bighearted, easy maturity. Maybe they are involved with the PTA or Rainbow Soccer, giving not only to their family but also to the larger community. *They have gotten over themselves.*

The difference between the happy couple and the sad, trapped one is partly a simple difference in attitude. The happy couple has mastered the generous spirit of the third quadrant; the sad one is still thinking in more self-centered, waxing Moon terms—terms which fail miserably here. Let's also recognize that the happy couple may have simply made better choices. Attitude alone, for example, cannot save a marriage between two people who are spiritually irrelevant to each other. The underlying principle here is that in this third quadrant starting with the Full Moon, we see the *epitome of manifestation.* The wisdom—or folly—of choices we have already made is now on the table, fully revealed. We get away with nothing. The karma has ripened. The results are in.

One corrective: in this example, I have used imagery of a very normal, middle-class tone. The third quadrant is by no means a sure indicator of that cultural posture! Add a strong Uranian element to the mix, for example, and we might see a local rock 'n' roll promoter struggling to keep a club open so that young bands have a place to cut their teeth. That would be the good news. The bad news might be a local rock 'n' roll promoter skimming the profits to buy cocaine in the hopes that he will be attractive to women who could be his daughters.

Let's take the third quadrant one big step further. Say that you have come upon a hard challenge in your life. Maybe you have received a scary medical diagnosis or things are looking ominous in terms of your job security. These Full-Moon-to-Last-Quarter people are the kinds of friends to whom you naturally turn for counsel, advice, and support. You sense that they have not only wisdom, but also enough magnanimity to welcome you and your problems into their hearts. This is a quadrant in which you find a lot of counselors, whether they have degrees from Harvard or they are sitting in rocking chairs on back porches in Appalachia. Carl Gustav Jung, born with the Moon in this third quadrant, presents us with a perfect illustration.

In terms of the soul-cages this third part of the lunation cycle presents, I have already mentioned hopeless enmeshment in "impossible" situations. We have seen despair. One might think of the tragic third-quadrant lives of Marilyn Monroe or Princess Diana. No one likes being trapped. We resent it. Freud said, "Depression is anger turned inward." That observation can be quite relevant in this third quadrant. But what if the anger is turned outward instead? That is another possibility. The third lunar quadrant presents us with many examples of people who have been engaged with others in highly destructive ways. Their own despair is made palpable in the lives of others. The brutal, murderous, and often-married English King Henry VIII is a frightening example. Worse, consider Adolph Hitler, Saddam Hussein, and Carlos the Jackal—all born with the Moon this third quadrant. In a twisted way, murder must be a profoundly deep engagement in the life of another human being. Always in astrology—and life—we need to be alert to these kinds of shadow-and-light reversals. Every front has a back.

Brighter examples with the Moon in this third quadrant abound. Think of the endlessly loving spiritual master Paramahansa Yogananda, who left such generous gifts behind him among us strangers here in the Western world. Think of U.S. Senator Ted Kennedy, who devoted so much of his life to trying to provide health care for the desperate and downtrodden, or Al Gore in his tireless efforts to save the Earth's ecosystem. Or Karen Silkwood, who was allegedly murdered because of her attempt to reveal lapses in safety procedures at a plutonium-fueled nuclear power plant.

Engagement with others and a willingness to put our little selves aside—or frustration, resentment and despair at our entanglements: those are the underlying evolutionary questions in this third lunar quadrant. What makes the difference between evolution and spiritual collapse here? What tips the scales one way or the other? As St. Paul put it in his first letter to the early Christians of Corinth, "If I have prophetic powers, and understand all mysteries and all knowledge . . . but have not love, I am nothing."

I cannot think of a better bottom-line summary of the core issue in this third part of the lunar cycle.

WANING INTO THE DARK

Black starry midnight, and a spectral glow insinuates itself into the eastern sky. A hundred breaths later, the horn of the waning half Moon clears the horizon. Slowly, as dawn approaches, it climbs higher. As it arcs upward toward its highest, brightest moment, the eastern sky fills with the gray glow of dawn, washing out the failing Moon's light. Defeated, the half Moon hangs pale as a ghost against the bright blue sky of daylight until it slinks, unnoticed, below the western horizon around mid-day. The next night, the Moon's battle against darkness is feebler. It rises later, has further shrunken in size and brightness. And it is even lower in the sky when the Sun King blows it away again. The third night, even feebler . . . the fourth night, feebler yet.

Again, listen to your ancestral DNA. A Last Quarter Moon is an entirely different beast than a waxing First Quarter Moon. In photographs, they look almost the same—literally, mirror images of each other. But in the human context, there is an emotional abyss between them. How would you feel, out there in the Olduvai Gorge a million years ago, with every advancing night swelling the darkness around you? The feelings are entirely different from the ones that arise in anticipation of the Full Moon. Our senses do not mislead us here; these feelings are the key to understanding the lunation cycle.

Formally, in this fourth and final quadrant of the lunar cycle, we see the reflective, withdrawing spirit of the waning Moon integrating with the subjective spirit of the dark hemicycle: abstract, transcendent, impersonal. The spirit is purely Yin. It has a natural resonance with the psychology of the Elder. The presence of death is vivid—along with the mystical scent of what possibilities might lie beyond it.

It is somewhere on the far side of difficult to experience how the world might feel to another person. Astrology, perhaps more than any other human discipline, allows us to glimpse life through the lens of alien senses, values, and imagination. Still, astrologers often speak with the greatest clarity and understanding when they discuss a configuration which they themselves actually possess. Dane Rudhyar was a solar Aries with an Aquarian Moon, thus born with the Moon in this fourth, Waning-into-Darkness quadrant. I value his insights into all the quadrants, but I especially resonate with his perspectives here.

The last quarter phase is, like the first quarter, a moment of crisis and repolarization; but the crisis now involves problems of consciousness and formulation, rather than issues dealing with the building of organic structures. The element of conflict is strong, at least at the ideological level; and if we consider the waning period of the cycle as an ebbing tide of biological-cultural power, we find that the breaking down of all idols and images likely then to occur tends to create physiological or societal crisis—illness and revolution.

Apart from his fourth quadrant Moon and three planets—Mercury, Saturn, and Uranus—in Water signs, Rudhyar's chart is dominated by Yang elements of Fire and Air. Actually, without factoring lunar phase into the equations, it might be a surprise that he pulled twentieth century astrology so far in the subjective, psychospiritual direction. Still, his natural Arian/Aquarian orientation to social, collective, outward realities comes through in most of his writing. We see it in the lines above, and we see it again here:

The symbolic personage who focuses upon himself a social drama and the martyr may well be born during these days preceding the new moon. They are the incorporation of the need of their collectivity for a new birth of spirit. They call down the creative spirit; they summon forth the future—even if it be through their own death.

No argument with anything Rudhyar posits here, yet his focus on "the collectivity" misses, in my opinion, the real core of the fourth lunar quadrant. Being both waning and dark, the orientation of consciousness indicated here is quite internal. *In this quadrant, something ancient and non-material within us is preparing to leave the world.*

Earlier, we looked at the cultural biases that have blinded us to the lunar cycle. One of them was our collective fear of death and dying. To grasp the Moon's waning into darkness, it is imperative that we get past that negative projection. We have strong medicine to swallow here, but if we open wide, we can complete our understanding of the Mystery of Four. Try thinking of it this way. A man is presented with grim medical diagnoses. He is projected to have about six months to live. He goes into denial, then anger, then depression. Perhaps he becomes debauched. Perhaps he uses people sexually or abuses them verbally. He gleefully and compulsively runs up his credit cards, knowing he will never need to pay them off. He laughs and says, "Let them send me the bill." As the clock ticks, despair gradually subsumes him. He stares out windows. He stops bathing. He is lost in bitterness. Thoughts of suicide gather in his mind. Perhaps he actually kills himself. Regarding religion, he either defends himself from it with cynicism—or clings to it in a doctrinaire way, using it as a shield against his own human feelings.

Most of us, by the time we enter midlife, have witnessed this uninspiring storyline. People do in fact often face death this way. If you can open your heart to it and consider such a person compassionately, with full acknowledgment of the thin line that separates every one of us from that hell-world, you have understood the Shadow side of the Moon's last quadrant.

Even when death is not on the immediate horizon, even when it is safely locked behind the lead walls of cultural denial, this underlying mood can arise poisonously in the consciousness of anyone born under this final quarter of the lunation cycle. All of the behavior and attitudes we just described can easily emerge in such individuals—self-pity, denial, bitterness, escapism, cruelty, selfishness, morbidity, a paucity of self-care. Yeats writes, "And after that the crumbling of the moon. The soul remembering its loneliness . . ."

What are the antidotes to this poison? Let's consider a second version of our story. Again, we posit a fatal medical diagnosis and six months of life left. What positive possibilities might arise? As synchronicity would have it, I downloaded an email from one of my students this morning just before I began writing. She was getting together with an old soul-friend who had been given a diagnosis of pancreatic cancer. Here are the words my student wrote:

> My friend looks terrific. You would never know all the hideous
> medical treatments procedures she has been through. Her story
> is remarkable. Having cancer finally gave her permission to re-
> ally take care of herself for the first time in her life. It's ironic.
> Previously, she would drive herself relentlessly with overwork,

always hyper-responsible and over-functioning. Now she enjoys herself so much more, and actually seems much less stressed. The gift of cancer. Bizarre.

Underlying these words are layers of ancient human understanding both in you, reader, and very obviously in the woman who is the subject of this email. I don't know her or anything about her astrological chart, and I will wildly project my own thoughts into her for the sake of our larger purposes here. She has remembered something we all forget too easily: she knows that the only thing any of us really possess is the present moment. She has cast off the deadening demands of the world—of the Moon's bright hemicycle. She is letting a sweet, primeval gravity pull her into the nurturing dark Her joy and equanimity reflect some intuitive sense of the *meaningfulness* of the end of her life—and at least a hint of the ancient human instinct that we are not simply these material bodies. *She is going home.* Intuitively, the veil between this world and the next has become transparent. She embodies the higher possibilities of the fourth lunar quadrant.

Now, imagine living every day that way. In that thought, we see the real meaning of this final quadrant: the wisdom of the present moment opens like a flower, whether we are dying or as healthy as a happy kitten nestled in a box with mama cat near a warm hearth. The stakes are obviously very high in this part of the lunation cycle. Yeats writes, "Hunchback and Saint and Fool are the last crescents."

Rudhyar himself was one of the first among the "modern" astrologers to use astrological symbolism to point beyond this world. He thus effectively illustrates the positive spirit of the Moon's fourth quadrant. I also think of two master fantasy-weavers who have opened the edgy door between this world and the next for many millions of people: Rod Serling, of *Twilight Zone* fame, and film maker Steven Spielberg. I think of Wolfgang Amadeus Mozart and Leonardo DaVinci, whose art eternally invites the light of another realm into this one. Another person born in the fourth quadrant is Annie Bessant, the early Theosophist, who helped bring deep metaphysical perspectives far closer to the mainstream of the exoteric Christian world. All modern spiritual astrologers in the west owe her a great debt, whether they realize it or not. In the present cultural stew, we could point to Deepak Chopra, who has underscored the power of consciousness in shaping physical health in the world of Integrative Medicine. At least 65 million kids have been carried into other worlds via *The Magic Tree House* series by young peoples' author Mary Pope Osborne, also born in this final quadrant. One of the most compelling illustrations for me personally is the Irish musician and bard, Van Morrison, whose music always "puts our feet on higher ground."

Naturally, there are dark expressions of this risky fourth and final quadrant as well. I think of Nazi monster Adolph Eichmann, condemning so many people to death in the dark satanic concentration camps. Or of that Shadow expression of the Pied Piper, Jim Jones, leading almost a thousand souls to follow him into death via suicide during the infamous Jonestown debacle in Guyana.

Frida Kahlo, the brilliant, tragic Mexican painter, was born with the Moon in the fourth quadrant. She left these words in her suicide note: "I hope the leaving is joyful, and I hope never to return." I can think of few statements that so perfectly encapsulate the spirit of the Moon's fourth quadrant—but I *can* in fact think of one more. It comes from the pen of one of my personal heroes, long-distance sailor Tristan Jones. He voyaged for a while with a young German, Thomas Ettenhuber, who died suddenly of a heart ailment. Eulogizing him in his book *To Venture Further,* Jones wrote:

> *We shall meet again, he and I, and laugh together again,*
> *even as we laughed together on vast oceans and dangerous rivers,*
> *at death's feebleness.*

No words I have ever encountered more clearly illuminate the highest potential of the Moon's closing quadrant, nor do I know any better ones with which to close this chapter.

9

THE MYSTERY OF EIGHT

In the widdershins realm of the Moon, I believe that the mystery of the number eight is the heart of the matter. Such a division is complicated enough to have plenty of fairly narrow individual meanings, and yet simple enough for the heart to grasp without putting the left brain hemisphere into overdrive. Many of you have naturally already skipped ahead, straight to reading about your own specific lunar phase. I confess that I would probably do that myself. But if you jumped the gun that way and feel you have gotten something out of what you read, I would very much encourage you to go back and read the earlier chapters about waxing, waning, bright, dark, and the quadrants, or at least the parts that are relevant to you. If you do that, you will not only grasp the system a lot more clearly, you will also learn a lot of specific practical elements of personal interpretation which do not figure in the next eight chapters, or in this one.

WHY EIGHT?

Astrologers are so accustomed to the number 12 that the idea of a system of eight phases seems a little jarring. As I recounted in Chapter Five, I did not like the idea very much myself at first. I tried making a system of 12 phases work. I got nowhere. One can always build card-castles in astrology—it is one of the plagues of the field. But my 12-phase card castles just did not stand up to the test when I tried to apply them to friends and clients.

Since I love his poetry so much, I experimented with the cryptic

28-phase system pioneered by William Butler Yeats and his wife, Geor-gie Hyde-Lees in *A Vision*. Pursuant of that, I tried to stand on the shoul-ders of Marilyn Busteed, Richard Tiffany and Dorothy Wergin, and later Martin Goldsmith, as they attempted to make rational, practical sense of the Yeats's system. Their approach made sense, more or less, for me. I respect that material and I recommend it if you are interested. But for me it was too heady. It lacked that simple intuitive "click" that has been a characteristic of just about everything I have found to be of lasting value in astrology. Maybe it is just that 28 archetypes are too many for me. I can handle it intellectually, but my heart gets lost.

In the end, I returned to Dane Rudhyar and the eight-phase system he introduced in *The Lunation Cycle*. As I recounted earlier, Rudhyar's system often worked pretty well—but it also seemed way off to me at times. Linking Rudhyar's work to the yearly pagan cycle of eight natural holidays seemed to put the corrective lenses on the eight-phase system. That marriage of Celtic tradition and the lunar phases is the subject of this chapter.

SEASONS

Spring, summer, fall and winter—the cycle of seasons. What could be more ordinary to an earthling? One can divide the year in other ways, of course. Weeks. Months. Financial quarters. Semesters. But the seasons are based rigorously on a natural cycle that can easily be observed. At the Winter Solstice, the night is as long as it can be. After that, daylight be-gins to gain ground. It is quite objective; you can check with a watch. The time between sunrise and sunset gets longer and longer. At the Spring Equinox, daylight and darkness are of equal length. Summer Solstice brings the shortest night of the year and the longest day. Afterwards, the days grow shorter until we come to another point of equilibrium: the Autumnal Equinox.

All this is naturally quite familiar. We learn it when are young—and, doubtless, humanity itself figured it out long ago, perhaps before we could even be called human. We were certainly motivated. These four turning points in the year had obvious practical application in terms of agriculture. And long before the idea of agriculture was a glimmer in some Neolithic woman's eye, migrations—both of game and of the tribe itself—were timed by these seasonal rhythms.

The four seasons sunk deep into our collective bones, in other words. They became the foundation of much mythology—the motif of dying and rising gods, for one example. In every society, the phrase "the springtime of life" naturally conjures up images of vibrant youth, full of hope and possibility. And who could fail to understand the more serious resonances of "the winter of her life"?

SEASONS LOCK WITH THE MOON

The Moon's cycle of phases takes about 29 days, start to finish. The cycle of seasons takes about 365 days. Their lengths are different, but might the two cycles resonate with each other? Might they be different expressions of the same archetypal structure? Astrologers have always thought in that fashion. For example, the cycle of Venus through the 12 signs and the cycle of Pluto through them take vastly different lengths of time, but they have the same archetypal stages. If we understand one, we have a good start on understanding the other. In secondary progressions—one of the most reliable workhorse techniques in astrology—the cycle of the day is made to equal the cycle of the year.

Could this same thinking be applied to the seasons and the lunation cycle? To the year and the month, in other words? Once I asked that question, the lock between them practically leapt out at me.

At the Winter Solstice, darkness is triumphant. The night is as long as it can be—extremely so in the higher latitudes of either hemisphere. And even when the Sun finally rises, it does not rise very high. Winter is the season of short, dim days, long shadows, and seemingly endless nights. Similarly, at the New Moon, there is no moonlight at all. It is the darkest night of the month.

To me, the connection between the New Moon and the Winter Solstice is compelling and obvious. I cannot imagine another way of thinking about the two of them. The darkest time of the month and the darkest time of year—they are like two mirrors facing each other.

Let's test it further. If the New Moon and the Winter Solstice have a natural symbolic linkage, we should see the system "click" with the rest of the lunar phases and their corresponding seasons.

Opposite the Winter Solstice we have the Summer Solstice: a time of maximum light. Opposite the New Moon we have the Full Moon: again, a time of maximum light. Bingo.

Try the same test more subjectively. Imagine people dancing for joy at the Summer Solstice—Midsummer, with all its revelry. Now imagine people dancing under the Full Moon. Any problem? Again, that mutual reflection is easy and natural. If we tried dancing outside at the Winter Solstice, we would freeze. If we tried dancing outside at the New Moon, we would stumble and fall. It's too dark to dance.

The two Equinoxes, with light and dark balanced, would then be made to correspond with the First and Last Quarter phases of the Moon. Again it works—at the lunar Quarters, light and dark are evenly balanced, literally, on the face of the Moon, just as daylight and darkness balance perfectly at the Vernal and Autumnal Equinoxes.

At the First Quarter, we are heading toward the brightness of the Full Moon. It resonates with the Vernal Equinox, when we are heading for the maximum light of Midsummer. At the Last Quarter, we are heading down into the Dark of the Moon—a natural resonance with the Fall Equinox, when we are bound for the dark and cold of Winter.

These correspondences hit me like a thunderbolt. Suddenly I knew where the treasure was buried—at least for four of the lunar phases. The treasure did not lie, for all their helpfulness, in the pages of Dane Rudhyar's *The Lunation Cycle* or in the work of any other living astrologer. It ran like a vein of gold through the seasonal mythology that has been the human heritage for at least a hundred and fifty thousand years.

We will get to the other four phases soon. Let's first weigh some of the gold we have already mined.

Cultures are different, and their mythology is not only diverse, but also endlessly evolving. What the seasonal cycle provides is something closer to the *template* upon which that mythology is structured. It is the key, the Rosetta Stone. Take, for example, the evocative mythic motif of "the return of the light in the hour of deepest darkness." It runs through countless tales told around Neolithic hearth fires and in modern Cineplexes. That is, fairly literally, what happens at the Winter Solstice. Humans have been happily celebrating it throughout our history. It represents the triumph of indefatigable hope in the face of seeming impossibility. In the Christian world, it is now celebrated as Christmas. And in half the movies you have ever seen, you can recognize the same motif—it looks very bad for the good guys, but wait . . . here comes a ray of hope, probably with his hair perfect, despite everything.

It is often alleged that the Church Fathers "co-opted" the ancient pagan holidays in order to better insinuate their new religion into the existing ancient cultures. There may be some truth in that, but it is also true that there is simply a very good fit—for one example, between the symbolism of the birth of Christ and the symbolism of the return of the light. By the way, there are those who might object that Christmas was simply the actual birthday of Jesus. There is actually no scriptural evidence at all for that common fallacy. In fact, the one hint the Bible does give us about the birthday of Jesus precludes the possibility that he was "a Capricorn." If we were raised in the Christian faith, we know these familiar words from Luke 2:8 in the old King James Bible, "And there were in the same country shepherds abiding in the field, keeping watch over their flock by night." The practical historical reality was that it was cold in Galilee in the winter and the shepherds tended to keep their sheep in folds at that time of year. They simply would not have been outside anywhere near the Winter Solstice—it would have been too uncomfortable for both them and the sheep. So the only hint we really have about when Jesus was born is that it was during the warmer months of the year, when spending the night outside watching the sheep freeze would not have been such a dumb idea—probably sometime between March and November.

One key here is simply that the cycle of the seasons, so vividly and easily experienced, provides a kind of skeleton onto which every culture hangs its mythology, customs, and holidays. And a second key is that the seasonal cycle is perfectly mirrored in the lunation cycle. At least by relating them to the Solstices and the Equinoxes, I realized we could now unlock some of the deeper mysteries of the Moon's phases.

We will get to the problem of the other four lunar phases in the eight-phase system momentarily, but first we must deal with . . .

THE AUSTRALIAN PROBLEM

This whole system would be so neat if it were not for those plucky Aussies! Not to mention South Africans, Chileans, Kiwis and the rest of the southern hemisphere crowd. While we are shoveling snow, whistling *Jingle Bells*, and thinking of reindeer, the Australians are firing up their barbies and reaching for their sunblock. (They are whistling *Jingle Bells* too, but that is another story.) The seasons are "upside down" in the southern hemisphere, and yet the dominant cultures there today are mostly northern hemisphere transplants. Aussies mail each other snowy Christmas cards while the sweat is pouring off their foreheads. This doubtless contributes to their fabled sense of ironical humor.

Two interlocked points arise: First, our inherited seasonal mythology still works fine in both hemispheres. You just have to put it six months out of phase for it to make calendrical sense. Second, that seasonal mythology has nothing to do with the actual seasons as they are experienced south of the Equator—in fact, everything is completely reversed.

I am sure that the indigenous seasonal mythology of the pre-European people of the southern hemisphere would offer rich veins of deeper understanding in all these matters, as would the forgotten or ignored mythology of various northern hemisphere cultures. Unfortunately, I am mostly ignorant of all that and will stick to more familiar ground. In doing this, I take comfort in knowing that Nature itself has provided the archetypal template, and that therefore no enduring mythology in either hemisphere could possibly stray very far from the seasonal cycle and still survive for very long. Prehistoric Celt or prehistoric Aboriginal, the yearly light and heat breathed the same way, just six months sooner or later.

ENTER THE CROSS-QUARTER DAYS

Convincingly, the New Moon locks up symbolically with the Winter Solstice. As we have seen, that creates a pattern that fits consistently with the other three major seasonal turnings, linking them to the lunar Quarters and to the Full Moon. But we still have to account for four more lunar phases if we want to work with an eight-phase system. We have one solid clue. We know that those extra four phases fit midway between the four phases we have already identified. Logically, the four remaining points of the yearly cycle would have to do the same. We would thus look for them halfway between the Solstices and the Equinoxes.

Enter the ancient people of Scandinavia, Finland, England, Scotland, Wales and Ireland. These groups—the ancestors of a great number of you reading these words—celebrated four more annual holidays under various names, but always falling exactly where we'd hope to find them:

midway between the Solstices and the Equinoxes. Collectively, these four holidays were called *cross-quarter days*. The term refers to how we celebrate them as we "cross" the center of each seasonal "quarter" of the year.

Nigel Pennick, writing in *The Pagan Book of Days*, describes the Solstice and Equinox holidays as masculine in nature, celebrating sky gods. Describing the cross-quarter days, he writes:

> The four remaining festivals of the natural year are recognized as more feminine in their quality, they are the earth-defined festivals, related to the cycle of plant growth and the changes of the seasons. Traditionally, these four cross-quarter days are known as the fire festivals. Each has a fire ceremony whose origin is of great antiquity. They were the most important festivals of the Druids, held on fixed dates in February, May, August and November.

As we will see, some of these holidays are still celebrated vigorously—consider Halloween. Others are mostly forgotten and unmarked, such as Lammas in early August. All of them cast an ancient, penetrating light on the lunar cycle.

With all due respect to Dane Rudhyar, he was just one human being looking at the world through his own eyes. He was conditioned by his culture and his times, as well as by his own personal experiences and philosophical biases. No one can escape that, at least not until after they have mastered walking on water, healing lepers, and raising the dead. Humanity—and the tribe of astrologers—has always seen more clearly when looking through many sets of eyes at once. That way, we let the paradoxes and ambiguities shine; we find a middle path; we see the bigger picture. Time weeds out some of the transitory cultural biases—sexism, for example, or faith in the efficacy of human sacrifice. It also weeds out personal quirks—what if, for example, someone born under the New Moon once cruelly abandoned you for someone else? Can you still interpret the New Moon clearly?

In the cycle of (mostly) Celtic holidays which we are about to explore, there are antiquarian elements that are no longer relevant to us. There are also more modern elements which have been added. For those recent additions, I make no apology—the "old ways" are still alive and breathing. They have never gone completely dormant. In some ways the modern "neo-Pagan" perspectives are more connected to what humanity has become than are the more historical readings.

The critical point is that whether we are taking the neo-Pagan perspective or the ancient one, the essential meanings of these holidays mostly shine through. And the reason is that they are not rooted in the philosophy of any single human being or of any one Age. They are rooted in the unchanging cycles of nature itself.

A FEW PRELIMINARY COMMENTS

In the pages that follow, we explore each of the eight holidays of the natural year in some detail. My intention is to let them stand on their own two feet without much attempt at interpretation. I will mention the lunar phase to which they correspond, but we will save the in-depth analysis of their connection with the lunation cycle for the following eight chapters. I will freely mix the traditional names of the holidays with later Christianized versions, especially where the latter cast a more familiar light on the essential core of the holiday, as is often the case—for most of us, "Easter" rings a more nuanced bell than does "Ostara." Occasionally I will include cultural perspectives from further afield, in the non-Celtic world. My aim is simply to bring the old cycle of holidays to life for you as effectively as I can. For more Simon-pure academic analyses of the strictly historical traditions of northern Europe, please see my list of recommended reading at the end of the book.

The calendar dates I give for these holidays are also approximations. Solstices and Equinoxes slowly drift though the calendar, riding the 26,000-year cycle that is currently driving the Age of Pisces into the Age of Aquarius. Check ephemerides or the computer for the exact date each year. Similarly, the cross-quarter days are properly celebrated when the Sun arrives at the midpoint (15°) of the Fixed signs, Aquarius, Taurus, Leo, and Scorpio—again, check for specifics each year. That would generally occur around the fifth day of the month, but by custom, these cross-quarter days are often celebrated on the first day of the month.

For the northern Europeans, the *eve* of the holiday was often the actual beginning of the festival too—a custom that remains alive and well today in the form of All Hallows Eve, Christmas Eve, New Year's Eve and so on. As Sarah Fuhro put in her fine *Mountain Astrologer* article, "The Four Fire Festivals" (Feb/Mar 2010), " . . . the Celts also began each new day at sunset. The necessity to experience the darkness of the womb or the tomb before entry into the light seems to be woven into this particular way of looking at things."

Finally, for natural seasonal correspondences in the southern hemisphere dates, add or subtract six months. Also, if you are living in the southern hemisphere, where I speak of "south," turn it into "north." But leave east and west where they are.

There is argument about where to start the traditional year. The Celtic cultures typically used Halloween, timed by the rising of the Pleiades. Others used the Vernal Equinox and the beginning of Springtime. For our purposes here, I am going to begin with the Winter Solstice because of its correspondence with the New Moon, which for obvious reasons we generally take as the start of the lunation cycle.

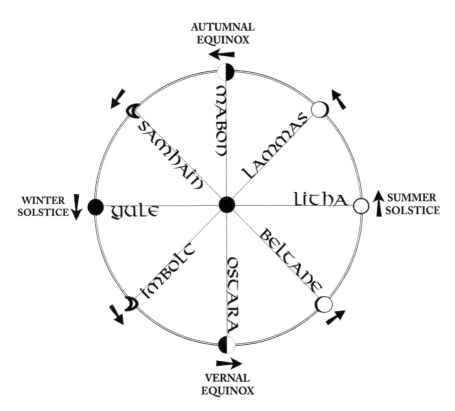

THE PAGAN HOLIDAYS

HOLIDAY: *Yule; Christmas; Sol Invictus; Saturnalia.*
Seasonal Place: *Winter Solstice*
Corresponding Lunar Phase: *The New Moon*
Approximate Date (Northern): *December 22*

The night is long and the Sun is low in the southern sky, even at noon. All life seems drained from the world—but then, when everything seems only to be getting worse, hope arises. The tide turns. Miraculously, the light begins to fight back.

The word *Yule* is related to "yoke," describing the point in at which the heaviness of the year is first perfectly balanced, and then begins to tip in a more encouraging direction. It is no wonder that in so many cultures, the birth of a major god was celebrated at this time. To the Romans, it was *Sol Invictus*, the feast of the Invincible Sun. The list of similar iconic religious figures whose births were celebrated around this time is long: Jesus is the most obvious illustration in our present culture. But we can add Mithras, Dionysius, Helios and Horus.

It is clearly a season of celebration: something extraordinary, super-human, and life-giving is being hatched into this cold, dark world. "A thrill of hope, the weary world rejoices," in the words of the Christmas carol—perfect, triumphant words for wintertime! In the modern Western world, the festival spirit expresses itself in Christmas feasting, but it also extends into the revelries of New Year's Eve—and an ancient Roman would not have been surprised to see our behavior around that time. They behaved the same way, and called it *Saturnalia.*

HOLIDAY: *Imbolc; Candlemas; Brigantia*
Seasonal Place: *Midway between the Winter Solstice and the Spring Equinox*
Corresponding Lunar Phase: *The Waxing Crescent Moon*
Approximate Date (Northern): *Early February*

The light of the world remains dim, but it is increasing day by day. Darkness still has hegemony over daylight, but its hold is visibly weakening. Of *Imbolc*, Nigel Pennick writes:

... the three-fold goddess is transformed from her winter aspect as the aged hag, veiled in black. She throws aside her black rod of wintry barrenness and is transformed into the radiant virgin bride, springing from seeming death into life.

New birth, a general freshening of life—these are Imbolc's themes. The word literally means "ewe's milk," and references newborn lambs. Susan Fuhro calls it "a festival of washing, of purification through fire and water."

Reflecting the transformation of the goddess, the seeds of vegetative life are stirring under the ground. There is still no manifest sign of them yet, but we know they are there, on the verge of beginning their upward journey through the soil, heading forth in a spirit of faith to meet the light and warmth that have not yet been born themselves.

At this point in the sacred year, the Celtic goddess Bridhe displayed her three great powers: that of healing, that of fire craft, and that of poetry. We can thus imagine ourselves experiencing healing by being set on fire with the transformative, cathartic power of poetry—or more broadly, of art in general. Hope is mounting, but the light has not yet broken forth. In Christian churches, we light candles—the priests called this ancient holiday *Candlemas*. It is a time of *holy anticipation*. The goddess is not so much pregnant as ready to be made that way. You can feel the rising tension of ecstasy not yet broken forth.

You may recall the 19-year Metonic cycle, which we discussed in Chapter Three. In her *Mountain Astrologer* article, Fuhro points out that the "Imbolc custom of floating nineteen candles on water marks the years in the lunar Metonic cycle. This nineteen year cycle is calibrated in stone circles, including the bluestone horseshoe at Stonehenge."

In our system, the re-booting of the Metonic cycle reflects a time of renewed commitment to the specific realities of our own spiritual path. This does not mean the formal pieties of religious practice, but rather something of a more instinctual nature rising up from our psychic depths, just like those *Imbolc* seeds.

HOLIDAY: *Alban Eilir, Ostara, Easter*
Seasonal Place: *The Spring Equinox*
Corresponding Lunar Phase: *The First Quarter*
Approximate Date (Northern): *March 22*

At last light has equaled the darkness. And light has the momentum; night now shrinks from the ever-higher, ever-brighter glare of the rising Sun. Everywhere the Earth is warming. The battle for life's dominion over death and frozen stasis is now fully engaged. Seeds sprout; animals are born. For all creatures, *now is the moment*. We commit. We enter the breach. We roll the dice, take our chances on life. No more hiding underground. No more sweet, safe womb. The time has come to take risks. And even though the waxing light provides encouragement, a 50-50 feeling pervades the air. Maybe you will live and maybe you will die—and there is only one way to find out.

At the macrocosmic level, day and night are equal; the Sun rises due east and sets due west. Reflecting that same tossed-coin feeling on the microcosmic level, the stakes are high and our chances of surviving feel about even. There are no guarantees. One creature's body is another creature's food. The goddess Bridhe, attracting a mate at *Imbolc*, is now pregnant—and will bear the child of a sky-god come *Yule* in nine months time. And for one more metaphor of gambling everything on faith, think of a Celtic woman long ago in those physically-challenging times contemplating the fact that she is now pregnant. What does she face? What are her chances? All she can do is to steel herself, take refuge in faith, and go forward. For now, dream-time is over. We are entering manifestation, ready for victory—or perhaps, as reflected in the Christian holiday of Easter, to be nailed to a cross.

HOLIDAY: *Beltane; May Day; Walpurgis Night*
Seasonal Place: *Midway between the Spring Equinox and the Summer Solstice*
Corresponding Lunar Phase: *The Waxing Gibbous Moon*
Approximate Date (Northern): *Early May*

Days are now markedly longer than the nights. The Sun rises higher and higher in the sky, shining down on the green and fecund Earth.

And there is no green like the green of May, before summer's scorching heat leaches the color's vibrancy. Flowers bloom, flagrantly sexual in their form and function. Fertility is everywhere. Even the humans have cast off their winter clothes, leaving their bodies healthy and alluring. Reading Marian Zimmer Bradley's evocative accounts of *Beltane* in her masterpiece, *The Mists of Avalon*, will make the holiday come alive for you—and the way it was originally celebrated is not for the prim. I downloaded a helpful paper by Merlyn, a modern Wiccan, from www.ladywoods.org. She writes:

> All other Beltane customs are minor compared with those that explicitly celebrate human sex and fertility. Up to the Protestant Reformation in the 16th Century, marriage vows were conveniently forgotten at Beltane in many rural European villages. Newly formed 'couples' went into the plowed fields at night to lie down together and copulate in order to ensure the fertility of the coming year's crops. The Catholic Church could not stamp out this ancient pagan tradition. It took the dour Protestants who suppressed May Eve celebrations in England by passing and enforcing laws against public gatherings around Maypoles with their accompanying dances and fertility rites.

The idea of a reinforcing resonance between human fertility and the fertility of the Earth is an ancient one that has existed in many cultures. We still, however dimly, grasp that our food supply originates in the fertility of plants and animals. In modern times, we tend to take that food for granted—which is, of course, folly. And in terms of our sexuality, as we saw earlier in this book, we tend to oscillate between pornography and Puritanism, and only rarely do we relate sex to reproduction. Compared to times gone by, we also tend to have a very different attitude toward pregnancy. Often, we are more concerned with avoiding it than with engendering it. But for most of human history, our collective survival was on far shakier ground, and making babies in some plenitude was encouraged. In those days, both the magical and *procreative* aspects of sexuality were cut from one cloth. There is, in Beltane, at once an honoring of that erotic and creative power that courses through all life, and a celebration of its wild, edgy and ecstatic dimensions as well. Prudish people are blind to it—but so is anyone who thinks of sex without relating it positively to fertility. Beltane is a festival of *co-creation*.

HOLIDAY: *Midsummer; Alban Hefin; Litha*
Seasonal Place: *The Summer Solstice*
Corresponding Lunar Phase: *The Full Moon*
Approximate Date (Northern): *June 22*

The term "Midsummer," the common name for this ancient holiday, often confuses people. For us in the modern world, the Summer Solstice represents the *beginning* of summer, not the middle of it. The reason behind the confusion is simple, if little understood. Traditionally among the Celts what was called "summer" actually began with the warmth of Beltane in early May, peaked at the Summer Solstice, and came to end in early August with the feast of Lammas. The rest of the seasons were similarly skewed, *peaking* when we now see them as beginning. Thus, to the Celts, "Midsummer" *was* actually the middle of summer.

Days are at their longest. The weather is clement. Food is plentiful. Life seems to want to take good care of us. "Summertime—and the living is easy," as George Gershwin put it in *Porgy and Bess*. "Fish are jumping and the cotton is high." Bonfires were traditionally lit at the highest points of various districts—hilltops and promontories—to celebrate and embody the life-giving heights which the Sun itself had reached. It is no accident that this holiday was linked to the nurturing Great Mother, called Cerridwen among the Celtic tribes. Fairs were held; social life reached a crescendo. At Midsummer, we were fully engaged in life and the world. With social culture purring along, people traveling to fairs and festivals, commerce occurring, folks dancing, theater and music stimulating the imagination, relationships forming—what happens? *Fun*, certainly! And plenty of drama and complexity too. Just think back to the senior prom at your high school—a ritual we typically celebrate between Beltane and Midsummer, and which reflects the same archetypes. Around the prom, there is excitement certainly, but also tears, rejections, drama, social jockeying, concern with status, and enmeshment in situations that seem to develop their own irresistible momentum. Welcome to Midsummer.

HOLIDAY: *Lammas; Lughnassadh; La Lunasa; Hlafmesse.*
Seasonal Place: *Midway between the Summer Solstice
and the Autumnal Equinox*
Corresponding Lunar Phase: *The Waning Gibbous Moon*
Approximate Date (Northern): *Early August*

The weather remains gentle. Although we notice the Sun setting earlier and earlier each evening, days are still longer than the nights. Despite the pleasant conditions, something slightly unsettling is in the air; some vaguely threatening change. It is still too far off to be called ominous. But we sense it. We huddle a little closer together, and maybe try to pretend we do not feel it. We know that summer—in every sense of the word—cannot last forever.

To the Anglo-Saxons, this cross-quarter day was called *Hlafmesse*, which means "loaf mass." It was literally a celebration of bread, which brings us to heart of the matter, at least historically: Lammas is a *grain festival*. As such, it is probably the most difficult of these cross-quarter days for modern people to grasp—and, probably for that reason, it is the only one for which there is not even a vestige of modern practice. We are accustomed to bread being available year-round. It is a staple; we do not think of it as a seasonal thing. We do not even typically think of it as a grain! And yet for our ancestors, the harvesting of the grain crops around this time of the year was an occasion of enormous significance. That grain might be all that stood between them and starvation in a few months' time. Even today in the Christian context, we sacralize bread in Holy Communion—we make it represent the body of Jesus. Through eating it, we visualize ourselves "communing," literally, with Christ. At a more secular level, but reflecting the same principle of *bonding-through-eating*, we speak of "breaking bread" with someone. That is a reference not only to having a meal together, but also to the *vast symbolism of soul-connection that is linked to shared food.*

If you can bring these symbolic threads together, you have understood Lammas. Jesus enjoys a "last supper" with his good friends. No one, except Jesus and Judas, knows what is about to happen—and yet no one at that famous table mistakes what is happening for grabbing a quick bite. Something heavy is about to occur. A cold, hard time is on the horizon.

Rituals of connection bind us together. By melding sweet, shared memory into the soul, they make us stronger in the face of the unknowable and the catastrophic. They prepare us for what might come. These notions of bonding and the strength it gives us are the soul of Lammas, the forgotten holiday.

HOLIDAY: *Alban Elfed; Mabon; Harvest Home*
Seasonal Place: *The Autumnal Equinox*
Corresponding Lunar Phase: *The Last Quarter*
Approximate Date (Northern): *September 22*

We reach the Fall Equinox. Night has been nibbling away at the daylight for three months, attempting to regain hegemony over the lifegiving powers of light. Finally it succeeds. Equilibrium is reached, and darkness is in the ascendancy again. From now on, we are bound into ever-deeper night. The cold will seep into our bones; life will be leached from the world, driven underground, into seeds, into houses, into burrows and caves—and, very possibly, into the grave. In ancient Greece, the Autumnal Equinox was the time for the celebration of the Eleusinian mysteries. Very little is known about them, except that they involved a symbolic passage into death and rebirth—from light into dark and then back into light. There is significant evidence that the ceremony involved wine mixed with psychedelic mushrooms (if you are interested, check out Ivan Valencic, *Yearbook for Ethnomedicine and the Study of Consciousness*, Issue 3, 1994, pages 325-336).

The quintessential point of the Autumnal Equinox is that here we are collectively facing the sobering reality of winter. Symbolically we are also facing that larger "winter" we call mortality. We need strength for that ordeal. We draw it from ritual, from our connections with each other, and from what remains of the abundance of food from our growing season. Speaking of this holiday, Merlyn of Ladywoods points out, "It is the Pagan Thanksgiving, the Middle Harvest when the fall fruits—apples, pumpkins, winter squash, and field corn for the cattle—are brought in from the fields and orchards."

We all know how to say "Eat, drink, and be merry . . ." And of course, as much as we might like to forget it, the rest of that familiar phrase is "for tomorrow you may die."

By the way, Mabon—the common neo-Pagan name for this holiday—is actually a reference to a character from Welsh mythology. He has great powers, and King Arthur is dependent on recruiting him for a critical mission. Yet Mabon was kidnapped when he was just three days old, and no one knows where to find him—except, that is, for the ancient Salmon of Llyn Llyw. One thing leads to the next, of course. (The tale is in the *Mabinogion*, if you want to find it.) The good guys eventually win. But the story, at the deepest level, is about the preciousness of interdependency, even when our own powers are great in proportion. Calling this festival "Mabon" actually only dates to about 1970. But the custom has caught on in the neo-Pagan world, and I echo it here.

HOLIDAY: *Samhain; Halloween; El Dia de los Muertos, All Souls' Eve*
Seasonal Place: *Midway between the Autumnal Equinox*
and the Winter Solstice
Corresponding Lunar Phase: *The Waning Crescent Moon*
Approximate Date (Northern): *Late October/early November*

We have come to the end of the kinder months of the year. Darkness has overcome the daylight, and it is gaining ground with each passing day. The fading Sun shines over fields gone fallow and barren. A chill permeates the air. *Samhain* Eve in the old Celtic calendar was New Year's Eve. It marked the end of the year—and of course the beginning of the next one. The slaughter of livestock was customary then, and the reasons were practical. First, our Celtic ancestors could finally gauge with some accuracy how many animals we had enough hay and grain to keep alive over the winter. And secondly, it was cold enough for the safe storage of salted or smoked meat. Thus at Samhain, the smell of smoke and slaughter was in the wind. It is helpful to remember that those animals did not come from impersonal factory farms. Our ancestors knew them, had looked into their eyes, scratched them behind the ears. Taking their lives so that our forebears might survive was not a simple act. No wonder this cross-quarter day became a Feast of the Dead. It was a time to remember one's ancestors—and to placate their spirits.

In historical northern Europe, surviving winter was dicey. In our weakened physical conditions, in the crowding and the smoke and the endless damp chill, one never knew what diseases would run rampant, nor who would live to see the spring. It made sense to be nice to the dead since we might be dining at their tables ourselves before long. Halloween, with all its wonderful demonology, is a delicious and authentic expression of this ancient cross-quarter festival. An even better one is the Mexican *El Día de los Muertos*, when the dead are greeted and welcomed as if they are still among us.

To our ancestors, at this time of year only the thinnest and most transparent of veils separated this world from the next one. Beings could peer through—and possibly slip through—in either direction. We celebrated our closeness to the spirit world. We challenged our tendency toward overdramatizing our own mortality. We affirmed the ultimate unity of all planes of experience, embodied and otherwise.

This completes our survey of the Pagan calendar. As I indicated earlier, I have not attempted here directly to relate that calendar to the eight phases of the Moon, wanting instead to present the cyclical Pagan worldview in its own right. As you read, you probably already sensed the basic structure of the monthly lunar cycle underlying this longer yearly cycle of seasonal holidays. In the next eight chapters, I'll explore each lunar phase specifically, making that linkage explicit and practical.

PART THREE:

THE EIGHT
LUNAR PHASES

The Eight Lunar Phases

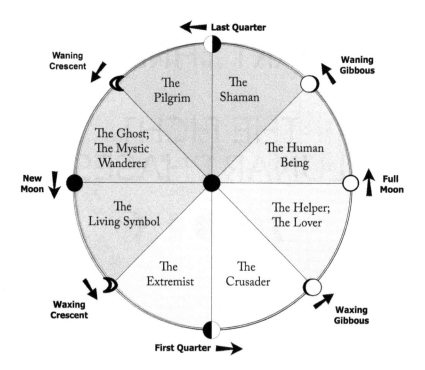

10

☽

PHASE ONE
THE NEW MOON

THE LIVING SYMBOL (THE LEGEND)
Sun-Moon Phase Angle: 0 - 45°
Pagan Holiday: Yule

Key Concepts: *Charisma. Star Quality. Presence. Nurturing qualities. Leadership. Guidance. Seductive Vagueness. Innocence and Naiveté. Becoming symbolic to others; making others into symbols. A Bringer of Gifts.*

The Mood

A dear friend asks a special favor. She intends to hike alone into trackless mountains on a spiritual vision quest. She will fast and meditate for three days and three nights. Only you will know even approximately where she is. All she asks of you is that you be awaiting her at the trailhead when she is finished. That will be on Tuesday at high noon. If she shows up, you drive her home. If she doesn't, you call the Mounties.

She is solid, mentally and physically. You respect her and you feel confident that she is not being foolish. You are honored that she has asked you to be the one to receive her back into this world.

Tuesday noon comes. You arrived at the trailhead an hour ago. To your relief, you see your friend walking down the mountainside toward you, intact. You rise to meet her. As she approaches, she is aglow. Her eyes, inwardly and outwardly, have seen something extraordinary. She has been in the Holy of Holies.

Instinctively, you keep silence. You respect her exalted condition. She is your friend; you have been silly with her, drunk with her, stupid with her. But now she is transfigured. She has seen something beyond this world.

She has been made both strong and fragile by it.

You await her cues with love, awe, respect, and anticipation . . . and a thousand questions you will not ask until the time is right. She knows something precious. She has brought something back from the Other Side.

The Theory

The New Moon is one of the two darkest phases, the other one being the Waning Crescent at the other end of the cycle, which we will explore in Chapter Seventeen. The two are entirely different. At the Waning Crescent, the natural inwardness and otherworldliness of the dark Moon are allied harmoniously with the withdrawing and transcendent qualities of the waning cycle. Here, at the New Moon, we experience a much stranger combination. The dark Moon's inwardness and otherworldliness merge with the out-rushing intensity of the waxing cycle. In fact, that out-rushing quality is at a peak of intensity. This is the sheer life-fire of the germinating seed. It is young, naive—and bursting with vital force. Think of Cerridwen giving birth to a sky-god's child—or of Jesus in the manger.

Your friend who undertook the vision quest left this world behind. She entered into communion with something beyond the concerns of personality and its realms of worry. Similarly, at the actual moment of the precise New Moon we see a symbolic door opening into the Otherworld. At that moment, the soul is one with the Divine—sitting in God's office, so to speak. In the language of the haiku, *Master has gone to the mountain. Cloud-hidden. Whereabouts unknown.* In other words, as all the mystics in every culture and time have reported, there simply are no metaphors adequate to describe this kind of perception. A person in that state is not a "person" any longer, at least not as we normally understand the term—to us, he or she is "cloud-hidden, whereabouts unknown." A "person" is a being conditioned to three-dimensional space, to chronological time, to the sense of being a distinct object in a field of objects. Not so the soul in union with the Infinite. She may appear as a three-dimensional creature, but there is a sense of something greater, deeper, bigger around her. We sense that she knows something, something that could be inexpressibly precious to us.

As the Moon begins to separate from the Sun, this numinous, magnetic spirit of the New Moon, while still rooted in the sweet darkness, also experiences an impulse to enter physical life. It embodies something precious, but so vast that it simply does not fit into this world at all. And the creature carrying it is illuminated—and befuddled.

Just as in the Winter Solstice, *a great power is emerging into the blinding dark.*

The Personality

Not every Capricorn is the same, and neither is everyone born under the New Moon. The rest of the chart naturally makes itself felt, as do soul differences, cultural influences, and so forth. But with those caveats understood, we can make comments about the typical personality dynamics of each lunar phase.

A person born under this first phase of the lunar cycle seems aglow with a kind of *understanding.* That understanding is human—there is typically warmth here. But it transcends being human. There is an impersonality to it. It seems to extend to the point that the individual has some special insight, some charismatic wisdom, some special relationship with God. Depending on other factors in the chart, people born under this first lunar phase may be introverted or extroverted, colorful or quiet. But when they speak, we notice them. We listen. We sense that behind their words is something more, some treasure from the Great Beyond. We may not phrase it that way, of course—but we trust them, value them, let ourselves be touched by them. We often, quite literally, want them to touch us.

And yet we never truly know them. Some elemental piece of their humanity seems unavailable to us—not "missing," but rather simply "elsewhere," on some other plane. They have one ear on the world, while the other ear seems to be attuned to an invisible Mothership up above the clouds. And some fraction of the messages they receive, they pass on to us—and some fraction of what they say, we understand . . . as we "understand" poetry or what Beethoven "meant" by his Ninth Symphony.

We project our own inner archetypes onto people born under this phase of the Moon. They become *living symbols*, legends in their own time within their community circles. For example, if I describe Elvis Presley or Ray Charles as "singers," what is missing from that statement? What does the word "singer" *not* capture about those two men? What is that elusive harmonic of *sheer living symbolism* which they carry?

That is the quality of the New Moon, which was present in each of their birthcharts.

The Shadow

Every front has a back. An elemental principle of evolutionary astrology is that there are positive soul intentions implicit in every astrological configuration—and that every configuration can be turned into a catastrophe with enough malice, ignorance, or greed. What is the potential Shadow dimension of the New Moon phase?

At the simplest level, we recognize that at this first phase of the lunation cycle, there is an inevitable naiveté about the world and the people in it. Blundering is a significant risk. So is rampant subjectivity—mistaking wishes and fears for reality. The imagination is so strong that it can run away with a person. Facts are not as important as ideas, and ideas take second place to hunches and intuition. Desire is compelling. Mix those qualities with naiveté and there can be a peculiar inability to foresee the seemingly obvious consequences of impulsive actions.

Going deeper, as we have seen, a person born under the New Moon often represents an archetype to his or her community. There can be a two-way street here. Such a person, looking out at the world, can potentially perceive only archetypes. In other words, there is a risk of seeing others more as symbols than as unpredictable, unique, three-dimensional human beings. As Dane Rudhyar put it in *The Lunation Cycle*, "People and situations are met, in most cases, without much regard to what they actually are *in themselves*; they become symbols." Thus, there can be a curiously innocent ignorance about the needs of other human beings—their need for pride, for attention, for respect, for time.

The Evolutionary Intention and the Karmic Predicament

One of the unique elements of evolutionary astrology is that we do not simply ask what an astrological configuration might mean. We ask *why* the person has it and what evolutionary purpose it might serve.

Why might a soul be drawn to incarnate under the New Moon?

Consider the emotional nuances of this advice: "Don't let mere impossibility stop you." At one level, the words are encouraging and inspiring. At another level, they are boneheaded. Most of the time, we benefit from knowing our limits and paying attention to reality-checks. But what exactly are our limits? We are never sure until we test them. A person who errs in the direction of caution and realism may actually be establishing destructive constraints on his or her potential. "You never know until you've tried." That too can potentially be dangerous advice, but it has led to brilliance and breakthrough.

A person born under this first phase of the lunation cycle, in a prior life, very likely allowed "realism" and "humility" to erode his or her capacity for excellence. In this life, he or she needs to have faith—to dive in and "just do it."

There is a necessary *selfishness* in such action. In a prior life, someone born under the New Moon likely allowed love and duty to take too much of a bite out of freedom. Sorting out that question is always a balancing act—loving others and loving ourselves are so often pitted against each other. There is no ultimate formula for getting it right. Like trying to balance on one foot, you do a lot of quivering and compensating.

In a prior incarnation, for this person, the balance went too far in the direction of compromise and generosity toward others. In this lifetime, there is a reaction against that prior experience. The soul carries an intention of establishing a certain quality of *enlightened selfishness*. If we want to "do the impossible," that kind of determination—even if it might be perceived as ruthlessness—is simply necessary. And, as with all things at the evolutionary cutting edge, there is inevitably experimentation—and thus, some failures, some excess. That must be taken as part of the context of learning.

The Secret of Happiness

With the Moon in its New phase, the secret of happiness lies in trusting the dictates of the heart more than those of reason. Find something that ignites the fire in your soul and hurl your life into it. Happiness is multi-dimensional, but do not worry too much about "finding balance." You are not about balance in this lifetime. You are about passion and commitment to something that feels bigger than yourself.

Examples

Richard Branson, Tom Cruise, Ozzy Osbourne, Queen Victoria, Val Kilmer, Pablo Picasso, Sigmund Freud, Agatha Christie, Benjamin Franklin, Mary Queen of Scots, Edgar Allen Poe, Elvis Presley (by 13', almost Phase Two), Ross Perot, Roy Orbison, Carlos Santana, Ho Chi Minh, Harrison Ford, George Clooney, John Wayne Gacy, Florence Nightingale, Georgia O'Keeffe, Antoine de Saint Exupéry, Scott Ainslie, Bobbie Fischer, Billie Graham, James Hillman, Brad Pitt, Ray Charles, Tom Hanks, Steve Jobs, Bhagwan Shree Rajneesh, Sting, Bruce Springsteen, Edgar Rice Burroughs, Muhammed Ali, Elton John, Dustin Hoffman, Teilhard de Chardin, Vaslav Nijinski, Richard Nixon, Sybil Leek, Kenneth Lay, Ivan the Terrible, Ken Wilber, John Maynard Keynes, Daphne du Maurier, James Arthur Ray, Michelle Obama, Annie Lennox, Yao Ming, Isak Dinesen, Paul Cezanne, Ringo Starr, Louis DaGuerre, Snoop Dogg, Joseph Smith, Emile Zola, William Shatner.

11

☽

PHASE TWO
THE WAXING CRESCENT

THE EXTREMIST
Sun-Moon Phase Angle: 45°-90°
Pagan Holiday: *IMBOLC/Candlemas*

Key Concepts: *Drive to accomplish and experience. Hunger. Imbalance. Success—and its costs. Presence. Natural Authority. Radiant, infectious hope in the face of darkness.*

The Mood

A new friend hands you a poem out of the blue and asks you to read it. By the end of the first quatrain, you are entranced. More than just elegant imagery adroitly conveyed, you sense living wisdom in these verses. There is a *power* at work here. This is the poetry of a great soul, not some embittered nihilist with a Ph.D. in English. When you finish, somewhat dumbfounded, you ask your friend, "Who wrote this?"

Her answer shocks you. "My 16-year-old son."

Later, feeling a little awed and nervous, you meet the boy. He is bright and sensitive—no surprise. But he is also a 16-year-old kid and acts that way. He's a little goofy. He mumbles. When you praise his poetry, he lights up. But he also seems slightly embarrassed. You tell him that his poem reminded you of William Butler Yeats—high praise. He responds, "Most of those old guys suck." You ask him if he has actually read Yeats. He shrugs.

Later you ask the young poet about his plans for the future. He tells you he plans to grow wealthy by writing poetry, and to have a famous band—he knows he can write music too, once he masters the guitar he plans to get soon. And then he intends to use his money to establish an ecological school on an island for underprivileged visionaries that will be the base for a world revolution that puts the global economy on a solid Green foundation, because the answers to all the Earth's problems are actually very obvious . . .

He is on fire. You agree with a lot of what he says, in principle. But he also sounds very young, with that classic mix of teenage fragility and one-dimensional certainty.

And yet . . . *he did write that soul-rattling poem.*

The Theory

The Waxing Crescent Moon dominates the evening sky, hanging like the proverbial sickle over the western horizon after sunset. It is a young Moon, beautiful, full of possibility. Like the New Moon which we explored in the previous chapter, we are still in the first quadrant of the cycle, still dominated by the alchemy of the early stages of the waxing cycle—still in Winter, by the pagan calendar.

Being in the dark hemicycle, we are looking at that element of the *otherworldly* or the *archetypal.* The emerging soul-impulse is still suffused with a sense of recent emergence from the Holy of Holies, still on fire with something that is fundamentally untranslatable into human terms. Being a waxing phase, there is a mood of outrushing intensity, an urge toward manifestation. The main difference between these two First Quadrant phases—the New Moon and the Waxing Crescent—is simply that the latter is closer to actual material manifestation. It is less abstract. The gun is loaded this time. As Nigel Pennick described it, here at the Imbolc cross-quarter day, the goddess "throws aside her black rod of wintry barrenness and is transformed into the radiant virgin bride, springing from seeming death into life."

A 14-year-old on a bicycle. A 16-year-old behind the wheel of a car with 200 horsepower. Do two more years of maturation compensate for that astronomical upping of the stakes? Logically, we doubt it. And yet we can only hope—and have faith. Sooner or later kids must learn how to drive. Will that 16-year-old have a few fender-benders? Almost certainly. Will he or she make some bad judgments? Again—count on it. But will the young person eventually become an experienced driver, as safe and responsible on the highway as anyone else? In most cases, even though our fingers are crossed, we have ample reason to anticipate that good outcome.

Idealism *must enter the world*. Pure, new ideas must at some point be physically "born." Youth is as necessary to the workings of the Great Tao as is wise elderhood. At the Waxing Crescent, this process is at an awkward stage—hence, my repeated use of the analogy to our teenage years. But there can be a seed of true brilliance here, and a willingness to roll up the sleeves and dive into the nitty-gritty process of bringing that brilliance into manifestation in the human world. As we saw in Chapter Nine, at this moment in the pagan year the Celtic goddess Bridhe displayed her three great powers: that of healing, that of firecraft, and that of poetry. Similarly, people born under this second lunar phase are sometimes extravagantly gifted. They can heal us; they can warm us, and they can uplift and beguile us with their arts.

But, regardless of their age, make sure they phone you at 10:00 p.m. and let you know exactly where they are, whom they are with, and when they will be coming home!

The Personality

Not every woman aspires to be a mother, and similarly not everyone born under the Waxing Crescent will have the same values or personality. Astrology is always about integrating many themes in the birth chart. Lunar phase is only one of them. Please take what follows in that light.

Born under the Waxing Crescent, the mood of the personality is characterized by an eternal *urgency*. Something has to get done; there is no time to waste. That is one reason why I call it the "Extremist." This underlying drive manifests in countless ways in the course of the lifetime: I must make the Little League team . . . I must finish work on the Jones account . . . I must get to the end of *The Tibetan Book of the Dead* before I lose consciousness here in the hospice . . .

Should we call this unceasing urgency "neurotic?" Let's not rule that out! But let's not be so quick to categorize it as pathology either. Imagine that you really *were* on a mission from God. There really *was* a flash of light at the foot of your bed. Something bigger than you has taken over your life. If you drive yourself hard in pursuit of it, should we dismiss that as "neurotic?" If it is, then probably most of the great artists, social activists, and geniuses of history are head cases. Not that everyone with the Moon in this phase actually *is* one of the great artists, social activists or geniuses of history! The point is that the personality of people born under this phase feels similarly driven.

Under the Waxing Crescent, we are moving away from the magic moment of soul-infusion that we call the New Moon, but we are still close enough to it to feel it and to be inspired by it. That sense of carrying something divine—or at least something more important than ourselves—has lit our fuse. In Rudhyar's words, "Here we see the new impulse for action . . . theoretically released at the new moon, as it challenges the old in a more or less intense struggle." Tellingly, Rudhyar adds, "This leads usually to self-assertiveness, faith in one's self and an eagerness to overcome obstacles in carrying out an inwardly felt command or vital urge."

There is a drive to accomplish great things—and often a fairly naive faith in how "obviously convincing" one's message will sound to the local community. The general population, of course, may not agree—or even notice. And the person carrying this lunar mark may not even detect the indifference. The Extremist's energy is not fundamentally a belligerent one, just enthusiastic. And the enthusiasm is in fact contagious—followers, assistants, and volunteers are likely to appear.

In keeping perspective, it is important to remember that sometimes people born under this lunar phase actually are the bearers of something authentically fresh and vital. They may depend heavily on others for practical support, and they may in fact be nearly incapable of sustaining interest in anything that lacks emotional urgency. Others may later have to tweak the vision to make it work. But the vision itself is precious.

The Shadow

Nothing in astrology is inherently good or bad. Consciousness and intention always shape the expression of the archetypes. What is the potential Shadow expression of the Waxing Crescent Moon phase? Simply said, there can be a strong theme of *neurotic compulsiveness* here. There are things in life for which it is worth paying a big personal price—struggling to save an ecosystem or the life of a child, for example. But that same intensity can be applied to video games or housecleaning. There it crosses the line into the Shadow realm.

In common with the New Moon phase, people born under this phase are instinctively attuned to the archetypal realm. With that attunement comes a diminished sensitivity *to individuals as they actually are* in all their infinite unpredictability and diversity. A person born under the Waxing Crescent must guard against seeing people as objects or as pawns in the game—he or she must, in a nutshell, guard against *oversimplifying* them. Even at its worst, there is typically not viciousness in this phase. It is simply pig-ignorance, mixed with a profound focus on larger aims and issues. Still, this orientation can lead to insensitivity toward, the taking-for-granted of, and, in practical terms, the exploitation of others.

What is the price of success? It is rare that anyone accomplishes anything of lasting value without making a great effort. And even if we do fall into some form of success without effort, it is unlikely that such success will have much spiritual meaning to us. We may appreciate its benefits, but it is unlikely to enhance our dignity or our self-respect. But success—in any sense, be it financial, artistic, mystical, or intellectual—always comes at a price. *It requires imbalance.* I remember reading an article once about people who had survived to the age of 100. The formula seemed to be to live a boring life! That is not for a person born under this phase. Where we truly enter Shadow territory is when we contemplate all this phase's potential wreckage of self, others, body, inner peace, and so forth—and simply see that the goal was not worth the destruction that attaining it caused.

The Evolutionary Intention and the Karmic Predicament

Why might a soul incarnate under a Waxing Crescent Moon? What underlying intention or condition is suggested here at the transpersonal level? Always, the analysis of karmic imprints in the present birth chart is a complex subject. Here, with our usual caveats about any kind of single-factor astrological analysis, let's hazard some speculation. The sheer emotional urgency of this phase of the lunar cycle suggests a compensation for opposite conditions in a prior lifetime.

Rudhyar says that people born under this phase "may be characterized in some cases by a deep, subconscious sense of being overwhelmed by the momentum of the past and the power of 'ghosts' or *karma*." Let's focus this idea more precisely. The presumption is that in a previous incarnation, a condition of stasis arose—that what was actually important in one's life slipped between one's fingers. There might have been simple laziness. More likely, there was a sense of one's hands being tied as a result of enmeshment in some defining set of social or cultural circumstances.

Possibly, this enmeshment was not ultimately real, as in the case of a person who cannot imagine life without daddy's money—and daddy charges a lot for those financial perks!

Possibly the enmeshment was actually inescapable—the poor woman from tribal Pakistan, married and pregnant at 14, who does not manage to become the voice of her generation, even though she had the innate potential to do so.

Either way, the same haunting sense of *a life not lived* courses through the karma. In the present life, the reaction is like seeing one's hair on fire. There is a sense of having no time to waste—in unconscious response to the reality of wasted time in a prior life. Think of the urgency of the innocent person, wrongly and hopelessly incarcerated, who breaks out of jail. That person can run all night long, propelled by both desperation and righteous reason.

In religion, people sometimes comment on the zeal of the newly converted. People born under this second lunar phase possess some of that same zeal. Having found what they take to be truth and freedom—and having a frightening gut-familiarity with the deadening prison of the opposite—lights a fire in the soul.

The Secret of Happiness

With the Moon in Waxing Crescent phase, the secret of happiness lies essentially in having something bigger than one's self to give shape, purpose, and direction to one's life. There must be a *mission* of some sort. And the cause must be a worthy one, or this energy collapses into neurotic, shortsighted selfishness. The mission does not always have to possess the quality of obvious altruism, as in crusading for some social good. Art can do it, for example. So can scientific or academic work, provided we feel it is genuinely important. Raising a family can do it. All that matters is that the effort reflects the best part of ourselves, and that it is somehow bigger than us.

Examples

Galileo, Clint Eastwood, Ann Frank, Anais Nin, George Patton, the fourteenth Dalai Lama, Eckhart Tolle, J.R.R. Tolkien, Stevie Ray Vaughn, Ian McKellen, Warren Buffet, Ronald Reagan, John Mayer, Simone de Beauvoir, Bill Cosby, Christopher Reeve, Rainer Maria Rilke, Neil Young, Ralph Waldo Emerson, Heidi Fleiss, Shirley Temple Black, Brian Wilson, Mae West, Twyla Tharp, Frank Lloyd Wright, Voltaire, Rex Stout, Dizzy Gillespie, Rush Limbaugh, Amy Fisher, Bob Geldorf, J. Edgar Hoover, Beyoncé Knowles, Frank Sinatra, Charles Manson, Britney Spears, Julia Child, Alfred E. Adler, Joan of Arc, Heath Ledger, Rembrandt, Maria Montessori, Alan Alda, Hans Holzer, Patti Smith, W.C. Fields, Fabio, Virginia Woolf, Philip K. Dick, Friedrich Nietzsche, Leonard Nimoy, Wernher von Braun, Judith Resnik, Herbie Hancock, Chay Blyth, Max Roach, Rudolph Giuliani.

12

☾

PHASE THREE
THE FIRST QUARTER

THE CRUSADER
Sun-Moon Phase Angle: 90°-135°
Pagan Holiday: OSTARA/Easter

Key Concepts: *Tension between self and group. Concern with justice. Battles. Group efforts; organizations. Sacrifice for group. The abstract, idealistic principles of the archetypal realm collide with reality.*

The Mood

On June 5, 1989, perhaps the most famous unknown man of the late twentieth century stood before a column of tanks in Tiananmen Square in Beijing, stopping them cold. After that, he disappeared. The presumption is that he was executed.

Karen Silkwood died in a suspicious accident after investigating claims of "irregularities" at the Kerr-McGee nuclear plant in Oklahoma.

Stephen Bantu Biko died in police custody in Apartheid-era South Africa after being arrested under an anti-terrorism law. His crime was organizing protests against racism.

Jesus went willingly and knowingly to the cross.

How many Tibetan monks were murdered, never breaking their vow of nonviolence? How many Native Americans charged the rifles and the cannons, knowing the futility of it and yet doing it anyway?

This heroic willingness to die for a principle—how dangerous it is to romanticize it, and yet what would the human spirit be without it? What would we become if we could not conceive of something more important to ourselves than our own lives? The energy of this *martyred hero* archetype intoxicates us. It has kept one religion alive and vibrant for 2,000 years. It sells tickets to movies. And it inspires *jihadis* to murder the innocent—and to murder themselves in the process.

How can we wrap our minds around this monstrous, heroic principle that defies both life and death at the same time?

The Theory

At the First Quarter—the half Moon—we leave the dark hemisphere and enter the bright one. As we explored in Chapter Seven, there is a vivid distinction between the energetic fingerprints of these two hemispheres. The dark hemisphere is about the *unmanifested realm*. It is about the world behind the one that we see with our senses, which is the one we share more or less with everyone else. In the dark hemisphere, we encounter archetypes and Platonic ideals. It is as if we were actually inside the mind of God.

Not so the bright half of the cycle, which we now enter. In the illuminated half of the Moon's journey, we are in the *realm of manifestation*. We are dealing with the mucky, ambiguous realities of actual embodied life. We encounter people who antagonize us and ideas which oppose our own—and both can perhaps enlighten us too. We must give up the comforts of certainty, clarity and pure idealism. To survive, we must become *political creatures*, engaged socially and cooperatively with people who see things differently than we do. We also recognize that what is to our advantage might not be to the advantage of another person. Thus, two ancient possibilities arise: *war* and *diplomacy*.

To understand the Moon's First Quarter, we need to add another dimension to our thinking: the fact that the Moon is also waxing. Here, at the midpoint of its waxing cycle, we could even make the case that the "torque" of the Moon's waxing energy is at maximum leverage—that there is no other moment in the cycle that so visibly embodies the outrushing fire of the first half of the lunation cycle.

At the First Quarter, in other words, *pure archetypal idealism collides with the brick wall of reality* at a tremendous velocity. A cynic might say, "So much for pure archetypal idealism." But that is not entirely accurate. Pure archetypal idealism is a powerful force. It can win, sometimes. Often it can at least make a dent in the monolith of existing social realities. And sometimes, those existing social realities are not simply evil or wrong. Sometimes they embody some wisdom too. In fact, *all* such outward realities themselves originated in the archetypal realm at some point. We might ideally see a process of synthesis here—one in which what emerges from this mighty collision is greater than either of its components. As Karl Marx put it, *thesis plus antithesis equals synthesis.*

And, at the Spring Equinox, as we saw in Chapter Nine, life commits to manifestation. It emerges into the light, comes out of the womb. There its enormous force encounters antagonistic realities. It eats—or is eaten. It must gamble; it must take its chances. It encounters friends, enemies, opportunities and blockages. How will all that turn out? No way to know except by leaping in.

It is time to roll the dice.

The Personality

Lunar phase is only one factor in astrology, and no human being can ever be understood through looking at only a single element of his or her makeup. Doing that is as simple-minded as assuming that all women or liberals or French people are the same. To be useful, what I write here about the personality dynamics of the First Quarter Moon needs to be placed in the larger context of a person's birth chart. You might, in other words, not find it to be true in an individual case. I do however believe you will see the truth of these principles if you look at a hundred cases.

Imagine an old sailing ship, dismasted and floating helplessly in the midst of vast ocean, driven by the whimsies of wind and current. The food and water are gone. The captain and her officers are huddled below decks holding a meeting about their dwindling options. You, the lowly cabin boy, are not invited. You are gazing out to sea. Suddenly you see land on the horizon! You rush down into the room where the meeting is happening, only to meet the glare of the captain. You must be silent. But you know something that could save all those aboard, something terribly urgent. You must speak—but you can't—but you must.

This same quality of tension underlies the consciousness of the person born in this third lunar phase. He feels he has something compelling to say, something of transcendent significance. And yet the circumstances are not receptive or conducive to him speaking. She knows something that can make a difference, but she will be killed (or otherwise punished) for saying it. Compelling urgency collides with restraint, not to mention with what appears to be blockheaded resistance. Thus, at the level of personality, we observe two major elements in the underlying mood of this third lunar phase: *urgency* and *frustration*.

There is in the First Quarter phase an essential sense of certainty about one's rightness. That is why I call it the "Crusader." Rudhyar describes "a feeling of self-exaltation when faced with crumbling old structures." There is compelling impatience with others' stubbornness. It is not so much a sense that other people are stupid or malicious; it is more like the feeling that they just don't see—all the captain and officers on that ship need to do is to *look*. They will see the land for themselves. But they are standing on ceremony and tradition, blinded by it.

Justice is a big theme in the First Quarter Moon phase. And of course, the vexation is that justice can be defined very differently by different people. That actual nuance is subjectively less clear in this lunar phase; the Crusader's certainty is too great. Battles are not so much desired as they are seen as inevitable or morally required. Emphatically, there is no inherent eagerness for martyrdom here—only an acceptance that there are, in fact, things in life for which it is worth dying.

Ultimately, the key is that people born under this third phase are actually carrying something potentially very powerful and transformative into the world. They are on fire with it. You would be too, if you could feel and see as they do.

They are willing to make a stand.

The Shadow

Every coin has two sides. Evolutionary astrology holds that there are positive meanings built into every astrological configuration. It also holds that every configuration can be turned sour with enough ignorance or fear in the mix. Let's consider the potential Shadow of the First Quarter Moon.

Moral righteousness, in its pure form, is of course laudable. But we humans *like* being seen as laudable, and that is where the darkness gets in. Self-righteousness can be intoxicating. And "right" ultimately has no meaning except in the context of "wrong." So with self-righteousness comes the need to make others wrong, and this is a big driver of the Shadow manifestations of the third lunar phase. Crusading self-righteousness can create unnecessary polarizations and oppositions between people and ideas. "If you are not with us, you are against us" is not always a constructive attitude. To work, it needs a little dose of "let's meet in the middle."

In its Shadow manifestation, the First Quarter Moon can see attacks coming from every direction. It can react with fear—or with fear's first cousin: violence. In the language of psychology, there can potentially be *paranoia* here.

Tolerance of ambiguity, an appreciation of subtlety, a recognition of the benefits of respectful dialogue—in the dark expression of the First Quarter, these ingredients are missing. Despite social mythology, many a good idea has actually been *improved* by a committee!

In setting the mood at the beginning of this chapter, we listed some heroic martyrs. These are honorable human beings who were willing to take a stand. Sometimes they actually win—think of Nelson Mandela. In our list, we saw only the ones who lost, or at least who died. But even there, we might ask the question, did Stephen Biko really lose? He died, but in a sense he actually won. And in doing so, he became bigger than life. As Obi Wan Kenobi said to Darth Vader in the first *Star Wars* film, just as he folded up his light saber, "Strike me down and I will become more powerful than you could ever imagine." And it is true. Look at Biko. Look at Karen Silkwood. Look at Jesus.

None of that is Shadow material—it is all connected with the noble side of this lunar phase. Where the Shadow enters the equations is in our *enthusiasm* for this kind of death-mythology. We can *romanticize martyrdom.* If you doubt that notion, just go to the movies. Probably half of them use this same ancient emotional trick. Under this phase, a person may pay a terrible price for not compromising . . . for not even listening. And they may slip into the belief that they are vindicated by their own destruction or rejection.

The Evolutionary Intention and the Karmic Predicament

In a lifetime prior to the present one, a person born under this lunar phase either made a terrible sacrifice for a principle—or failed to do so. The obvious problem with that statement is, of course, that it seems to apply to 100% percent of the human population! Actually, it is more precise than that by far. The majority of us are simply never faced with such a do-or-die situation.

Would you give your life for your child? Most parents would say yes without hesitation—and of course take great comfort in the high probability that the question will remain hypothetical. In all likelihood, their noble resolution will never be put to the test. Thus, the existence of this lunar phase in the present birthchart does speak fairly precisely about a prior life drama that left a mark on the evolving spirit: this person actually did have to make such a decision. We do not know from lunar phase alone which way they went. That answer may lie in the birthchart. To sort it out; I would recommend the more complex kind of karmic analysis described in my book *Yesterday's Sky*.

To die for something—or to fail to die for it. Either eventuality leaves us wounded. And "dying" is only the most dramatic way of saying it. The situation can take less lethal forms. Perhaps our financial security came into tension with an issue of principle. Or our good reputation was maintained by a lie—or destroyed by a brave truth.

If a person born under this third lunar phase stood his or her ground in the prior life, there is some residual martyr-karma. An attachment to that emotional drama formed. The person must be wary in this life of unnecessarily repeating a pattern of self-sacrifice, like a moth drawn to a flame.

If the person failed to stand up in the prior lifetime, it becomes pressingly important that he or she take on some meaningful cause or mission in this lifetime, and do right by it. But "doing right by it" does not mean martyring one's self. In principle, it is helpful to have something in our lives that feels bigger than our penny-ante personal needs and appetites. But that does not mean that we are eager for self-punishment—and it certainly does not mean that we have fallen under the dark spell of the "romance of martyrdom."

The Secret of Happiness

With the Moon in First Quarter phase, one secret of happiness lies in *successfully* bringing an important principle into manifestation. I emphasize "successfully" in order to distinguish this path from all variations on the theme of noble death or the dignity of martyrdom. Simply said, it is time to *win one*. And when ideas "win" in this world, that victory is almost never perfect. That is a given. Manifestation in the three-dimensional world always involves some degree of compromise—and that is the coin of the realm in the Moon's bright hemicycle. For example, did the hippies win or lose the "culture wars" of the 1960s and 1970s? Has feminism been a success or a failure? Has psychology actually helped people, or should we believe James Hillman's assertion in his book titled *We've Had a Hundred Years of Psychotherapy and the World Is Getting Worse*? For thinking people, none of these are easily answerable questions, at least not in black-and-white terms. After each one, we could simply write: *Discuss*.

To have made one's values felt in this world. To have left a mark. To have made a difference. That is what counts here. Part of the secret of happiness for a First Quarter person lies in recognizing and taking joy in smaller and more subtle victories.

At a purely practical level, the secret of happiness in this phase resides in learning how to work with other people in the context of their institutions and their customs. It is there that the necessary compromises occur—and there that we sometimes experience the delight of our own ideas being further enlivened, strengthened and improved as a result of their being forwarded to "the Committee."

Examples

T.E. Lawrence ("Lawrence of Arabia"), John Fitzgerald Kennedy, Benazir Bhutto, Bill Wilson, Jimmy Swaggart, Paul Verlaine, Joseph Campbell, Carlos Casteneda, Rembrandt, Timothy Leary, Neil Armstrong, Art Bell, Oliver Cromwell, Charles de Gaulle, Legs Diamond, Jay Leno, Linda Lovelace, George W. Bush, Shirley MacLaine, Nelson Mandela, Robert Mapplethorpe, Jonas Salk, Martin Scorsese, George Steinbrenner, Eminem, Dylan Thomas, Jack Kevorkian, the Marquis de Sade,

Aleksandr Solzhenitsyn, Adelle Davis, Jerry Brown, Richard Idemon, Wayne Gretzky, Gianni Versace, Norman Vincent Peale, Donovan, Jimmy Hoffa, Sam Abell, LeAnn Rimes, John McEnroe, William Randolph Hearst, Patsy Cline, Elaine Pagels, Michelle Pfeiffer, Aretha Franklin, Dennis Lehane, Albert Schweitzer.

13

☽

PHASE FOUR
THE WAXING GIBBOUS

THE HELPER (THE LOVER)
Sun-Moon Phase Angle: 135°-180°
Pagan Holiday: *Beltane; May Day*

Key Concepts: *Service. Identification with group ideal. Sexual energy. Joint expressions of creativity. Creator-audience synergy. Support offered to a person or a principle. Generosity. Teamwork. Partnership.*

The Mood

An astrology friend of yours feels that the phases of the Moon have been given short shrift in the literature. She has been working on the problem, reading and exploring and thinking about the charts of her friends. She invites you over one evening to sit down with some charts and some cappuccino. You love and respect her—and as it happens you have some ideas of your own about lunar phase.

Your friend proposes that people born under the waxing Moon are extroverts and people born under the waning Moon are introverts. You hear that and you sense that while there is some truth in what she is saying, her idea is a little off the mark. You pull out the chart of a mutual friend with a waxing Moon, Joey, who is actually quite introverted.

"Hmm," says your friend. "Maybe other factors can overcome the waxing Moon." You agree. With that simple insight, you have perhaps taken your understanding a step further. Your friend becomes pensive. After a moment, with a little smile, she points out that "Joey, while he's definitely introverted, is not exactly *shy* about it."

You both laugh at the obvious irony of the remark. But when you have stopped laughing, you realize that your friend has said something profound. Joey is quite emphatic about how being introverted is not a psychiatric disorder. If people complain to him about his not going to a party, he stands up for himself forthrightly.

Now your friend is stumped. What does Joey's behavior mean about the waxing Moon? She thought she understood it, but now your bringing up Joey has made everything more complicated. It is your turn to be brilliant. You point out that maybe the waxing Moon does not mean extroversion . . . not exactly. Maybe it means something more like "active" or "forward" in expressing whatever our nature *happens* to be.

Ah. That is an insight that stands up solidly to the test, as the two of you paw through the rest of the charts on the table. You and your friend have *co-created* something. Neither one of you could have gotten there without the triggering insights provided by the other. *Your two minds have become one, and something greater than either of them has arisen from the union.*

The Theory

At the Waxing Gibbous Moon, we have come to the last phase of the waxing cycle. A kind of culmination has been reached. The waxing Moon's out-rushing impulse to bring archetypal principles into manifestation has now entered as fully as it possibly can into the bright hemisphere—the hemisphere that represents the three-dimensional world of men and women, with all its flaws and compromises and possibilities. The archetypes are becoming fully embodied, fully human.

We can best understand this fourth phase by seeing it in contrast with the last one. In the previous phase—the First Quarter—we saw a battle emerging. The sheer perfection of the New Moon's Platonic ideals resists being sullied by political deal-making. It sees attacks coming from every direction. There is an underlying spirit of *aversion* in it. We also recognized how, in the previous phase, the path of wisdom entails the acceptance of the idea that other people carry positive potentials, as well as potential threats, to the purity of our principles. We can learn from others and improve what we have brought into the world with our visionary imaginations. This idea—*that strangers are not necessarily the enemy*—is positive evolutionary advice under the First Quarter.

Under this present phase, the Waxing Gibbous Moon, that same advice is unnecessary. Such cooperativeness is implicit in the psychology of the fourth phase. Here, we have gone over the waterfall. We are fully committed to the world, engaged interdependently with the human family. Strangers are not the enemy. Instead they are fascinating, creative, full of surprises—and sexy.

As we learned in Chapter Nine, the festival of Beltane was unabashedly erotic. Humans engaged *procreatively* with each other—and that rhymes with "co-creatively," which is helpful to note because it gives the sexual concept room to breathe. Sexual relationship tends to press people toward development of their human potentials, broadly defined. Together, we are typically stronger, better and wiser than we could be alone. Often we simply have to grow in order to stay together. That is one reason why I call this fourth phase the "Lover." But the processes of exchange and mutual triggering which abound in this phase exist outside the sexual realm as well. Co-creation, along with the exchange of insight, vitality and a strong current of psychic energy are the essence of the Waxing Gibbous Moon. The dangers that arise have to do with the risk of losing one's self in the world or in relationship. Where *aversion* can get us into trouble in phase three, in phase four it is *desire*.

The word "compromise" says it all. Without compromise, we cannot exist in society. We cannot engage in synergy with other beings, or even avoid conflict with them. And yet, compromise can go too far. We all need to compromise. And yet we do not want to *be compromised*.

Those are both good ideas! But where exactly is the line that separates them?

The Personality

Gemini may indicate curiosity, but some Gemini folks are curious about baseball while others are curious about astrophysics. Just as not every Geminian is the same, neither is everyone born under the Waxing Gibbous phase of the Moon. The rest of chart plays a role, as do sociological and cultural differences and, most importantly, karmic differences. Take the following profile of the Waxing Gibbous personality in that light. Your mileage may vary!

As I mentioned earlier in this book, when I was developing the ideas you are reading about here, my first step was to put together a list of people in my own life, people I really felt I knew. If my Moon phase theories did not work with them, I would discard the theories. And as I described in Chapter Five, there were a lot of false starts. Theory can get you in a lot of trouble.

But one thing that never gets you in trouble, although it will sometimes seriously surprise you, is reality. And, in looking at my list of people born under the Waxing Gibbous Moon, one pattern jumped out. I have been fortunate in that helpers have always stepped up to the plate to support my work—for example, by administering my teaching programs. I was struck by the number of people to whom I feel great gratitude for that reason who were born under this fourth lunar phase. This led me to one fundamental insight into the personality traits of this type of human being. He or she feels a strong impulse to engage with the world through *service*. As Dane Rudhyar says, "They may devote themselves to a . . . personality . . . or cause . . ." Thus, as well as "Lover," we can call this phase the "Helper."

Underlying this insight is a more fundamental one. As the root archetypal ideas born under the New Moon reach this stage of manifestation, they are "compromised"—which, as we have seen, can mean enriched, tempered, and improved—through their interactions with the minds of others. In this Waxing Gibbous phase, there is much delight in that kind of interaction. The root idea is no longer something we possess personally. There is less ego and less "self" in our inner equations. We are co-creators now. We are motivated to engage imaginatively and energetically with people whose visions resonate with our own. Whether they are helping us or we are helping them becomes a moot point. The point lies in the *synergy*, and in relishing the unexpected paths down which it will lead us. We want to help others shine, and to be swept along in ecstatic fellowship.

The social or collective impulse is typically strong in fourth-phase men and women. Not all are extroverts by any means. But they are people who prosper in connection with others, thriving on the exchange of information, interest and enthusiasm. They are often *team players* or *networkers*. Even the shyer members of this tribe tend simply to *know* a lot of people.

Sexual connection is, for most of us, the most intense kind of human interaction. Beltane, the pagan holiday resonant with this lunar phase, was deeply oriented to sexuality and fertility, as we saw in Chapter Nine. The wild abandon of the traditional May Day spirit could easily be confused with the notion of "meaningless sex." If we attempt to define that term, the definition really comes down to the kind of sex that is simply about the needs and impulses of the body. In *meaningful* sexual expression, there is a sense of "many of my bodies" interacting with many of yours—the emotional body, the spirit body, and so on. In meaningful sex, with its possibilities of cross-fertilization at every level, we perhaps see the purest, most characteristic expression of the Waxing Gibbous Moon—and of Beltane. Correspondingly, the classic fourth-phase personality is not only sexual, but also romantic and affectionate.

The Shadow

As always, there is potentially a dark side to the equations. There is no astrological energy that cannot be perverted, or reduced through ignorance into something awful. The Waxing Gibbous phase of the Moon is no exception. It too has a Shadow side.

We have been playing with the word "compromise" quite a lot. As the Moon swings outward into the bright hemisphere, it must engage with the world. Ideals cannot ever become real without some degree of adaptation and deal-making. That is not just bad luck; it is closer to a fundamental law of the universe. It is connected with the requirements of translating multidimensional realities into three-dimensional contexts. In this process, something is always lost. If we cannot accept that, we become lost ourselves, irrelevant idealists living in a world of theory—that, or we get crucified! But here, in the Waxing Gibbous phase, we are extremely extended into the world. Instead of touting the necessity of deal-making, we accept it—and begin to reckon with its darker potential. Virtually everything you need to know about the Shadow side of the Waxing Gibbous phase is embraced in the unpleasant and truly negative aspects of the word "compromise."

In this phase, in our very open-mindedness, we can lose our moral compass. In our zeal to be nonjudgmental, we can fail to make important discriminations between that which is healthy and that which is sick. We can enter into "contracts" that are hard to exit—relationships, habits, professions, communities and subcultures. We are particularly vulnerable to being negatively impacted by inappropriate sexual partners—and when I say "inappropriate," I am not talking about motorcycles, dirty words, and tattoos. I mean *spiritually* inappropriate, as in partners who are simply unworthy of us or otherwise bad for us.

The Evolutionary Intention and the Karmic Predicament

What kind of karmic or evolutionary situation could lead a person to incarnate under the Waxing Gibbous phase? As always, there are many possible answers to that question, but they do have certain common denominators. Fundamentally, we see here a strong soul intention to let oneself be touched by others. To listen. To take in the unpredictable, surprising mystery of other people. Underlying such a present soul intention was a prior-life situation of emotional isolation or containment. Perhaps we brought it on ourselves through fear or misanthropy or egotism. Perhaps it was thrust upon us by circumstance—in a prior lifetime we were a lonely priest, or a lonely lighthouse-keeper . . . obviously, the range of specific possibilities here is vast. We may have prior-life experiences of being part of a highly repressed, choreographed, and formal culture, where keeping one's humanity out of view was the norm. Whatever the story, there is a strong reaction against it in this lifetime. There is a soul need to be "fertilized" by the consciousness of other beings.

Typically, with the Moon in this fourth phase, the soul intentions should not be separated from sexuality. There are, of course, exceptions—the real point here is not sex *per se*, but rather the exchange of strong energies with other human beings. One can do that without "meaningful sex" or any sex at all. Similarly, one can perhaps cross the Atlantic in an inner tube, but why bother when you've been handed tickets for a luxury stateroom on the *Norwegian Wind*? Sex is mostly helpful here. Why not use it? Astrology is, at root, a pagan system. Inherent to its symbolism is an appreciation for the mystical and evolutionary possibilities built into the sharing of consciousness in sexual union. Implicit in the Moon's being in this fourth lunar phase is the notion that the soul benefits greatly from that experience in this lifetime. Underlying this reality is the implication that in a prior lifetime, there was some shaming of sexuality or repression of it, which must be undone—and which can only be undone, needless to say, "with a little help from your friends."

The Secret of Happiness

With the Moon in its Waxing Gibbous phase, the secret of happiness is very much connected with lively, surprising and meaningful relationships. Partners and friends play a big role in this. So do appropriate and engaging teachers of all stripes. We experience uplift and joy when we are part of a vibrant collective, and especially so if we can play a helpful role within it. We need to experience a genuine feeling of welcome in our hearts toward other people who inspire it naturally. Nothing is forced here—the specific natures of the other people spontaneously do half the work!

Our happiness is also mightily enhanced in this Waxing Gibbous phase if we see a corresponding welcome in the eyes of these people when they see our faces coming around the corner. We need to feel loved and appreciated. The secret of happiness here, in a nutshell, is that you cannot do it alone.

Examples

Bono, Camille Paglia, William Shakespeare, Aleister Crowley, Xaviera Hollander, Edith Piaf, William Wordsworth, Rudolph Valentino, Dante Alighieri, Mike Tyson, Lord Byron, Melissa Etheridge, Jack Kerouac, Swami Muktananda, Harry S. Truman, Hillary Clinton, Donald Trump, Dino DeLaurentis, Dylan Bennet Klebold, Jimmy Page, James Leininger (reincarnated WWII fighter pilot), L. Ron Hubbard, David Copperfield, Noel Coward, Arnold Schwarzeneggar, Magnus Carlsen, Bill Gates, Paris Hilton, Sid Vicious, Antonio Vivaldi, Babe Ruth, Christian Dior, Catherine Zeta-Jones, Ralph Nader, Prince Charles, Pope Benedict XVI, Janis Joplin, Ansel Adams, Robert Hooke, Nicole Kidman, Marvin Gaye, Ernest Hemingway, R.D. Laing, Johannes Kepler, Isaac Newton, Mario Cuomo, John Irving, Dan Brown, Jack Nicholson.

14

☽

PHASE FIVE
THE FULL MOON

THE HUMAN BEING
Sun-Moon Phase Angle: 180°-225°
Pagan Holiday: *Midsummer; Litha*

Key Concepts: *Committed or inescapable involvements of all sorts. Familial complexities; divorce. Life-long bonding. Wedlock as deadlock. Caregiving. Art and creativity made manifest. Nurture. Outward expression of light and dark. "Damned if I do and damned if I don't." Drama.*

The Mood

You have always wanted to skydive . . . sort of. On the other hand, *are you totally insane? Volunteer* to jump out of an airplane? No way, José!

A friend's birthday comes along. It has a zero in it, so you feel like you owe him something special. At the party, one thing leads to the next and at his instigation, you agree to accompany him in a parachute jump the following weekend. And suddenly there you are, flying at 13,000 feet in a DeHavilland *Otter*, contemplating two miles of thin air between you and the hard, cold, unforgiving ground. Your Aries friend, whom you blame for your being in this predicament, has just jumped. You *mostly* hope his 'chute opens safely and he lives to see another birthday. You are next in line—and there is someone pressing behind you, eager to go. How in the name of all that is holy did you find yourself in this situation?

There is nothing that gets us into more trouble in this world than that single, fatal word "yes." And you said it. You agreed. And here you are.

What can you do? You jump.

Yes.

With that single word, we enter chapters of our lives whose outcomes we cannot foresee or control. With yes, we marry or commit. We have children. We take jobs, move to new cities. We enter friendships. We become someone's lover. We succumb to temptation. We volunteer for sainthood. *And we never really have any idea what we are getting ourselves into!*

The alternatives? Say no to everything—and have fear be the defining force of your life? Or say "maybe" to everything—and live in a cold, colorless, halfway-house of a world forever?

With "yes," we entangle ourselves in life. We make ourselves vulnerable. We learn. We grow. We get wounded, perhaps irremediably. We prosper—and we get into situations that shred our souls. Only our wisdom can make the right call. But our wisdom is flawed. We do not know what the future holds. We haven't been there yet.

Nothing for it but to jump.

The Theory

We have reached a critical juncture in the lunation cycle. That literally could not be more obvious—the Moon is Full. It has reached its brightest, most dramatic moment, dominating the night from sundown to dawn. Moon-wise, the pedal is to the metal. This is it. The Moon can do nothing now except fade. In our technical language, the critical observation at this stage is that the Moon, now halfway through its cycle, begins to *wane*. We have reached the end of the out-rushing, forward logic of the waxing Moon. We begin the long homeward journey. We have begun to head back toward the archetypal realm, to the Divine, to death—to all the natural endings and disappearances that permeate this realm of impermanence we call life.

With the onset of the waning phases, we can expect some *calming*. We can expect more *reflectiveness*. But here at the Full Moon we also find ourselves at maximum extension into the world.

In our analogy with the human life-cycle, at this fifth phase we are now resonant with the natural psychology of midlife and its attendant spiritual crises. Where *naiveté* was the demon that stalked the waxing cycle, the demons we start to face now are feelings of *defeat, despair*, and *hopelessness*. In understanding the Full Moon, it is imperative to remember that we are only at the *beginning* of the waning cycle. Those vitiating demons will be stronger later—just as the archetypal principles and the *expressions* of naiveté arising at the New Moon become more pronounced and evident as the waxing cycle advanced. Now, at the outset of the waning cycle, we have reached a kind of culmination. Climax and victory may be sweet, but something deep inside us understands that the next day will not dawn quite so brightly.

Beyond the duality of waxing and waning, at the Full Moon we are also at the *midpoint of the bright hemicycle*. This is a critical insight, as it indicates that we are fully extended into the world of manifestation. As Dane Rudhyar put it, "What was mainly *felt* in the past is now *seen*." Everything is on the table, out there. We are, at this point, *enmeshed in our own creation*. The New Moon vision, having accelerated headlong into the world, having compromised—and been compromised—is now fully what it is. Warts and all, in other words.

And escaping that creation promises, at best, to be a lot more difficult than was getting into it in the first place. Likely, we cannot escape it at all. Our choices bind us. *Having leapt from the airplane, second thoughts are futile.*

In relating this lunar phase to Midsummer, we recognize the sense of *peaking* that arises now—the days are long and warm, people are social. We have festivals. Relationships are forged. Everything is brought into visible manifestation. And, again, there is nothing easier to escape than it was to enter. That goes for careers, responsibilities, addictions, relationships, good habits, bad habits, self-created health issues—you name it.

The Personality

Name any astrological configuration and ask a group of astrologers what it means. You will get answers, and most of those answers will hold water across broad populations of people whose charts possess that signature. But you will always find some people for whom those observations do not really resonate. That is to be expected, since no single astrological factor completely determines the shape of a personality, any more than your gender or nationality or race determine your personality. To understand a person, we need a full birth chart. In what you read here, we are focusing on the personality dynamics of the Full Moon, broadly defined. The real art of a good astrologer is to weave them into the rest of the chart.

Make it real. Just do it. Bring it to fruition. Put it out there. Why not? Those are the motivational themes of the personality under this fifth lunar phase. This could be understood as ambition. It might be seen as extroversion. But neither of those concepts really captures the feeling. Perhaps the most precise terms would simply be *generosity* or *expressiveness* or even *faith*. The urge to leave tangible evidence of our inner lives in the hands of the world is compelling in this phase. It is not so much the idea that if we are not noticed we do not exist—although that can indeed be a less-evolved response to the Full Moon. It is more along the lines of thinking, "If I leave no mark of my existence on this world, what was the point of it all?" Depending on individual factors, this mark of one's existence can take many forms—creative output, professional work, volunteer work, a healthy family. But whatever form it takes, it will represent a crystallization of what we believe and what we value.

In psychology circles, the phrase "thank you for sharing" has become an ironical cliché. Often nowadays it is employed cynically, with its meaning reversed. We might use it, for example, when a blustering, opinionated fool has finally run out of wind. And yet there are situations in which its positive sentiment would be absolutely sincere. Someone, for example, tells us in humble and open terms what it felt like to meet the Dalai Lama—or to meet and forgive her estranged father. We are genuinely moved, and we appreciate it. People born under the Full Moon have the ability to invoke that kind of gratitude in us. Their sheer *humanity* is contagious. When they share their hearts, it can be moving. *They have the ability to get us to identify with their emotions.* There is a quality of the "fully human" about them—thus my decision to label this Full Moon phase "The Human Being." Furthermore, they care; they tend to be nurturing, at least toward those whom they love, and often more broadly, even to strangers.

With the Moon opposite the Sun, two equal forces are pitted against each other. This sets up a resonant dynamic in the minds of fifth phase people: they, too, find they must *balance opposites* in their lives. Thus, they naturally possess a *tolerance for ambiguity*. They see the other person's point of view. They are inclined to accept life's paradoxes. Faced with "damned if I do and damned if I don't" situations, they are not surprised. They tend to accept them as the natural state of things. Thus Rudhyar fairly praises their "objectivity and clear consciousness."

Sitting on the razor's edge, maintaining their balance this way, it is as if Full Moon people are fully incarnate, fully manifest in this ever-imperfect world. They accept flawed reality as it is, and they try to make a difference within the context of those givens. In a sense, they are life's consummate realists.

The Shadow

Nothing in the context of evolutionary astrology is inherently positive or negative. Consciousness, imagination and intention always shape the outward expression of the archetypes. What Shadow expressions of the Full Moon might we encounter?

Remember jumping out of an airplane a couple of pages ago? Well, you've really done it now! Once you take that first big step, gravity and luck are holding all the aces. Your skill is significant too, but it is in third place. You are up and you are heading down. Deal with it.

People born under the Full Moon constantly feel this same underlying mood: a sense of inevitability, a sense of fate or destiny. The feeling that life is a runaway train. The feeling of endless improvisation in the context of free-fall. Gravity rules.

They have created the reality they inhabit—that, at least, would be true philosophically. But their human truth is one of not really feeling any clear certainty in their bones about how they got into their situations—their families, their relationships, their jobs, and so forth. It is as if it all "just happened" somehow. Yeats, as you may recall, described them as, "Estranged amid the strangeness of themselves."

One possible Shadow manifestation here is a feeling of *entrapment*. There can also be a sense of *paralysis*, like a deer in the headlights. This can lead to feelings of *dissociation* from immediate reality, and in the darkest expressions, a refusal to take any responsibility for one's choices. The tolerance for ambiguity which we discussed in the previous section can come into play negatively here too, manifesting as *indecision* and endless halting between courses. Sheer stasis looms.

Relationship figures very strongly in Full Moon psychology, both positively and negatively. We have all witnessed impossible romantic liaisons that refused to die—the same battles, the same dilemmas, the same impossibilities, endlessly recycling. Sometimes, to keep on performing this mime, people change partners while retaining the basic patterns. Other times, they simply repeat the same sequences with the same partner. In either case, it is the same script no matter who is playing the opposite role. This stasis reflects outwardly the inward Sun and the Moon, which are equally strong, ever opposed, and locked in their tidal tug-of-war. Thus, we observe not only a lot of drama in the Shadow expression of the Full Moon—but, more specifically, *drama that threatens never to end and never to change.*

The Evolutionary Intention and the Karmic Predicament

The karma of simple stasis is one of the hardest ones to resolve. Stuckness has no dynamic energy. By its very nature, it is not going anywhere. We have all been stuck in various ways. Generally, we get ourselves going somehow. If we fail in that, and thus die in such a static condition, one possibility is that we reincarnate under the Full Moon—and quickly bring the old entrapped, stuckness back into manifestation, unchanged.

We could die that way a second time. But obviously, that is not the soul's intention.

Thinking positively about the Moon in its fifth phase, the underlying spiritual strategy reflects an intention to bring the unresolved karma into concrete manifestation. We have promised again to meet the people with whom we created those stable, if unsatisfactory, patterns in the past. *We have resolved to reproduce the situations that stumped us in a prior life.*

There is genuine wisdom in this approach, despite appearances. Reproducing those former situations does not mean that we stay stuck. It is more like we get a second shot at answering the questions. Remember our pagan affirmation of the goodness of incarnate life. The purpose of a human life is not to transcend it, but rather to use it—and to celebrate and enjoy it, if possible. Those are attitudes appropriate to the bright hemicycle, which the Full Moon epitomizes. In a sense it means *maxi-*

mum incarnation. The affirmation in this fifth phase could simply be *bring it on.* Don't be afraid. Don't be guilty. Don't recriminate or judge. Let's just have a second look at it—again, "warts and all." Nothing is left abstract, or safely in the realm of philosophy.

We live it out, or we die trying.

The Secret of Happiness

For those born under the Full Moon, the secret of happiness lies in a sense of jumping wholeheartedly into life—in not being intimidated by it. To be bold enough to love as if we have never been hurt. To attempt to live our dreams and our aspirations.

We must find some mechanism for *self-expression* too. There is an imperative to leave something of what we thought was sacred, or important or beautiful behind us in this world. That can be a painting or a symphony or a wise child grown to sane and flowering adulthood. It can be as simple as having made a difference in someone's life—and knowing that the circles of benefit that radiate outward from that act of kindness are limitless.

Our happiness in this lunar phase is also mightily dependent upon recognizing situations that are truly stuck, not amenable to any real evolution, and *resolving not to prolong them.* Definitive exits, often without mutual agreement and without agreed-upon interpretations of "what happened," are typically necessary to the evolution in this phase. Aren't we just creating more karma that way? Sure—but at least it is different karma! Drama that moves forward is part of how we evolve; it serves life. But drama that goes nowhere except back to Square One serves only the Dark Lord. Time to put an end to it, with no regrets.

Examples

Michael Jackson, Sandra Bullock, Robert Plant, Harold Pinter, F. Scott Fitzgerald, Susan Boyle, Ted Kennedy, Paramahansa Yogananda, Robin Williams, Al Franken, Federico Garcia Lorca, Johnny Depp, Thomas Merton, Gabriel Garcia Marquez, William Blake, Christine Jorgensen, Robert B. Parker, Michael Crichton, Johann von Goethe, Sigourney Weaver, James Cameron, Gene Roddenberry, Cat Stevens, Ken Burns,

Tina Turner, Kit Carson, John Coltrane, Saddam Hussein, George Gershwin, Ed Sullivan, Margaret Mitchell, John Travolta, Coco Chanel, Steve Irwin, Gustave Courbet, Abbie Hoffman, Gene Wilder, Chris Rock, Jorge Luis Borges, Giuseppe Verdi, David Bowie, Sue Grafton, Nat "King" Cole, Jeane Dixon, Patty Hearst, Anna Freud, Charles Jayne, Tommy Hilfiger, Michael Crichton, Taylor Swift, Jeremy Irons, Maurice Jarre, Graham Nash, Percy Bysshe Shelley, Antonio Salieri, Thor Heyerdahl, Francis Ford Coppola, Quincy Jones, Gore Vidal, Dr. Dre, Alexander Graham Bell, Louis Braille, John Dee, Robert de Niro, Gen. Stanley A. McChrystal, Chick Corea.

15

☾

PHASE SIX
THE WANING GIBBOUS

THE SHAMAN
Sun-Moon Phase Angle: 225°-270°
Pagan Holiday: *Lammas*

Key Concepts: *Deep inner work. Acceptance and Surrender. Caring. A poignant sense of life's brevity. Psychic intervention in others' lives. Assistance around death, dying, and crisis. Loving Relationships. Attunement to "primitive" wisdom. Death and rebirth. Gratitude. The loss of self-importance. Mature perspectives.*

The Mood

The wealthy, perpetually over-extended Chief Executive Officer of a major corporation learns that his doctor "found an anomaly" in the results of his physical examination. He is called in for further tests. The physician expresses serious concern—and also regret that the follow-up laboratory results will take a week to arrive.

It is a hard few days for our hero. He is dealing with the possibility that he might have only months to live—and that leads him to face the reality of death in general. His perspective is altered.

The results come in. The anomaly was nothing—just a glitch in a lab procedure. The C.E.O. is as healthy as the proverbial horse. But the medical scare has changed him. He describes it as a wake-up call. He realizes that his job is not feeding his soul, that it pays him only money. He sees his future too clearly—another decade of banging his head against the corporate wall, followed by a few years of golf, expensive whiskey, television, then, inevitably, death.

Next time we tune in, that C.E.O. is building inexpensive homes in Haiti, working for Habitat for Humanity. He has left his job behind, cashed in his chips. His friends joke that they are going to call the Vatican. But he doesn't think of himself as a saint. He genuinely feels that he is doing exactly what he wants to be doing. They think he is altruistic. He doesn't feel that way himself. In a world in which everyone dies, he feels he is simply being realistic. Helping beleaguered Haitians means more to him than worrying about third-quarter profits.

When people tell him that Haiti is hopeless, our Chief Executive Officer has a strangely inarticulate reaction. *How do you explain that hope is a condition of the human heart, not of the material world, and that the heart never needs to be hopeless?* How do you explain feeling *gratitude* that there are places in the world like Haiti, places that mirror for the human heart the extent of its capabilities and the power of its faith?

He does not even try. He hammers another nail, with a smile on his face.

The Theory

The waning part of the lunation cycle, begun at the moment of the Full Moon, is now solidly established. The homeward journey is underway, heading back toward the archetypal realm or the Divine or God . . . or whatever you want to name it. In the symbolism of the human life-cycle, we are now past midlife. We are closer to death than we are to birth, and we feel that temporal reality in our bones. A certain detachment from worldly concerns arises. The excitement of endless, youthful expansion—or the illusion of it—now gives way to a more reflective mood, one in which wisdom stops miles short of cynicism, but draws certain understandings from it. The appetite-driven possibilities that once excited us—power, sex, fame—lose their luster. We are beginning to understand that everything born must die. Today's rock star is tomorrow's talk show joke. Power slips between our fingers. Our looks fade. Money buys pleasure, but not happiness. We have turned toward home, toward Eternity. Something in us welcomes that change of orientation.

That is half the puzzle. Here is the other half.

At this sixth lunar phase, we are still in the bright hemicycle. Thus we are still extended outward into the realm of manifestation, caught up in our relationships and the existential structures we have created, just as we saw under the Full lunar phase in the previous chapter. The sheer momentum of those relationships and structures carry us forward. We continue to be enmeshed in them, as if they were rushing white water into which we had fallen. The idea of escape may be emotionally tempting, but it hovers somewhere between highly impractical and flat-out impossible. We have mixed feelings about the brick wall of reality that defines our lives—not simple resentment and entrapment, although those feelings are possible here. But more dominantly, we feel something akin to *acceptance* and *surrender,* as we accept without much protest the existence of gravity or the inevitability of aging.

Putting the pieces together, in the Waning Gibbous phase our attention is *simultaneously focused upon the outward social world* and *upon eternity.* Think of our C.E.O., seeking a larger framework for his life. We are still engaged with others, while we are becoming less engaged with our own personal hopes, needs, and dreams—even though their results are manifest all around us.

In the face of these mature realizations, we seek *communion with kindred souls*—in the spirit of Lammas, we want to *break bread* with them. This simple, present-tense act of *authentic connection* feeds our souls. It pleases us to share that bread, and to nourish others and bond with them as we sense the gathering darkness on the horizon.

A man becomes a dentist and practices for twenty years. The thought enters his mind, "Maybe I should have become a recording engineer." What can he do? Start over? That is not out of the question, but the practical challenges are daunting. He has a marriage and three school-age children. He has a home. The wistful thought enters his mind, "Maybe I should have married my college sweetie instead." But he knows that while people sometimes try going back in time that way, it rarely works out. And maybe he actually loves his three kids and his wife. Maybe being a dentist isn't so bad. *Maybe the Road Not Taken will never be taken and we need to find a way to live with that.* And maybe this bittersweet wisdom about the brevity and finitude of life is a more solid foundation for our souls than exciting promises about a perfect future and all the hair-on-fire Answers in the world.

Most deeply, maybe the purpose of life doesn't actually fit complete-ly into that little box labeled Your Personal Happiness.

The dentist invites his wife out to dinner. They arrange a babysitter. Together, they break bread.

The Personality

Virgo may indicate a certain taste for precision and exactitude. True to form, some Virgos are careful house-cleaners. But others live in material chaos—yet their hard drives are studies in orderliness. Just as not every Virgo is wired the same way, neither is everyone born under the Waning Gibbous phase of the Moon. The condition of the rest of the birth chart makes itself apparent, as does ethnicity and, most notably, karmic differ-ences. Please understand the following profile of the Waning Gibbous personality in that light. It is a profoundly significant factor in a person's chart, but it must take its place in the larger context.

Imagine that, like our Chief Executive Officer a few paragraphs ago, you were faced with a medical death sentence, but one which would not claim you for a year or so. Accepting that emotional challenge, even in your imagination, is a good way to begin to understand the Waning Gibbous Moon personality. The visceral, underlying sense of *limited time* permeates the psychology of this lunar phase. In our opening story, that diagnosis proved spurious, but its effect upon the C.E.O.'s psyche was immediate and powerful. How would you personally face that kind of reality? People's possible reactions are, of course, all over the map. One reaction, easily understood, is of extreme selfishness—a feeling that this is our last chance and so we had better "get it while it's hot." We will look at that possibility more carefully when we consider the Shadow expres-sion of this lunar phase.

For many of us, the impact of such a medical death, while certainly emotionally bracing, would be more beneficial. Suddenly, for example, time with our loved ones is so much more precious to us. We feel gener-ous toward them. We take time with our partners, our soul-friends, our children. We want to know who they really are. We want strong heart-bridges linking them to us. Correspondingly, the sixth phase personality is often loving and engaged, able to look past its own needs enough to truly see and appreciate others in a three-dimensional fashion.

Because of the way synchronicity permeates our lives, people born under this phase of the Moon will often see human mortality and fragility expressed outwardly, perhaps in the form of deaths which occur at emotionally close range. They may, in other words, lose people close to them in dramatic ways. They may be actively involved in the deaths of others. There are obvious murderous Shadow possibilities here, although such cathartic involvements are more typically benign—we counsel the dying or the bereaved, or otherwise help in such extreme times. Often, such people have good instincts about what to say to those facing death, or to those left behind.

Like our C.E.O., the person born under the Waning Gibbous Moon often feels a strong pull toward making the world a better place. There is an urge for some *larger framework of purpose* in life. To call this "altruism" is accurate enough—altruism is often a characteristic of people born under the Waning Gibbous Moon. But the word implies a kind of saintly motivation, when actually what we see here is closer to a sense of *enjoying* and *deriving personal meaning* from deep engagement in the lives of other people. Dane Rudhyar frames this sixth-phase generosity in the following terms: "Such a person tends to want to demonstrate to others what he or she has learned or experienced. Thus an individual of that type often acts as a disseminator of ideas—as a popularizer of what has impressed him most forcibly . . ."

Among evolved sixth-phase people, there is an instinctive feeling about how to help others prepare for their own evolution—and perhaps for their own mortality as well. In my own circles, I have seen many people born under this phase who became involved in profound soul-interventions with others. They may, for example, be psychotherapists or astrologers or psychics—although calling them "medicine people" in the Native American fashion really captures it more effectively. That is why I chose to label this lunar phase "The Shaman."

One of the hardest elements to express in terms of the psychology of this phase of the lunar cycle is its *sweet sadness*. A sense of the transitory nature of all worldly happiness is built into the entire waning lunar cycle. That poignant feeling sprouted in the previous phase—the Full Moon—

where the waning cycle began. Here, in the Waning Gibbous phase, it is surfacing more compellingly into consciousness. Even in teenagers born under this phase, one often senses the kind of humble, accepting wisdom that more typically expresses itself in men and women after midlife.

The Shadow

Every coin has two sides. A core idea in evolutionary astrology—in fact, in all spiritually healthy forms of astrology, in my view—is that there are affirmative soul-intentions built into every astrological configuration, and that every configuration can be turned into a calamity with enough spite, laziness, or rapacity. What is the potential Shadow dimension of the Waning Gibbous phase?

Not too many lines ago, I raised the question of how a person might respond to having only a year left to live. While there are many positive benefits that might come to us from such a reminder, we also recognize that it could engender an extreme—and ultimately desperate—form of selfishness. The root issue here is simple enough to grasp: If our working assumptions are that everything in life is meaningless except appetite, that we simply *are* our physical bodies, and that when we die the lights go out, then a terrible, amoral voracity arises. We want money—and we don't care how we get it. We want sex and we don't care whom we hurt. We want fame and power—mostly because they lead to sex and money.

The human imagination becomes tragically constrained in this dire situation. Compassion is banished. In our list of Waning Gibbous Moon examples below, you will find the twentieth century's Prince of Darkness himself, Adolf Hitler. You will also find Carlos the Jackal. Sadism is a form of engagement with others, as is murder. So is abuse in general. The cold, cruel, driven desperation that is the hallmark of the Waning Gibbous Shadow is ultimately an outward crystallization of the psyche's relationship with itself. The brutality is aimed inward as well, in other words. Depression and apathy can arise throughout the waning cycle, and they are part of the Shadow profile of this lunar phase too. But *active sadism* is its unique signature in that regard. We are at the end of the bright hemicycle. We are still "into relationships." Under the domain of the Shadow, that becomes a chilling line.

The Evolutionary Intention and the Karmic Predicament

Why might a soul incarnate under the Waning Gibbous Moon? What are the evolutionary purposes behind such a birth? Throughout the waning cycle, there is a general theme of "finishing business" with other beings. To be deeply engaged with the evolutionary journeys of other people, to the point that we are willing to sacrifice something of our own needs and intentions for their sakes—this kind of love, while potentially dangerous, can also clean up the karma of indebtedness toward others. The soul-intention here is as transparent as glass. We simply aim to *pay our karmic debts!*

There is more, of course. At some point, every evolving soul must get over its self-importance and diminish its self-involvement. Navel-gazing spirituality and self-obsessed psychology do serve their purposes, but in this lunar phase the intentions are more spiritually mature than that. The gradual erosion of self-importance and self-involvement are the evolutionary targets. In making other people's needs temporarily more urgent to us than our own, we chip away at our egocentricity. The result is that the monumental edifice of our sense of separation and specialness casts a less blinding shadow across the eyes of the soul.

The Secret of Happiness

With the Moon in the Waning Gibbous phase, the secret of happiness in a nutshell is to live every day as if it were your last day on earth. That is a lofty ideal, and thus probably unreachable in practical terms. But the wisdom in those words is the North Star we must follow. When we realize how brief our time on earth is, our entire perspective changes. We stop worrying so much about trivial things. In our motivations, the creation of purpose and meaning begin to replace the endless "almost there" of the satisfaction of appetite.

With our self-importance diminished, life's inevitable slights, unfairness and insults become nothing more than background noise. Authenticity, genuine human connection, and a sense of the "power of now" all loom larger. The spirit thrives.

We begin to get the joke that makes the angels smile.

Examples

Carl Jung, Alan Watts, William Butler Yeats, Mother Theresa, Bob Marley, Albert Einstein, Loreena McKennitt, Peter Jackson, Jimi Hendrix, Marilyn Monroe, Princess Diana, Allen Ginsburg, Al Gore, Gus Grissom, Steven Hawking, Hermann Hesse, Adolph Hitler, Martin Luther, Vladimir Putin, Vincent Van Gogh, Bill Clinton, Henry VIII, Edmund Hillary, Paul Simon, Jules Verne, Tammy Faye Bakker, Brigitte Bardot, David Byrne, Carlos the Jackal, O.J. Simpson, Johnny Cash, Arthur Conan Doyle, Stephen Jay Gould, George Harrison, Louis Armstrong, Robert Bly, Stonewall Jackson, Valentina Tereshkova (first woman in space), Yehudi Menuhin, Robert 'Buz' Myers, Vaclav Havel, Elizabeth Claire Prophet, Gen. David H. Petraeus, John Paul Sartre, Helen Gurley Brown, Stephen Stills, Andy Warhol, Brigham Young, George Washington Carver, Sally Ride, River Phoenix, Prince, Condoleeza Rice, Yasser Arafat, Don Imus, Mitt Romney, Stephen Jay Gould, Tupac Shakur, Antonio Banderas, Winston Churchill, Uma Thurman, Tammy Wynette, Dwight Yoakham, Frank Zappa. John Steinbeck, James Dean, Walter Cronkite, George Lucas, George Clooney, Kurt Vonnegut, Yo Yo Ma, Keith Richards.

16

○

PHASE SEVEN
THE LAST QUARTER

THE PILGRIM
Sun-Moon Phase Angle: *270°-315°*
Pagan Holiday: *Mabon*

Key Concepts: *Sensing the smell of home. Sweet sorrow. Longing. Romantic tragedy. Solitude. Art as an inner search. Service. Theater; ritual. \Graceful endings. The art of saying goodbye. The air of death and finality.*

The Mood

Reluctantly, an introverted woman agrees to go to a party with a friend. Across the crowded room, standing thirty feet away, she notices a man whom she has never met. She gazes at him, feeling an inexplicable pull. After a few heartbeats, he looks up. Their eyes lock. Something electric passes between them. Both turn away, a little embarrassed. The woman turns to her friend and says, "I think I just saw the man I am going to marry."

Meanwhile, the man steps outside for a breath of air. He is shaken by the intensity of what he just experienced. How could a total stranger seem so familiar? A friend of his joins him on the patio, commenting that he looks as if he's just seen a ghost. Nodding toward the crowded room, the man says, "Actually, I think I've just seen my next wife."

Bravely, he steps back inside. Six weeks later they are married.

Here's the hook. The man is eighty-two years old. Last year he had quadruple bypass heart surgery. The woman is seventy-eight. She has survived cancer twice.

Death is the third partner in their marriage, always present in the background. To lose this precious bond so soon after finding it would be a tragedy beyond the compass of the heart. And yet, the uncertainty of their time together is a fierce gift as well. Little annoyances are released without a second thought. The quality of their attention to each other is exquisite. Every meal, every evening stroll, every conversation has the vivid preciousness of a first kiss—or a last one.

The French tell us that hunger is the best sauce. And there is no sauce on today better than the knowledge that we may not see tomorrow.

The Theory

A corner is turned as we enter the Moon's Last Quarter. After four phases of glaring brightness, we can rest our weary eyes: We have at last returned to the dark hemicycle. We now leave the realm of the manifest and the outward. We begin to disentangle ourselves from the visible world—the realm of objects, of people, of community and institutions. We return now to the province of the inner world. Our orientation becomes archetypal, abstract and principled, potentially spiritual. Consciousness is directed inward now, away from all the unexpected serendipity and distraction of shared experience. Material detail is lost; the three-dimensional reality of other people dissipates. Replacing it is a vastly more graphic and immediate sense of the Platonic realm from which all ideas and images arise—the Holy of Holies, the archetypal realm, the *dharmakaya*, God . . .

In that blinding inner light, all the treasures of outward experience are forgotten. All phenomena become trivial in comparison to this quintessential purity.

This place is familiar; we have been here before. Long ago, in the first two phases of the lunar cycle, consciousness was suffused with the scent of that mythic realm as well. Back then, we were on fire with it, eager to bring it forward into manifestation. We felt a need for other people to know about it too. Little did we know then that, in our zeal to carry this "Holy of Holies" energy forward into the world, we were simultaneously turning our backs on it. We were riding the surging wave of the waxing cycle out into the world.

Now everything is different. We are carried back inward by the receding wave of the Moon's waning cycle. The resonances are with old age, not with youth's enthusiasm. Our naiveté has been tempered into something closer to wisdom. That tempering, which happened in the burning cauldrons of experience, has taken its toll. We are wise, but we are tired as well. Where foolishness was the soul-enemy in the dark part of the waxing cycle, now the enemies become *resignation* and *despair.*

If we defeat those enemies, we see this world with a penetratingly neutral clarity, free of desire and aversion. We "cast a cold eye on life, on death," as William Butler Yeats put it. We see it the way a foreigner might see our own country—which is to say with a bemused lucidity spawned by a detachment that we, as citizens, could never entertain. If you want to know about the sea, don't ask a fish. And if you want to know about life in this world, ask someone who has one foot in the next one.

The Autumnal Equinox festival of Alban Elfed or Mabon marks the passage into the dark half of the year. It may be the "Pagan Thanksgiving," as we learned in Chapter Nine, but this feast is more poignant than mere "Turkey Day" gluttony. We have today . . . or at least this moment.

Tomorrow? We will see.

The Personality

People born during the Last Quarter differ from each other, just as do Capricorns, Cubans and chiropractors! This is just one factor in a person's individuality. The rest of chart naturally makes itself felt, as do age, soul differences, cultural influences, and so forth. Still, lunar phase is a major element in the psyche. It would take an avalanche of countervailing factors to outweigh the following set of underlying moods and attitudes.

When I was a little boy in the long-lost 1950s, I saw a Norwegian woman interviewed on television. She had recently visited America. The interviewer was pumping her for "booster" comments about how wonderful America was. Even then, I could almost sense him wanting to ask, "Aren't our toasters amazing? What about our blenders and our automobiles?" The Norwegian woman, deadpan, answered him, "I liked America . . . but everyone there feels they have to be happy all the time."

The personality associated with a Last Quarter Moon is not of necessity miserable or depressed. That would be a misleading view. But it is *poignant*. There is a sense of Autumn about it, of the sweetness of good things that must surely pass. Like our elderly lovers in the opening images of this chapter, this sense of life's transitoriness adds depth and passion to our love affair with the only thing we ever truly possess—the present moment. And yet, as we contemplate the present moment, we realize that we can never really possess it either. As soon as we look for it, it is gone—replaced by another one, equally slippery. At its best, the Last Quarter personality embodies a wisdom that is at ease with this quality of *impermanence*. There is a richness in it, an appreciation for subtlety. We know we are merely pilgrims passing through this world.

The flaming—and often ungrounded—idealism of the waxing phases of the lunar cycle long ago gave way to the more reflective, humble, tolerant perspectives of the waning cycle. In this seventh lunar phase, there is an *acceptance of imperfection*. Yet despite that, in closing back into the archetypal realm, there is simultaneously a kind of gravitational tug toward the perfect. There is no contradiction here: While the present is accepted as flawed, faith arises. There is a confidence in the notion that time—and infinite patience—can work wonders.

Flawed wisdom, hard-won.

Those four words capture so much of the spirit of this seventh lunar phase. We have bled to understand certain principles—impermanence, the brevity of life, the transcendent reality of the present moment. Our "teenage" certainty that we are always Right is shattered, and good riddance! But these more elemental certainties we have forged are precious to us. As Dane Rudhyar described people born under this phase, "In personal as well as social relationships, they tend to force issues on the basis of some more or less important principle which they feel they must uphold, perhaps at all costs."

There can be stubbornness here, or great conviction. Yet we can also observe a certain humility, as if we get our own joke. It's the kind of humility more likely encountered in older people who have experienced defeats as well as victories. Reflecting that piece of the Last Quarter phase, Rudhyar adds, "In some cases, they are able to display an irony or sense of humor which they can put at the service of their Cause . . ."

As usual, Rudhyar is putting his more Airy and Fiery spin on the phase, emphasizing its social and collective aspects. To me, the Pilgrim hears the call of another world. The affairs of this one have less gravity. There can be compassion, but this burgeoning non-attachment is the key concept. The Pilgrim knows that he will soon set sail for another land entirely.

In terms of relationships, a man or woman born under this phase often possesses an acute sense of *necessary endings*—that certain relationships must be undertaken, explored, even endured, despite an emotional certainty that they will not last. The mental healthiness of that philosophy may seem difficult to comprehend. Try thinking of it this way: Imagine that you have a sister or a brother to whom you have not spoken in twenty years. You hit a turning-point birthday. You begin to reflect on the passing of time and the uncertainty of life. A feeling arises in you that perhaps you should make contact with your sibling and try to bury the hatchet while you still can. Your not liking each other very much pales before that instinctive evolutionary necessity: *be truly done with it!* In this seventh phase, we feel a similar need to jettison that kind of baggage. Bottom line, under the Last Quarter Moon, sometimes *we must engage in order truly to disengage*.

As we move into the mysterious, uncontrollable dark of the final two lunar phases, feelings about the inevitability of certain endings become compelling. Faced with them, we seek *mechanisms of transcendence*. How do we handle loss? What about death and failure and impossibility? What are the precise methods? What tools can help us in that monumental work? Immediate necessity compels us toward practicality here; we want to know how to do it, specifically, step by step. Thus, there can arise a focus on *ritual*, with or without a religious framework. Cathartic experience calls. It is a time for *magick*.

As one illustration, I have seen a great number of stage actors born under this seventh phase, reflecting the transformative possibilities of serious theater. Still, even though theater is public, we must recall that being in the dark hemicycle here, the level of social, outward engagement is lessened. Because of that, the collective, social aspect of art is not emphasized so strongly. Thus in the Last Quarter phase we often encounter the *unrecognized, solitary artist*.

Contemplating such an individual from the perspective of this lunar phase, we realize that art in all its forms is a spiritual discipline. It creates momentous evolutionary change in the individual who practices it, even if no one else ever appreciates it or even sees it. To grasp the enigmas of this seventh lunar phase, we must honor the private, metamorphic mysteries of all the world's unpublished poetry. We must listen for the songs that have never been sung by anyone but the singer. We contemplate the soaring accomplishments of the human imagination known only to the angels and the walls.

The Shadow

All the symbols in astrology represent beauty and horror. Nothing is inherently good or bad; the goodness or badness comes from what we make of the energy. What is the potential Shadow dimension of the Last Quarter phase? When someone is born under this phase, with what demons must they wrestle if they are going to manifest the actual soul-intention of the configuration?

Don Juan, the half-mythic Yaqui sorcerer in Carlos Castaneda's books, once said that there are "four enemies of a man of knowledge." The first is fear. The second is power. Those two are fairly self-explanatory, and we might easily relate them to the perils of the waxing lunar cycle. The third enemy is clarity—and that is a tougher one. Usually we value clarity. But here I believe Don Juan was referring more to an attachment to clarity—the compelling charm of being right all the time! And we could make a case for its resonance with the third quadrant of the lunar cycle.

The fourth enemy of a man of knowledge is the most mysterious one. Don Juan simply called it "old age." But I think he meant something more than geriatric issues. With "old age" comes the threat of laziness or sloppiness, a sense of just not giving a damn anymore. We might develop a feeling of defeat, of hopelessness, of the best being over and used up. We might simply indulge in feelings of tiredness. All these attitudinal soul-cages are the Shadow of the seventh lunar phase. No matter what our chronological age, if we are born under this phase, we must battle the *demons of resignation.*

This seventh phase is attuned to the perceptual wavelength of ideals compromised, decent people defeated by treachery, and the triumph of fools. The simple notion that "the good guys do not always win," so incomprehensible in the waxing phases, is now woven into the fabric of our experience. How do we live with such unfair realities? One bad answer is cynically—and taking *refuge in cynicism* is another trap for people born under the Moon's Last Quarter.

The Evolutionary Intention and the Karmic Predicament

Why might a soul incarnate under this seventh lunar phase? What are the pre-existing karmic conditions that call forth such a manifestation? What are the underlying evolutionary intentions?

Coming to this stage of the journey, a Pilgrim soul is nearing the final chapter of what we might presume to be a series of incarnations all dealing with certain recurrent themes. There is a feeling of the *pressing necessity to finish things*. Outwardly, that may entail projects or relationships, but ultimately it is the inward dimension of completion that is most compelling. Often it is the higher grades of school that present the hardest courses and the greatest challenges. That is the case here. Tiredness must be overcome, commitment and discipline renewed. The stakes are high. We must be wary of "snatching defeat from the jaws of victory."

Let's imagine that wherever you go, people fall to their knees. They believe you to be God incarnate—Funjar the Wonder Boy, as Garrison Keillor once put it. What does that actually make you? Of course the right answer is nothing at all—your actual spiritual condition is a purely internal reality, independent of the opinions, positive or negative, of other people. A person born under the Last Quarter possesses the strong soul-intention fully to internalize that liberating insight. There is an aim to go beyond the seductive power of worldly titles or status in all categories, most especially the spiritual ones. In the words of His Holiness the Dalai Lama, "Drop the titles. You don't need to call yourselves lamas or roshis. Drop the costumes." Here, we need no one's approval. And the foundation of that high state is *letting go of our judgments* and assessments of the conditions of others. We must stop judging, so that judgments—coming or going, so to speak—become as irrelevant to us as yesterday's weather report in Mongolia.

The Secret of Happiness

With the Moon in the seventh phase, the secret of happiness lies primarily in the inner world. The "mechanisms of transcendence," as we put it earlier, must be mastered. Energetic release, creativity, effective ritual—all can contribute significantly to a sense of well-being. A deep attention to the present moment, coupled with an acceptance that "all things must pass," brings ease to the mind.

Outwardly, the main element here lies in *clean endings*. We must finish business with people, insofar as they will allow it. And when they do not allow it, simply knowing that we genuinely tried is often enough to allow us to release the past. A cornerstone of happiness in this Last Quarter phase lies in penetrating the illusion of significance that we attach to our "diagnoses" of other people, especially ones who have hurt or offended us. As they have no idea what is in your heart or your mind, similarly you accept your ignorance about theirs.

Examples

Pema Chodron, Fritz Perls, Pedro Almodovar, Rev. Rick Warren, George Washington, Barack Obama, Mohandas Gandhi, Van Morrison, Amelia Earhart, Julia Roberts, Steven Spielberg, Oprah Winfrey, Wolfgang Amadeus Mozart, Sean Penn, Evel Knievel, Adolph Eichmann, Mark Hamill, Leonardo da Vinci, Jim Bakker, Annie Besant, Max Ernst, Chet Baker, Jodie Foster, Michael J. Fox, Victor Hugo, Bob Fosse, Billie Holiday, Charles Dickens, Mary Pope Osborne, Sir Edmund Hillary, Angelina Jolie, Kevin Costner, Mick Jagger, Henry Miller, Andrew Wyeth, Keanu Reeves, Thelonius Monk, Colin Powell, Lenny Bruce, Michael Jordan, Terrence McKenna, Harvey Milk, Ezra Pound, Walt Disney, Rubin "Hurricane" Carter, Paul Hogan, Claudia Schiffer, Salvador Dali, Sonia Sotomayor, Thomas Edison.

17

☾

PHASE EIGHT
THE WANING CRESCENT

THE GHOST; THE MYSTIC WANDERER
Sun-Moon Phase Angle: *315°-360°*
Pagan Holiday: *Samhain; Halloween.*

Key Concepts: *Deep psychic sensitivity; possible imbalance. Alternate descriptions of reality. The Anthropologist, observing us. Hypersensitivity. Ghosts and spirit visitations. Creative, visionary imagination. Awareness of ancestors and the dead. Clean, definitive endings.*

The Mood

Enter Alfred Hitchcock and cue up some creepy music: It is two o'clock in the morning on a dark and stormy night. You are lying alone in the bedroom of a Victorian bed-and-breakfast, sound asleep. Lightning flashes and three seconds later, a peal of thunder startles you into full wakefulness. Your eyes get wide. You sit bolt upright in the bed. There, at its foot, shimmers the diaphanous form of an old woman. She looks lost and confused. She turns to stare at you. You can't see her feet—they trail off below her into misty nothingness. She died in that same room in 1917, back when she owned the house. She is now a ghost.

You say, "Hello."

The hairs on the back of your neck are standing up. You are seeing a ghost, after all! But, by reflex, you greet her. The existence of spirits in other dimensions and states of being does not stand so far outside your instinctual view of life. You stare at her as she peers back at you.

Five minutes earlier in the next-door room, the same thing happened. A peal of thunder awakened the gentleman in that bed too. He faced exactly the same apparition. He rubbed his eyes. He blinked. And she disappeared.

He said to himself, "I must have been dreaming." Or, "Maybe it was something I ate." By morning, he forgot all about it. Seeing a ghost is so far outside his system of beliefs and expectations that his mind discounts it. A week later the memory is erased. It is as if the event never happened.

With the Moon in this final phase, the veil between the worlds has grown translucent. Presences are everywhere. Strange energies and ambiences abound. Mystery is woven into every moment. All conventional descriptions of reality and all our pat explanations of the world, such as science and reason, are breaking down. The dead are never far away. Heaven, Hell, and the Land of Faerie are folded into the three dimensions everyone else seems to believe constitute the totality of reality. Wisdom—and madness—loom at the fingertips. And you, like that diaphanous old woman, are just a pilgrim passing through this strange, brief world.

The Theory

The circle is closing. We have come to the last phase of the lunation cycle. After a long, dark night, the feeble sickle of the Moon rises in the east—and is soon washed out by the rising Sun. It is over; the cycle is complete. From the Moon's point of view, we have reached the End of Days—and of course, in good cyclical Pagan fashion, we have also reached the threshold of a new beginning. The Moon will soon disappear into the invisible, archetypal realm, dissolving itself in the Great Mystery for three nights. Then it will re-emerge as a Waxing Crescent, thereby rebooting the ancient cycle.

All along, we have contemplated the interplay between two polarities: the cycle of light and dark, and the cycle of waxing and waning. Here, in phase eight, the whole system is winding down. We have waned utterly into darkness. Let's reflect on the meaning of this descent into the heart of all mysteries, this maximum withdrawal from the realm of light.

The key is to reflect upon the moment of the New Moon itself, which is the epitome of all enigmas. In it, we have gone beyond anything comprehensible in terms of the logic of this three dimensional world. It is as if we are inhabiting the great singularity from which the Big Bang of modern cosmology burst. That event gave rise not only to the physical universe but also to the laws that govern it. Within it, those laws did not yet exist. Thus, understanding it is—quite literally—impossible. It is not simply that we do not understand it. It is that we cannot. The laws that underlie our very ability to understand do not apply there.

And, equally literally, at the moment of the New Moon something exists but we cannot see it. The New Moon gives no visible evidence of its existence. We conjecture its presence, but we cannot prove it. The parallels with the Divine are obvious. As the Buddhists say, Enlightenment is beyond all descriptions and characteristics. Or as thinking Christians, Jews, and Muslims acknowledge, one cannot ultimately prove the existence of God through logical means.

Whatever that fierce mystery might be, at the Waning Crescent Moon we are rushing headlong into it. We have gone over the waterfall, surrendered to the tug of the mystical current.

The bright hemicycle dominated by the Full Moon represents the material world and all its phantasmagoria, temptations and possibilities. But now we are as far away from all that as we can be. In the Waning Crescent, we have turned our backs utterly on this physical world, almost to the point of having forgotten that it is there at all.

Dane Rudhyar refers to this eighth phase as the "Balsamic" Moon. It is a reference to incense—balsam—rising up from the altar to the realm of the gods and goddesses. Smoking balsam is a beautiful, diaphanous metaphor that nicely captures the transcendent feeling of this last lunar phase—and also to the possibility of a simple "smoky" loss of focus.

All along, we have observed a natural resonance between lunar phases and the human life-cycle, with the New Moon phase corresponding to childhood and so on forward through the stages of maturation. Here at the final phase of the cycle, we would naturally hypothesize a link with the psychology of extreme old age.

How does life look from the perspective of a wise old man or a wise old woman? The more you can intuit an answer to that question, the more deeply you will understand the positive face of the Waning

Crescent Moon. And let's balance that perspective with another question. How does the world look from a less lofty geriatric perspective? Not the wise old man or wise old woman, but rather the old fool, bitter and broken. How does life look from that point of view? Ask your drunken, angry old uncle—that is, if you can get a word in edgewise. That is the Shadow dimension here.

Samhain, the cross-quarter day which corresponds to the Waning Crescent Moon, adds Pagan wisdom to our understanding. Just think of Halloween, our modern version of that ancient holiday. In it, we *practice the presence of the dead.* We engage actively and intentionally, if playfully, with the spirit world. To the old Celts, this was the end of the year. We are invited to surrender to the gathering, inviting dark of wintertime. We "go gently into that good night." *We recognize that we are not, and have never been, fully and finally at home in this narrowly physical and three-dimensional world.*

The Personality

Just as not all Pisceans are interchangeable, not everyone born under the Waning Crescent Moon is cut from the same cloth. The rest of the chart naturally makes its presence felt, as do an array of other non-astrological factors—soul differences, social influences, and so forth. But with that caution internalized, we can make some general comments about the personality dynamics of people born under this last phase.

We might start off with a perennial show-stopping question, *what is reality?* There are many people in the world to whom our just voicing such an inquiry would sound flaky. To them, the nature of reality is "obvious." To pursue any questions about it would be a waste of time—something to occupy airheads and dreamers. And while there is no shortage of airheads and dreamers born under this final lunar phase, none of them would be blockheaded enough to dismiss our question!

What *is* reality, actually? Intuitively, eighth phase people understand that "reality," as the word is customarily understood, is at best a simplification. Ultimately, it is no more than a cultural agreement. It is a social contract that allows human society to exist and human conversations to happen. But that social contract also deludes us all, encouraging us collectively to frame mystics as harebrained, our dream lives as "just dreams," and apparitions of the spirit-world as "our eyes playing tricks on us."

To people born under this last lunar phase, the questions about the nature of reality are not merely philosophical curiosities. They are a pressing daily concern, constantly in the backs of their minds as they attempt to adjust to functioning in the "normal" world of daily life—all the while routinely entering other relativistic frameworks. This is why I call them the "Mystic Wanderers." As Castaneda's Don Juan put it, they "move fluidly between the worlds."

I also call them "Ghosts," because that is the way they feel a lot of the time—as if they were ghosts in this physical world. And of course, in a way, they are absolutely correct in that assessment. We are all "ghosts in the machine;" people born under the Waning Crescent simply grasp that truth more readily. As consciousness enters the final two phases of the lunation cycle, it goes beyond three-dimensional space. It goes beyond time itself—and once time is gone, cause-and-effect ceases to have meaning. The entire logic by which we consensually make sense of the world collapses. Dane Rudhyar says: "At times the individual feels himself possessed by a 'social destiny,' or led by a superior power. He is more or less aware of being a kind of shrine (or 'field') in which something greater than his personal selfhood is taking place . . . "

In the light of that, it is no accident that we find born under the Waning Crescent both Neils Bohr, the seminal figure in quantum mechanics, and Uri Geller, the spoon-bending psychic. Are both of these men perhaps demonstrating the same phenomena? Let's add Rod Serling who, with his *Twilight Zone* television program, invited the invisible realms into living rooms all across the unsuspecting 1960s English-speaking world. And Deepak Chopra, who perhaps more than any other popular figure in recent history has brought the power of mind and consciousness to bear upon our understanding of sickness and health.

Here is another dilemma that easily sits alongside questions about the ultimate nature of reality. *Where do we go when we die?* As before, this conundrum gives jitters to people who want to cling to three-dimensional views of reality. To them, death either means "game over," or it triggers vague platitudes about heaven and hell. Either way, they quickly try to dance away from the subject. Yet all through history, human beings have reported contact with the dead. Reports of ghosts and hauntings abound the world over. To people born under the eighth lunar phase, the dead are a presence. To some, this is a straightforward truth—many tell matter-of-fact stories, for example, of encounters with ghosts or of being contacted psychically by loved ones around the time they pass away. To others of a more conventional nature, this sense of the presence of the spirit-world (and its inhabitants) is more vague—an uneasiness arising at the flash point where their intuitive experience clashes with the more orthodox descriptions of reality they have internalized.

A characteristic of the Waning Crescent phase—and of lucid old age—is a long memory. For obvious reasons, the older person simply has more to remember than the younger one. Also, when we are young, naturally more of our mental energy goes into planning and visualizing possible futures. Following the parallels between the human life cycle and the lunar cycle, we recognize that here in the eighth phase, memory wields a tremendous gravitational field.

Typically, for people born under this last phase, the *ability to remember* is simply good—details, dates, food eaten, and clothing worn are often recalled even after the passage of years. But there is also a sense of being haunted by the past, as if it were not really over. And if time is an illusion, who is to say that the past is indeed over? Perhaps "the past" is simply one more arbitrary construction within the context of consensual reality.

Ego is beginning to dissolve in this Waning Crescent phase. That dissolution is what allows these extraordinary perceptions we've been describing to enter consciousness. The fall of the ego-wall also invites a tremendous surge of *creative imagination*—a rich inner life, which may or not be expressed outwardly. Dreams are vivid, life-altering, and often disturbing. These people must heed the call of the "other" world—and I prefer that term to the more conventional "inner" world, since the tone of this eighth phase points *beyond* the Self at least as much as it points *into* the Self. The mystical call is pressing, and to heed it is to turn somewhat away from human society—to turn away from the world defined by "beauty's cruelty and wisdom's chatter," as William Butler Yeats put it.

Thus, for men and women born in this phase, quiet time alone is essential to their sanity. For them, a "busy and productive" outward life takes a dangerous toll, since it sets them in combat with their own natures. They may sustain a driven pace for a while, but psychological damage arises in the long run. In short, they need some form of spiritual practice, however they choose to frame it. And note that this is about actual spiritual practice, not just metaphysical beliefs—their actual experience compels the belief! They are not learning to "believe" it; they are learning to live it.

The Shadow

The most basic principle of evolutionary astrology is that life is about choices, not about a passive acceptance of some predetermined "fate." There are healthy possibilities built into every astrological configuration. Simultaneously, every configuration can be made into a disaster just by adding enough stupidity, self-centeredness, or confusion. What is the potential Shadow dimension of the Waning Crescent phase?

The most dramatic dark possibility is naturally not the most common one. It is, simply stated, *madness*. Quite possibly, people born under this phase can lose their grip on reality. But, as we explored earlier, what exactly do we mean by "reality"? It is a truism that most of history's great mystics would be deemed psychotic by the standards of conventional academic psychiatry. That judgment is unfair to the mystics, to put it mildly. Reality is vastly more complex than the descriptions of it generally offered in university departments of psychology. Actually, for a better description, walk across campus to the physics department! The vision of a multidimensional, consciousness-influenced, quantum-mechanical universe emerging in those corridors nowadays is closer to the actual experience of a person born under this final lunar phase.

Soberly speaking, the frontier between prosaic, everyday, three-dimensional consciousness and the spirit-world is not always a peaceful or safe one. Inhabitants of this "Balsamic" lunar phase live on that churning borderland. This is not church-on-Sunday spirituality; this is active mysticism, with all its perils—and sometimes the conventional psychiatrists are right! A mind navigating the knife-edges between the worlds can become unbalanced. It can encounter things it fears, project these inner demons onto the canvas of this world and attack innocent surrogates—think of Jim Jones and the infamous Jonestown mass suicide. He came into the world during this final lunar phase.

In a nutshell, people born under the Waning Crescent Moon can lose their grip, not only on consensual reality, but also on the actual fabric of the more subtle and transcendent realities, which have their own steadying laws and logic. Consensual reality—that more or less agreed-upon sense of what is real—allows human beings to communicate meaningfully with each other and to support each other. We might make a similar case for the inner realities. Spiritual teachers in every tradition—not to mention the angels, guides and spirits who support us—understand these principles and use them to help keep their students' minds stable. If we lose our bearings there, as well as in this prosaic physical world, we have truly entered a realm of madness.

Losing their grip on *any reality at all* except their own inner demonology, people born under this last lunar phase can slip by degrees into frightening states. In mild forms, it is simply the mistaking of fears and wishes for "what is happening." In extreme forms, this condition crosses into the realm of obvious insanity.

These are the radical situations of Shadow expression. More moderately, for a person born under the Waning Crescent Moon, there can be a simple awkwardness about getting around in the conventional world. He or she, for example, can get lost easily, even in a familiar city—or apply four-dimensional logic when behind the wheel of a three-dimensional automobile. It goes further. The eerie sense of not sharing the general assumptions of society can trigger feelings of *alienation.* That can lead to *escapism* in all its forms. Criminal behavior can emerge.

Naturally, the sense of being "at the end of things" is quite real here—we are literally at the end of the lunation cycle. As Dane Rudhyar describes a person born under this phase, "He tends to sense a character of finality in all important relationships he experiences." There are positive aspects to this "last chance" feeling—but negatively, in the Shadow's domain, it can correlate with a fatalistic sense of *defeat* or *impossibility* in human partnerships. There may literally be dramatic endings—shattering breakups, sudden deaths.

Add all that mortality to the stew, and the possibility of morbidly dwelling in the vividly-remembered past is underscored. The vulnerability to depression, resignation and despair—elevated in general in all the waning phases—reaches a crescendo in this last phase. The alchemical transformation of those fierce truths into wisdom and compassion is higher ground. Surrendering to them is the soul's cage.

The Evolutionary Intention and the Karmic Predicament

Why might a soul incarnate under this eighth lunar phase? Spiritually speaking, there is a sense of placing a very large bet on the table. The deep intention is nothing less than a breakthrough into a whole new stage of the evolutionary journey. It is as if the person has said, *"Let me wash my hands, once and for all, of these issues with which I've been struggling for a thousand years."*

Whatever has been put off will now present itself. In essence, the soul declares, "Bring it on," adding, "and take what you want from me." Under this contract, strong, dark emotions will be faced directly and without filtration, unless escapism intervenes and cancels the process. People with whom we have business to finish from prior lifetimes will be as thick as penguins on an ice floe. We agree to have little respite—even in sleep, the work will continue through the medium of the hyperactive and often disturbing dream-life.

Built into this lunar phase is a further intention. It is for nothing less than a breakthrough in consciousness. There is no more optimal launching pad for Enlightenment than the Waning Crescent phase of the Moon. That is why the stakes are so high.

The Secret of Happiness

With the Moon in the eighth phase, the secret of happiness for the Mystic Wanderer or the Ghost lies hidden squarely in the domain of the psychic landscape. The blandishments of the material world may tempt us, but they deliver little in the way of real joy. To be happy, we need a rich, active kind of solitude. Simply spending time alone can be of some help, but better still is time spent in meditation, dream work, and the inward "yoga" of creativity. And yet, even here we must be cautious: the inner landscape can lead to self-absorption, which generally spirals down into self-pity and despair. True spiritual practice is the only effective medicine there. Positively, we must become "ghosts" in this world, knowing that we will soon leave it and practicing that perspective every day. We must recognize that our true identities and our only true home are more akin to that luminous emptiness that underlies our minds than to anything material or even cognitive.

Memory is intense and raw; the person born under this last phase must learn to balance the deeply felt presence of the past with a cultivated detachment from it, as if it were nothing more than a dream or a movie. Spiritual practice helps with that too.

There is an ancient formula in Vedanta—Atman and Brahman are one—which means that the soul and the Divine are ultimately inseparable and indistinguishable. In other words, *if we go deeply enough into ourselves, we come out into the universe.* One can spend a long time thinking about an idea like that. For those born under the Waning Crescent phase, that meditation is the ultimate key to a sense of well-being, sanity and happiness.

In the end, there is no one here but us ghosts.

Examples

Bob Dylan, Deepak Chopra, Jane Roberts, Stevie Wonder, Federico Fellini, Rod Serling, Whoopi Goldberg, Cate Blanchett, Maximilien de Robespierre, Dane Rudhyar, Michelangelo, John Belushi, Salman Rushdie (by a few minutes, close to New), India.Arie, Christa McAuliffe, Ludwig van Beethoven, Tiger Woods, Marlon Brando (by a hair, nearly New), William Faulkner, Rosa Parks, Havelock Ellis, Abraham Lincoln, Tristan Jones, Steve Fossett, Les Paul, Gérard Depardieu, Scarlett Johansson, Miguel de Unamuno, Ayn Rand, Jeffrey Dahmer, Sarah Palin, RuPaul, Andre Charles, Rob Hand, Bernard Madoff, Jim Jones, Frida Kahlo, Cesar Chavez, Edwin Hubble, Neils Bohr, Pancho Villa, Immanuel Velikovsky, Uri Geller, Reinhold Ebertin, Leonardo DiCaprio, Brad Steiger, Hugh Hefner, J.D. Salinger, Dave Brubeck, Joe Cocker, Charles Darwin, John Barth, Glenn Ford, Steffi Graf, Stephen Foster, Joan Grant, Peter O'Toole, Nicholas Rimsky-Korsakov, Andre Segovia, Algernon Swinburne, Kahlil Gibran (there are questions about the accuracy of his birth date), Lech Walesa, Greg Allman, Diane Arbus, Henri Matisse, Isabel Hickey, Arthur Rimbaud.

PART FOUR:

THE BIGGER PICTURE

18

INTEGRATING THE MOON'S PHASE, SIGN AND HOUSE

A New Moon in the natal chart, as we learned in Chapter Ten, suggests a personality shaped by the following energetic vectors: *Charisma. Star Quality. Presence. Nurturing qualities. Leadership. Guidance. Seductive Vagueness. Innocence and Naiveté. Becoming symbolic to others; making others into symbols. A Bringer of Gifts.*

There are a lot of ways to do all those things! And not every person born under the New Moon will display all of these qualities equally. In some, the rest of the chart will underscore the charismatic elements. In others, the nurturing sweetness will be emphasized. As ever, the great art in astrology—and what separates the masters from those who simply learn to parrot lists of key words—is the capacity to *synthesize* the messages of all the symbols into a coherent, breathing whole. With lunar phase, this process of synthesis begins with integrating two more elements that shape the Moon's actual expression: its sign and its house. And of course, planetary aspects further sculpt the lunar phase, just as they flavor everything else in astrology.

Twelve signs and twelve houses. That is 144 possible combinations. And there are eight lunar phases, each of which could potentially occupy any one of those 144 niches. Right there, we see it would require 1152 separate descriptions to cover all of the sign-house-phase bases. Even keeping them brief, that is a project that would require a volume thicker than this one—not to mention a more patient author! And even that total does not include planetary aspects to the Moon, which would exponentiate the possibilities beyond the scope of any book that weighed less than your grandmother.

What I am going to do here in this chapter is to work strictly with the New Moon, using it as an example, and hope to illustrate the *principles* that will allow you to tie any lunar phase into any astrological context.

THE ELASTIC NEW MOON

Like all the other lunar phases, the New Moon has intrinsic meaning. It is not subtle; it makes itself vividly evident in the character. But, as with everything else in astrology, its essential qualities are elastic, expressible in many ways. Just knowing that someone was born under this "Living Symbol" phase of the lunation cycle empowers us with insight. The first steps in placing those insights into the realm of uniqueness and precision is to integrate them with the equally urgent impact of the Moon's house placement and the way it is toned by the sign it occupies.

Here are some examples of that principle in action.

Rock star Bruce Springsteen is certainly charismatic and has clearly become symbolic to many people. Many human beings, from politicians to religious leaders, fit that description, but Springsteen has lived it out through his *artistry* and *performance*. His natal New Moon, standing 22° 42' ahead of the Sun, lies in Libra (aesthetic sensitivity) and in the fifth house (self-expression; performance; stagecraft). Consistent with that larger astrological context, he has expressed his New Moon through his art. We would not be able to deduce that fact from knowing only that he was born under the New Moon, but we can see it easily and clearly when we include his lunar sign and house factors.

Queen Victoria was also born under the New Moon. She left the mark of her enigmatic, withdrawn personality upon an entire age. She ruled England at the height of its power for sixty-three years. The final forty of those years, after her husband died, were spent mostly in isolation. She epitomizes the New Moon notions of leadership and of becoming symbolic to others, but she accomplished all that more through seductive vagueness than through presence or charisma. Needless to say, no one would mistake her for Bruce Springsteen. In Queen Victoria's natal chart, we find a very pure New Moon—it lies only 1° 35' ahead of the Sun. Both are in Gemini and in the twelfth house, with the Moon just a couple of degrees above the Ascendant and the Sun a little higher, more solidly in the twelfth. Inevitably, the withdrawn, indefinite components of the twelfth house are particularly evident in the shaping of Victoria's New Moon. Her Gemini influences emerge dramatically when we contemplate her effective leadership during the rapid transformation of England from an agrarian economy into the world's first industrial dreadnought. In a nutshell, Queen Victoria could *learn* and *improvise:* classic positive Gemini characteristics.

Controversial Indian guru Bhagwan Shree Rajneesh's New Moon lies in the eighth house in Capricorn, conjunct both Venus and Saturn. His enthusiastic encouragement of human sexuality, along with his penchant for Rolls Royces, seem to capture a major part of his outward reputation—and they are reflected clearly, on one hand, in his Venusian and eighth house elements (sex) and, on the other, in the status-conscious dimensions of Capricorn and Saturn. For these reasons, and others, he became symbolic to many people.

Another charismatic, symbolic New Moon religious leader of a very different bent is Billy Graham. His Moon lies in Sagittarius and the ninth house (both connected with religion) and is conjunct fiery Mars, reflecting his passionate oratory, his belief in sudden transformations of character, and his emphasis on simple, straightforward faith.

And so it goes. What we learned in the previous chapters about each of the eight phases is broad and abstract—like any other single factor in astrology. These factors only come to life when we stack them up like pieces of colored glass along with the rest of the elements in a given chart. We peer through the stack and we see a unique hue—something a lot more alive and singular than a "New Moon" or "Virgo" or anything else. Context is everything.

By the way, if you are relatively new to astrology and are not yet conversant with the basic meanings of various Moon placements in sign and house, you may want to review the tables at the end of Chapter Two, or immerse yourself in my first book, *The Inner Sky.*

PULLING PHASE, SIGN AND HOUSE TOGETHER

In an effort to make astrology simpler, someone might be tempted to ask which has more impact, the phase of the Moon or its sign and house? That is like asking which is more important, your heart, your lungs or your brain? Bottom line, you need all three. But juggling three complex and independent ideas all at once is daunting. What you need is a map. Here it is:

*The **sign** the Moon occupies symbolizes:*

○ an underlying mood

○ a core set of needs and values

○ an experience-coloring attitude toward life

*The **house** the Moon occupies symbolizes:*

○ an outward arena of pressing emotional preoccupation/concern

○ a locus of instinctual behavior

○ an area of life dense with developmental experiences

*The **phase** of the Moon symbolizes:*

○ a reflexive emotional posture relative to the needs of the Moon's sign and house

○ an instinctual strategy for fulfilling those needs

○ a set of attitudinal assumptions which underlie and flavor all perceptions and experiences

The Boss

Let's apply these principles by looking at the chart of Bruce Springsteen. He was born on September 23, 1949 in Freehold, New Jersey, at 10:50 pm. As we saw a few paragraphs ago, his birth chart shows the New Moon in Libra in the fifth house.

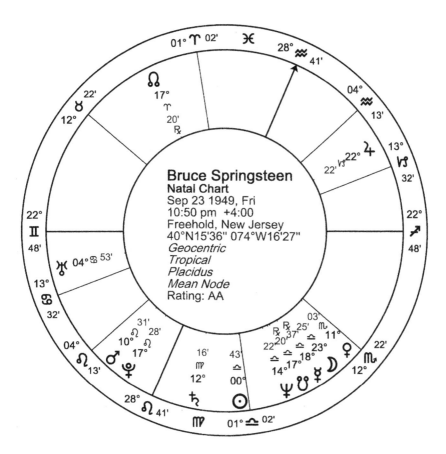

Let's analyze Springsteen's lunar influences more deeply, starting with the sign. With his Moon in Libra, his *underlying mood* is empathetic, with an instinct to connect with people emotionally and a strong sense that paradox is implicit in all situations. His *core needs and values* center on finding a peaceful middle ground, seeking justice, linking himself authentically with selected others, while harmonizing hues, shapes, sounds, and relationships. His *experience-coloring attitude toward life* is that of the artist and the seeker of fair solutions, both of which are flavored by his great sensitivity to irony and ambiguity. These are all textbook Libran qualities, and that sign shapes or underlies Springsteen's *reflexive emotional state*.

What about the Moon's house? Here, everything becomes less psychological and correspondingly more concrete, visible and behavioral.

With the Moon in the fifth house, *an outward arena of pressing emotional preoccupation and concern* for Bruce Springsteen is creativity in general. To feel good, he must be expressing himself creatively in some sense of the word, even if it is just entertaining the family at the dinner table with a funny story.

"Am I happy in the moment?" That's another fifth house question which presses upon him—and, from a far deeper evolutionary perspective, there's an underlying pain in the fifth house that calls for constant soothing.

That is why happiness—or the lack of it—is such an issue. As a result, there can be a preoccupation with pleasure, which can be addressed in healthy ways, such as creative self-expression—or in less healthy ones.

Going further, the fifth is the classic "house of children." At the literal level, his kids are naturally a big area of emotional focus, identification and concern to Springsteen. Less visibly, there is a strong relationship with his own "inner child" and the need to protect and preserve him. That inner child dynamic ties in again with the elemental fifth house need for uplift, release, and entertainment. If kids are not having a good time, they tend to feel that something is seriously amiss.

Just think of a five-year-old pitching a screaming fit in the grocery store just because he is a little tired of shopping and wants it to stop. We would expect to see some of that unreasonably demanding, even whiny, quality in the adult Bruce Springsteen. More positively, I would also imagine him simply to be good with children. His major secret there is that he is still, in many ways including good ones, basically one himself— he identifies with them naturally, seeing them as short *people*. And kids respond to that.

A *locus of instinctual behavior* for Bruce Springsteen, as is obvious from his life, is the stage—a classic piece of fifth house architecture. He seems to have been born to it, as anyone who has ever seen one of his indefatigable performances can attest.

Pulling sign and house together, in Bruce Springsteen's Moon we see the classic signature of the *artist* expressed just about clearly as it can possibly be expressed in astrological language. The Libran *aesthetic instincts* express themselves outwardly through fifth house *performance behavior*. We also see a powerful impulse toward the establishment of relationship, along with a warning regarding youthful naiveté in that intimate area of life. Illustrating this pitfall, Springsteen rather famously married "a beautiful princess" (Julianne Phillips) in haste, then found himself in *flagrante delicto*, back in the bed of his old girlfriend, Patti Scialfa. Divorce—and much tabloid "performance" of his personal life—followed. Twenty years later, he is still married to Patti, and she is the mother of his three children, with whom he appears to be quite engaged.

Much of the foregoing material is fairly conventional psychological astrology—the familiar alchemical merging of planet, sign and house. It can take us a long way.

Let's bring in the third layer—lunar phase. Bruce Springsteen was born, as we saw earlier, with the Moon 22° 42' ahead of the Sun. That places him solidly in the New Moon phase. (His Sun, by the way, was also in Libra and on the fifth house cusp, reinforcing everything we have been contemplating so far.) Using our formulaic first question about phase, what is Springsteen's *reflexive emotional posture* relative to the needs of the Moon's sign and house? In New Moon fashion, he is a *leader*—quite literally, the leader of the E-Street Band. From nearly the beginning, their music has been about *his* songs and *his* vision. Other musicians are swept along in those powerful currents, and they go mostly willingly.

Band members began spontaneously calling him "The Boss," and my impression is that this is mostly an affectionate title. The strange, inexplicable thing is the way the nickname caught on with the general public as well. Everyone could feel that he was truly "the Boss," despite the fact that Bruce Springsteen displayed almost nothing in the way of autocracy, self-importance, or affinity for conservative social structures.

There is a paradox behind this element of New Moon leadership. As we learned in Chapter Ten, a first-phase person is caught up in his own visionary process, fascinated by it—and, to a significant degree, has turned away from the three-dimensional world of real people in their actual realities. *Others become as symbolic to him as he becomes to them.* As a double Libran with Gemini rising, we might view Bruce Springsteen within the conventional tropes of astrology as friendly, fun, sociable, straightforward, communicative, extroverted and empathetic. I suspect that those words describe him reasonably accurately a lot of the time. But with his Moon in New phase, I also postulate a much more withdrawn, even mysterious, aspect to his character, one which would not be discernible through conventional forms of astrology. He is not easy to get to know.

Despite his streetwise persona, I furthermore imagine Springsteen to be inexplicably naive about people at times—genuinely surprised at the grittiness and duplicity of the world. Closer to the bone, I would imagine that those most intimate with him would be shocked at his sheer cluelessness about them at times. If I were Bruce Springsteen's astrologer, I might take the risk of wondering out loud if he ever found himself looking at an old friend—or even his own child—*and for five seconds not being able to recall the person's name.*

I immediately emphasize that my astrological impression is that Bruce Springsteen is a genuinely affectionate man and a good friend to those whom he loves. But the New Moon personality, as we learned, lives not in this world but in the archetypal realm. From time to time, such people float away from what we would call "reality." As Springsteen sang in his song *Jungleland*, "the poets down here don't write nothing at all. They just stand back and let it all be." Being called back to the mundane realm, out of the Holy of Holies, into this world of specifics and identities, startles New Moon people. And that is why it sometimes takes them five seconds to remember anyone's name—including their own.

Earlier I posited a second formulaic question for analyzing the contribution of lunar phase to the Moon's overall role in the chart. What is the person's *instinctual strategy* for fulfilling the aims of the Moon's house and sign? Springsteen's ultimate orientation of consciousness is rooted in his reflexive fascination with the world of archetypes. That is the realm of the New Moon. It is from there that he pulls his vitality. Fundamentally his back is turned to the world, while his eyes are focused on something the rest of us cannot see. And when he feels the New Moon's hunger to express itself and he finally turns his face toward us again, he is aglow with his vision.

We find the numinosity irresistible. Hence he functions in a leadership role, not because he desires it so much as because of his hunger to bring what he has seen out into expression—and the way his hunger combines with our collective desire to be lifted up by what he has seen. Thus, Springsteen's charisma and magnetism are actually an interactive phenomena, composed as much of our own fascination with him as any desire on his part to be seen.

A FAST MOON

In Chapter Two, we explored the meaning of a fast Moon versus a slow one. We learned that the Moon's average speed forward through the zodiac is 13°10' 35" per day, but that it varies rather widely. At the moment Bruce Springsteen was born, the Moon was setting speed records, moving at the surpassing and unsustainable rate of 15°03' 55" per day. For most people, the Moon is naturally moving at something more like an average speed, and so the fast/slow distinction is often moot. Springsteen, as an extreme case, provides us with a good test case for our theoretical construct.

Again, as with everything in astrology, each factor must exist in the context of the others. Qualities suggested by one symbol are sometimes cancelled or mitigated by another. Other times, as we will see here, they are strengthened. In Chapter Two, we learned that in general, a fast Moon suggests that a person is *alert,* and *quick to trust* and to *connect* interpersonally. He or she is *initially revealing, quick to process and digest information.* We saw that such a person would quickly *adapt and adjust* to new circumstances. By reflex, he or she would have an inclination to say "yes" rather than "no." Behaving in *manic* ways is a possibility.

Anyone who has ever seen Springsteen perform has witnessed a magnificent demonstration of the power of a fast Moon! The sheer speed and vitality of his performances are legendary. But because of the New Moon phase signature, I would soft-pedal the idea that Bruce Springsteen would be initially revealing. We have also learned that his New Moon birth adds some characteristic complexities to his intimate life—so we would not say he was quick to trust and to connect, although the potentially naive aspects of those fast-Moon qualities are likely to be strongly evident. I would suspect that he has sometimes been quick to trust the wrong people and slow to trust the right ones.

By the way, in Chapter Three we also explored the Moon being "Out of Bounds" by declination. That quality is not part of Bruce Springsteen's astrological make-up. When he was born, his Moon was in only 9°40' south declination, well within the 23.5° North or 23.5° South limits and thus not Out of Bounds. We check "Irrelevant" there—at least as far as his natal chart goes. But Springsteen's Moon *progressed* Out of Bounds between the summer of 1966 and the fall of 1971. During that time, he graduated from high school—then, in perfect Out of Bounds fashion, he broke the rules, dropped out of college and launched himself into a series of bands in which his unique style and vision as a poetic outsider were forged. Just a few months after his Moon returned from "the wilderness," he was discovered by a talent scout for Columbia Records. He returned from the Out of Bounds condition with his New Moon charisma inspired, radicalized—and charged with archetypal *ju-ju*.

In these last pages, I have gone into Springsteen's lunar phase in more detail than I did with the sign and house of his Moon. That is only because this book is fundamentally about the lunation cycle. But had his Moon not been in artistic Libra and the self-expressive, performance-oriented fifth house, the story would have been utterly different—he could have been Queen Victoria!

We must let *all* the voices of each person's Moon speak, then we listen to the chorus as a whole.

19

◗

THE PROGRESSED
LUNATION CYCLE

Watching the progressed Moon chase the progressed Sun around the birth chart is like watching a turtle chase a snail around a racetrack. You definitely want to bring a sandwich. The Moon is chugging along at about one degree per month, while the Sun takes about a year to get through a single degree. As they progress, the Moon gets ahead of the Sun, swings around, then slowly catches up from behind. Thus *progressed lunar phases are formed*. It works in the progressed chart in exactly the same way that it works in the sky, just much more slowly. As we pass through about three decades of time, we all experience the complete series of progressed lunar phases. With unmistakable power and relevance, they define the chapters of our lives. In this indirect way, all of us experience the energies of each of the eight phases at various times no matter the phase under which we were born.

By the way, watching the progressed Moon itself—without regard to progressed phases—pass through the signs, houses and aspects in the chart is one of astrology's most fundamental techniques. It is also a large subject which I have covered in detail elsewhere—specifically in the ninth chapter of the second edition of my book *The Changing Sky*, and in Chapter Seven of *Measuring the Night, Volume Two*. The latter is out-of-print and hard to find nowadays, but the former is quite available. Here, rather than repeating that material, I will concentrate on progressed lunar phases.

TIMING

As we saw earlier, the transiting Moon requires twenty-seven days, seven hours, forty-three minutes to return to any arbitrary starting point. As we move into progressions, days become years, so this works out to about twenty-seven years and four months for a "lunar return" to occur—that is, for the Moon to get back to where it started (a subject I'll consider in detail later in this chapter). But by then, the progressed Sun has moved forward about twenty-seven more degrees.In order fully to overtake the Sun, the Moon has to cover that extra distance as well—and at a speed of about one degree per month, that takes slightly over two more years. This makes the cycle between one progressed New Moon—the progressed Sun-Moon conjunction—and the next one come out to about twenty-nine and a half years. As a result, successive progressed New Moons occur just about exactly one full sign apart. We get two or three of them in a typical life span. The first such progressed New Moon will occur "at random" sometime in the first three decades of a person's life, and after that the rest are like clockwork. (That initial "randomness," by the way, depends simply on what the lunar phase was at your birth. Obviously, if you were born at the Full Moon, it takes the Moon half a cycle—over fourteen years—to progress around the chart and catch up with the Sun ... to get to the "starting line" in other words.)

Because both the Moon and Sun speed up and slow down as they progress, the actual timing of the specific phases varies. On average, each progressed lunar phase lasts for slightly over three years and eight months. The entry of the progressed lunation cycle into each new quadrant occurs every seven years or so, plus a little bit. Because of the wiggliness of the speeds involved, to know exactly when each phase begins, you need to do the calculations.

ENTER THE COMPUTER

I am not much of a computer jockey, and there are a lot of different astrological calculation programs out there. Each one looks a little different and takes some getting used to. In this section, for those of you who, like myself, might need a little hand-holding, here is the basic idea of how to get your computer to tell you what you need to know in terms of timing the lunar phases.

You go into the part of your calculation program that makes lists for the dates of ongoing astrological events—all the dates of your exact transits or progressions and so on. For Moon phase purposes, you are looking for *Progressed-to-Progressed* aspects. Be sure you are not looking at Progressed-to-Natal ones!

Open up your options there in the Progressed-to-Progressed category and *kill everything except the Sun and the Moon*. Disable the rest of the planets, the sign and house entries, parallels, stations—basically everything you can. Strip it down.

Look for the area of the program that allows you to choose which aspects will be reported. This is the critical step, so hunt until you find exactly what you are seeking. What you are after might be called "Hard" aspects, as distinct from "Ptolemaic" or "Standard" or "Complete." Another way to say what you want is "eighth harmonic aspects."

Depending on the program, you may have to make a customized aspect set, which you can then save for future use. The bottom line is that you want to enable the following five aspects between the progressed Sun and the progressed Moon, *and no others*: the conjunction (0°), the semi-square (45°), the square (90°), the sesquiquadrate (135°), and the opposition (180°). Notice that you are not using the familiar trines and sextiles. They have nothing to do with the eight-phase system.

Run it from the date of birth into the distant future—be optimistic about your longevity! You should get something that looks approximately like the table on the right.

Here is how to interpret what the "Hit List" is telling you.

First, *double-check that you are looking at Progressed-to-Progressed Moon-Sun aspects!* If you goofed and left the program defaulting to Progressed-to-Natal, you will make a monkey out of yourself.

The first line shows a Moon-Sun *opposition* which occurred for this person on

☽ ☍ ☉	07-20-1961
☽ ⊼ ☉	10-05-1964
☽ □ ☉	02-22-1968
☽ ∠ ☉	11-10-1971
☽ ☌ ☉	10-31-1975
☽ ∠ ☉	12-11-1979
☽ □ ☉	12-24-1983
☽ ⊼ ☉	08-14-1987
☽ ☍ ☉	11-09-1990
☽ ⊼ ☉	01-12-1994
☽ □ ☉	07-03-1997
☽ ∠ ☉	05-15-2001
☽ ☌ ☉	06-15-2005
☽ ∠ ☉	07-26-2009
☽ □ ☉	06-21-2013
☽ ⊼ ☉	12-14-2016
☽ ☍ ☉	02-17-2020
☽ ⊼ ☉	05-12-2023
☽ □ ☉	12-19-2026
☽ ∠ ☉	12-18-2030
☽ ☌ ☉	01-31-2035

July 20, 1961. The second line shows a Moon-Sun *sesquiquadrate* which occurred about three years later, on October 5, 1964. The third line shows a Moon-Sun *square* on February 22, 1968.

Now think about it—a square aspect, indicating that the progressed Moon was 90° from the progressed Sun, could refer to the Moon being 90° ahead of the Sun (the First Quarter), or, equally, to the Moon being 90° behind the Sun (the Last Quarter). Squares are squares, in other words. At least in conventional astrology, it is the same aspect either way. But we know there is a huge difference between the meaning of the First Quarter Moon and the Last Quarter Moon. How can we sort it out?

Easy. The answer is staring right at you. Go back to the first line: In '61, there was a Moon-Sun opposition. Unlike the squares, oppositions only happen *once* in the lunar cycle. When the progressed Moon and Sun are opposed, it is *always* the Full Moon. Since the square of '68 happened just a few years *after* the Full Moon, we know that it could only be the *waning* square—the Last Quarter Moon. That is the one that happens right after the Full Moon. (The First Quarter is the one that occurs right after the New Moon.)

The fourth line tells us there was a Moon-Sun *semi-square* on November 10, 1971. We now know that had to mark the beginning of the Waning Crescent phase. And, sure enough, the next aspect is the conjunction, occurring on Halloween 1975. Like the opposition, there is only one conjunction per cycle. It has to be the progressed New Moon.

The key to sorting out waxing and waning phases in the progressed lunation Hit List is to scope out the sequence by picking out the New Moon and the Full Moon. Let them alert you to whether the other phases are waxing or waning ones.

As we learn to follow the progressed lunation cycle, we will be relating what we have learned already about lunar phase in the natal chart—a permanent feature—to the ever-changing cycle of progressed phases. In the eight chapters prior to the last one, we divided everyone up into eight neat little boxes. The reality is that we are always changing. All the lunar phases are relevant to us all eventually. Against the backdrop of our natal charts, seasons of development are projected. That is what we are beginning to explore here. One practical note: In the above example, a progressed Full Moon occurred on July 20, 1961. That tells us that on that day the progressed Sun and the progressed Moon were exactly 180° apart. As we learned in previous chapters, that opposition marked the *beginning* of the Full Moon phase. For this person, the *Full Moon period* started on July 20, 1961 and continued until the Moon entered the Waning Gibbous part of its cycle on October 5, 1964. That entire period of three years and two-and-a-half months would bear the developmental signature of the progressed Full Moon.

These dates, by the way, are all for the lunation cycle of Irish rock star Bono, of the band U2. We will be looking briefly at the meaning of some of his progressed phases later on in this chapter, along with a variety of other examples.

Let's explore the eight phases again, this time from the progressed perspective. As ever, remember that the finest astrologers are the ones who have learned the skill of integrating many simultaneous trains of astrological thought. We may be experiencing a progressed New Moon while, independently, Uranus is transiting through an opposition to our natal Sun. That is a different situation than one in which the New Moon is happening while Neptune transits over Venus. And, of course, a progressed New Moon occurring in the seventh house might indicate a new beginning in terms of a relationship, while one in the tenth house might indicate a new start in the career. Throw in Gemini versus Virgo versus Capricorn, and you get the picture. It is complicated. And that is good! That is why astrology can be so specific. What follows are just guidelines—a starting point for your more integrative work.

THE PROGRESSED NEW MOON

The Progressed Moon Between 0° and 45° Ahead of the Sun

You may not have noticed it, but you have recently communed with the gods. They have given you marching orders for the next three decades of your life. Trouble is, they did not give them to you in English. They spoke to you the same way they speak to each other—direct thought-transfer. Telepathy. They planted an emotional zipped file deep in your heart. How can you unpack the message? You have to look in the right place, in the right way. In human terms, this new guidance is encoded in you as a *feeling*. A new set of *whimsies* is arising in you. You have to trust them and act on them.

The stakes are high. If you are able to receive and trust this new message, you will change the course of your life. You will find a meaningful path forward, one that is consistent with your continued happiness. If you are honest with yourself, you will realize that you *need* such a new path. There was nothing wrong with your old one—not any more than there was anything wrong with kindergarten. But you have graduated. You are ready to move on. But where? In what direction?

Only your heart knows. And that is enough.

What is beginning now may be obvious or it may be subtle—but either way, its true significance will only be revealed gradually over the years as the Moon progresses away from the Sun, out into the bright phases of full manifestation. Your task now is simply to *trust the feeling* and to act on it—in a nutshell, your task is to *get started*.

You will likely feel considerable uncertainty and insecurity. There is a good reason for that—you really *do not yet know what you are doing!* Take comfort in the fact that such doubtful feelings are normal, a sign that everything is going exactly as it should. You can *feel* what to do. That is enough. All you really ever have to know is where to put your foot next. Your heart can tell you that.

A curious feature of this New phase in the progressed lunation cycle is that often the new beginning is visible there quite obviously—but only retrospectively. You see it lucidly as you look back on the period from the viewpoint of many years into the future. But when you are in the midst of creating it, you typically do not have a very clear idea of what you are doing or how important it is. You are trusting instinct and feeling. You are improvising as doors open.

Examples

○ Carl Jung made his final break with Sigmund Freud and experienced the visions that shaped the rest of his work.

○ Rainer Maria Rilke met Auguste Rodin, triggering his poetic vision.

○ Stephen King, in the darkest hour, got a contract and a big advance for *Carrie*, his first novel.

○ John Lennon (and the Beatles) arrived in New York City, triggering Beatlemania in the U.S.A.

○ Christopher Reeve played *Superman*.

○ Adolph Hitler became Fuhrer of the Nazis.

○ Tiger Woods experienced his sex scandal.

○ Miles Davis played in his first jazz combo at age sixteen.

○ Pedro Almodovar released his breakout film, *Women on the Verge of a Nervous Breakdown*.

○ Agatha Christie published her first novel.

○ Bono answered an advertisement for a band, which became U2. At his next New Moon, he was *Time* magazine's Person of Year.

○ Joseph Campbell began work on his monumental, four-volume work, *The Masks of God*.

○ Walt Disney released his masterpiece, *Fantasia*.

○ Brad Pitt gained notice for his performance in *Thelma and Louise*.

○ Edith Piaf was "discovered" and began performing.

○ Bill Gates took a leave of absence from Harvard to form Microsoft.

PROGRESSED WAXING CRESCENT

The Progressed Moon Between 45° and 90° Ahead of the Sun

If you feel confused about what to do now, look back into the previous phase. The basic answers to all your questions are there, encoded in feelings you had then, in choices you have already made, and possibly in bridges you have burned. Each one is *symbolic* of what you are becoming. And none are as yet truly crystallized and clear—that is the source of your confusion. What is happening right now is that the New Moon vision is attempting to extend outward into the world. It is feeling its way forward, out of the abstract, archetypal realm toward the realm of concrete reality. It is not there yet. The seeds have sprouted, but the sprouts are still under the ground. You still really don't *know* what you are doing—and that is not nearly as big a problem as it appears to be. As with the New Moon phase, you can *intuit* your way forward. But now everything is more real—including the doubts and insecurities. It is as if you are playing for real money this time. The challenge is to keep nursing the vision toward full manifestation, and to *maintain your faith in it.* You are invited to take concrete steps, and they are often steps that afford no exit and no retreat.

Keep your eyes open for allies. Almost guaranteed, you will begin meeting people now who will prove pivotal to the expression of your vision. You cannot make it real without their help. Let them into your heart, your life, and your thinking. They are important triggers for the realization of your dreams and strategies. But do not compromise! As soon as you feel discomfort in that regard, pedal back a bit. *You may feel impatient, but there is no real rush—you have time.* Read that sentence again.

Examples

○ J.K. Rowling finished the manuscript of *Harry Potter and the Philosopher's Stone*, found an agent, was rejected by twelve publishers, then finally got her first publishing deal.

○ Rainer Maria Rilke served as Auguste Rodin's secretary.

○ Miles Davis got his first recording contract.

○ Carl Jung experienced mystical fainting spells as a boy, triggering his interest in psychology.

○ John Lennon met Yoko Ono.

○ Julia Child met her husband Paul.

○ Bono married his wife, Ali, while U2 developed a major following.

○ Al Gore became Vice President.

○ Joseph Campbell died—and became famous a few months later as *The Power of Myth* aired on television.

○ Paramahansa Yogananda met his guru, Sri Yukteswar.

○ George W. Bush invaded Iraq.

○ Benedict XVI became Pope.

○ Eckhart Tolle experienced his "inner transformation."

PROGRESSED FIRST QUARTER

The Progressed Moon Between 90° and 135° Ahead of the Sun

The rubber meets the road. Up until now in the present lunation cycle, your outer life has been a womb or a husk within which a vision was quietly taking shape, gathering allies, experimenting tentatively with manifestation. There have been concrete events, of course, and some of them were of lasting significance. But the real growth has been occurring in the depths of your inner, psychic world. In the Pagan context, you have been in the Winter cycle—the real action has been hidden down in the roots and the seeds. Underground, in other words. Now, at the First Quarter, is the time for *definitive commitment.* Time to put your money on the table.

The battle is joined! Please forgive the military metaphor, but it is aptly evocative here. Previously, you have had the luxury of tentativeness and elusiveness. You could hedge your bets. Life has not expected you to take an irreversible stand, any more than we would compel a child or teenager irrevocably to declare a marriage vow, a career choice, or even a political affiliation.

But now all that has changed. It is time to put your vision into action. Time to *act as if you believe in it.* Time to burn bridges, to cross the Rubicon, to bet the farm. *And when you do all that, you will meet resistance.* Expect that.

Competition is one of the basic qualities of existence, even if we have little competitiveness in our own natures. Your vision—the style of life you have chosen and intended—will be challenged, both by emerging inimical circumstances and by human beings with contrary visions. This is a cliché, but do try to reframe "bad luck" as "a challenge." Do not be passive, in other words.

Overwhelmed emotionally by the onslaught of the Orcs upon Helm's Deep in *The Lord of the Rings*, King Théoden asks, "What can men do against such reckless hate?" And brave Aragorn answers, "Ride out and meet them." That is the right attitude, more or less. But unlike in the movies, some degree of compromise will be compelled upon you, like it or not. Make those compromises strategically. You cannot win all of these battles—but there are some you must win. Choose them wisely. You cannot please everyone. Few of us make it through this period without accruing some enemies or rivals. But above all, just put it out there. Your knees may be knocking together, but *take a stand!*

Examples

○ Martin Luther King, Jr. planned his historic March on Washington.

○ Dane Rudhyar had a kidney removed at age twelve, and one cycle later published his revolutionary book, *The Astrology of Personality.*

○ Oprah Winfrey debuted *The Oprah Winfrey Show.*

○ Princess Diana met and married Prince Charles. ⊠ Adolph Hitler twice tried and failed to get into art school.

○ Agatha Christie disappeared for eleven days after learning about her husband's affair.

○ John Lennon experienced the breakup of the Beatles.

○ Germaine Greer published her controversial feminist book, *The Female Eunuch.*

○ Michael Jackson died.

○ Paramahansa Yogananda took formal vows as a Swami.

○ David Bowie's left eye was paralyzed in a fight.

○ Free on bail before serving jail time for "obscenity," Lenny Bruce died of a heroin overdose.

PROGRESSED WAXING GIBBOUS

The Progressed Moon Between 135° and 180° Ahead of the Sun

Our vision is launched. We see it crystallized around us in the reality of our lives. Choices are beginning to come to a focus. The first fruits are born. We have been through the fire. We have made helpful, worthy allies. *We have also found out who our friends are*—probably in both the pleasant and unpleasant senses of that phrase.

But we are still waxing. We are not yet at full bloom. Now the evolutionary work lies in opening up to serendipity, to the unexpected, and to the *creative force of the collective.* In that alchemical cauldron, our vision will grow and change. Hopefully, we will hold onto the core of it and not become totally lost in the world. But, equally hopefully, we will be open-minded and flexible. We welcome synergy into our life. Others see things we do not see. Others have skills and connections we lack. Compromise can improve things, just as it can destroy them. *Thus we are now invited to find the middle path, cooperating just enough with just the right people.*

Opportunities of both a helpful and destructive nature abound. Often they come walking into our lives on two feet. At some level, you are learning *team-building* skills. And you have entered the full-bloom confusion of the reality of human relationships, so:

○ *Just because you like someone does not mean they will be of any real positive help to you.*

○ *Just because you dislike someone does not mean their criticisms or contradictory perspectives cannot be lifesaving for you.*

○ *Just because someone is trustworthy by nature does not mean that you will benefit from trusting them.*

○ *Just because someone is mad or a scoundrel does not mean that he or she is not a link in the chain by which your vision is hanging.*

Outwardly, there is a sense of riding a rising tide in terms of reputation, profession, public relevance and public receptivity to what we have to offer. Inwardly, our characters are reaching toward a kind of mature expression. Often, that maturation requires an external trigger, generally in the form of human contact. One dimension of that piece of the puzzle is that sexual energy tends to run high at this time, as we allow ourselves to be "entered" in every sense of the word. Walls must come down for soul to flow into soul in that ancient erotic mystery. And of course people can enter each other in countless other, non-sexual ways as well—intellectually, practically, emotionally. More broadly, there is a tendency for *extreme forces* to enter the life now. We are swept along in collective currents of change. Is it really "our" vision any longer? Or are we singing a duet with another person or with a community?

Examples

○ Barack Obama was elected President of the United States.

○ Elvis Presley made his first public performance in a singing contest at a state fair. He won $5. A few months later, for his eleventh birthday, he was given his first guitar.

○ Bill Clinton had his affair with Monica Lewinsky.

○ Brad Pitt split with Jennifer Aniston and dated Angelina Jolie.

○ Bruce Springsteen released *Born in the USA*, and refused a $12 million offer to use his songs in an ad campaign for running shoes.

○ Frida Kahlo suffered her legendary, horrific bus accident.

○ Salman Rushdie went into hiding—and gained international fame after a *Fatwa* was declared against him.

○ Hillary Rodham Clinton ran for President and became Secretary of State.

○ Michael Jackson released *Thriller*, the best-selling album of all time.

○ Charles Manson orchestrated the Tate-LaBianca murders.

○ Thelonius Monk appeared on the cover of *TIME* magazine.

○ Billy Graham invited MLK to join him in the pulpit in New York.

PROGRESSED FULL MOON

The Progressed Moon Between 180° and 225° Ahead of the Sun

The New Moon vision of a decade and a half ago comes into full display now, wholly birthed into the community. Depending on our natures, this may happen on a grand scale or on a modest one—and much of that depends on the nature of the original vision. If one has a vision of, say, marriage and family, that may indeed come to pass now. But you will probably not appear on the national news for it. If you had a vision of changing the world, then this might be your hour in the public spotlight.

"Fame" is a word that has occasional relevance to the progressed Full Moon, but "manifestation" is a better one. So is "entanglement." So is the idea of having stepped into white-water rapids—a river that may look to others as if it were of your own making, but the subjective reality is often of being pulled along by external, social forces. The dominoes are falling. Feelings of "fate" often loom large in the mind now—fated meetings, fated events, good fortune, bad fortune. Our vision—and our life—has in a sense become communal property. Others are invested in it in practical and emotional ways. They have expectations of us. Generally, those expectations do not feel *disharmonious* with our own intentions, unless our original vision was a serious soul-compromise. But there is still a curious feeling of *estrangement* from events, even events others might consider enviable. We are, as Yeats put it, "estranged amid the strangeness of" ourselves. Other wills and other lives are dancing with our own.

You probably still have a personal life. That is your home base. But there is also something of an entity we might call *You, Inc.* out there, running on its own logic with its own momentum. Your life has taken on a quality of *symbolism* in the minds of others. Not to be hyperbolic, but you have entered the mythic realm. Maybe you are a "star." Maybe you are on television. Maybe you find yourself the head of the local PTA. Maybe you are simply "mom" to three rambunctious kids—even then, your life has taken on the symbolism of the Full phase. At some level, you are what you look like to others.

For most of us, what I am about to write is a relative long shot, but I have noticed a pattern of people dying under the progressed Full Moon, especially when their deaths seem to elevate them to mythic status in the minds of others. One would never "predict" death based on this configuration. In fact, in my opinion, predicting death in general is not ethical astrological practice. But death is one way a person might enter that symbolic, mythic realm that the Full Moon embodies.

Examples

- J.K. Rowling's *Harry Potter and the Deathly Hallows* broke the record as the best-selling book of all time, selling eleven million copies in the first day of release.

- Elvis Presley died.

- John Lennon was murdered.

- Christopher Reeve married.

- Monica Lewinsky was involved in the sex scandal over her relationship with Bill Clinton.

- Young Frida Kahlo met Diego Rivera.

- Adolph Hitler was awarded medals for bravery in World War One.

- Loreena McKennitt self-released her first album, *Elemental*.

- Oprah Winfrey got her own show in Baltimore, *People Are Talking*.

- Paramahansa Yogananda came to the United States and founded the Self-Realization Fellowship.

- Jim Jones triggered the mass suicide at Jonestown, Guyana, then killed himself.

- Rubin "Hurricane" Carter's murder conviction was overturned after he had served twenty-two years in prison.

- Walt Disney opened Disneyland.

PROGRESSED WANING GIBBOUS

The Progressed Moon Between 225° and 270° Ahead of the Sun

The world's backyards are full of half-built sailboats. The world's desks are full of half-finished novels. Most of us have a backlog of abandoned projects. Why? Is it laziness? That is not always the right answer. Truly lazy people typically do not even *start* ambitious projects such as those! Pressed about losing steam, a person will often say, "I lost interest." That is understandable and may very well be accurate and the best course of action. Time changes us. *The person who started that project no longer exists.*

Maybe in every moment we are doing our honest best. If that is true, then a few moments later we have probably benefitted spiritually from our virtuous efforts. *Our best is now a little bit better than it was just a moment ago.* But we are still stuck with last year's dream. Furthermore, we usually have other people involved, at least emotionally. Everywhere we go, supportive friends ask us how the novel is coming along. We have partners in that sailboat-building project. They have put their life savings into it. What can we do? Mix up some more epoxy. We cannot let them down.

Welcome to the progressed Waning Gibbous phase. It is time to *keep on keeping on.* Your original New Moon vision is now getting old. It has been modified by "committees" through the previous three bright-cycle phases. Perhaps you hardly recognize it anymore. *Perhaps you hardly recognize the life you have created for yourself.* Maybe the person who signed those contracts is foreign to you now. Much depends upon how skillfully you compromised in the previous phases—and how skillfully you recognized and refused certain compromises that would have been spiritually fatal. There is a good chance that your vision has been improved through the input and help of others. There is a near-certainty that it is more grounded in reality.

A good strategy now is to consider finishing the sailboat or completing the novel. Your heart may not be fully in it, but it still *is* your vision. Fight the doldrums of indecision. Finish what you have started, knowing that you are doing it as much for other people as for yourself. *Break bread with them;* listen; accept. Draw energy from the interactions. Notice and appreciate the benefit you are bringing into the lives of people about whom you care—or even ones about whom you do not care, just for the sake of the principle. Even that more abstract kindness has a certain spiritual merit. You are becoming a *symbol* in other people's minds. What is overtly great about you does not excite *you* that much anymore. That is because it is no longer under active development. It is mostly a gift for others now, not so much for you yourself. Engage; trust; relate generously. Behave in ways that give you a feeling of soulful pride and integrity, of big-heartedness. Go forward knowing that soon you will experience completion and release—and a fresh start.

Examples

○ Christopher Reeve had his crippling accident.

○ Barack Obama worked as community organizer in Chicago before entering Harvard.

○ Martin Luther King, Jr. won oratory contest at age fifteen.

○ Al Gore was elected to the House of Representatives, then, one cycle later, released *An Inconvenient Truth.*

○ Julia Child finished her signature *Mastering the Art of French Cooking.*

○ Amelia Earhart flew for the first time—as a passenger with a barnstormer.

○ Sonia Sotomayor became a U.S. Supreme Court Justice.

○ Michael Jackson started performing at age six.

○ Military psychiatrist Nidal Malik Hasan murdered thirteen people at Fort Hood.

○ Timothy Leary had his first psychedelic experience.

PROGRESSED LAST QUARTER

The Progressed Moon Between 270° and 315° Ahead of the Sun

A friend of mine got a ride in a Navy interceptor. They took off from the flight deck of an aircraft carrier and shot into a dizzying vertical climb, like a rocket. At something like fifteen thousand feet, the pilot cut the throttles and kicked the tail around so that they were pointed nose-down. Then he told my green-around-the-gills friend to look at the altimeter. *The needle was still going up.* The explosive thrust of their climb was still hurling the plane butt-first toward heaven, despite the nose-down orientation.

Butt-first toward heaven! At the progressed Last Quarter you may find yourself in a similar situation, at least emotionally. You have cut your thrust, but you are still going up. The twenty-year momentum of your vision carries you forward, even though you are beginning to feel curiously disengaged from it. Allow that disengagement to happen without your interference or help, and keep your eyes peeled for opportunities to rest and reflect. There is a fine art here of dropping things naturally without ever actually pushing anything away that is not ready to drop. Be as unselfconscious as an apple tree letting go of its apples. Things may fall apart. Let them. In practical terms, watch for opportunities to *delegate responsibility* and to *pass on the torch.* It will not be long before you are in a new stage of life with new possibilities. Meanwhile, you have a chance to clean up loose ends. Be especially attentive to *necessary goodbyes.* In show business, there is a saying, "You meet the same people on the way down whom you met on the way up." If you treated people insensitively or unfairly at earlier stages of the cycles—and to some extent we all do—you will often meet them again now and have a chance to offer apologies or acts of kindness. And however they react, let them be. Above all, avoid the temptation to waste your time diagnosing other people.

All of this assumes that you have done a reasonably courageous and honest job of responding to the earlier phases—that you had a worthy vision, in other words. If your response back then was weak, there is often a rising feeling of *pointlessness* and *emptiness* at this seventh phase. Like old age, it is not for sissies. And even if we have done well, the old vision is now at least somewhat tired and played out. Distinctly, our treasure is no longer in this world. The wise strategy is to begin to look for treasure in the next world. That can point to a renewed interest in spiritual matters, and it can also simply signal an increasingly psychological and internal perspective.

Pursuant of those inward lines of development, cathartic behaviors of all sorts are greatly beneficial now, especially those that occur at the interface of *art* and *ritual.* Those two words have different overt meanings, and yet the act of making art *is* a cathartic ritual, and all ritual can be understood as the generation of evocative metaphor—which is, in turn, a pretty effective definition of art. The underlying reasoning here is that you are *disentangling yourself from your own creation*, preparatory to releasing yourself into a new beginning. Giving it outward, symbolic form seems to help with that process of release.

You will likely experience poignant emotions during this progressed lunar phase. There is a sadness in it—a sweet sorrow. Think of the natural mood of old people, with so much of life behind them and so little ahead. Naturally this mood is not as giddy as that of youth, but it is not a pathological condition either. It is possessed of a quality of *clarity*, and it is optimized for reflecting honestly and accurately on the accomplishments and the failures of the previous phases. This integrative reflection is precious; it is the deepest heart of the evolutionary meaning of this Last Quarter lunar phase.

Anyone can have experience. But to *digest* the experience honestly and courageously—that is what separates wisdom from scratchy old home movies running endlessly in one's head.

Examples

- O   Bill Gates started his first philanthropic foundation, the William H. Gates Foundation.

- O   John Lennon met Paul McCartney, and his mother was killed by an automobile.

- O   Martin Luther King Jr. was ordained a minister and, one cycle later, assassinated.

- O   Sonia Sotomayor entered private legal practice.

- Bruce Springsteen got his first recording contract and made his debut album.

- Exiled Thich Nhat Hanh was allowed to return to Vietnam for the first time in many years.

- Elvis Presley had his first big hit, *Heartbreak Hotel*, which sold a million copies.

- Ted Kennedy experienced the Chappaquiddick accident.

- Keith Richards kept days-long vigil by his dying mother's bedside.

- Barack Obama became editor of the *Harvard Law Review* and graduated *magna cum laude* from Harvard.

PROGRESSED WANING CRESCENT

The Progressed Moon Between 315° and 360° Ahead of the Sun

You have come to the end of the cycle. With penetrating self-knowledge and a dollop of faith, you will realize that you are actually happy about that—the way a wise person is content with the approach of the end after a long, meaningful life. Why stick around? You are finished here. Such a liberated attitude does require faith, of course. Do what you can do to bolster that spiritual self-confidence now. Sit quietly. Meditate. Use whatever metaphysical or transpersonal methods work for you. Probably you will find yourself encountering various spiritual teachers and teachings, along with assorted reasons to appreciate the mysterious, multidimensional journey of life. That could mean psychic experiences, miraculous events, inspiring deaths—magic in general.

Deep down you are *ready* to move on to something new. You just do not yet know exactly what it is. Familiarity makes us feel secure, but overfamiliarity is boredom, the spiritual Gulag. It is time to *let go of familiarity*, time to abandon the tyranny of the Known. There is a feeling of endings in the air now. Relationships, beliefs, homes, professions—everything is on the table, often whether we like it or not. Sometimes these endings hit us from outside, without any conscious choice on our own part. As in the previous phase, things fall apart. Try to trust the notion that even events that appear to take the form of catastrophic loss or tragedy have layers of meaning and necessity woven into them, although it may be a while before you can appreciate that perspective. You may find meditative time practically forced upon you by delays, accidents, illnesses, waiting games.

New beginnings are happening now too, although you will probably not fully recognize them as such until later on. Many are purely internal and intuitive. The visionary world is pressing upwards out of the unconscious mind, giving you gifts. Hints and harbingers of them may appear in the physical world. They may emerge as insights. They may come in dreams, which are often incredibly active and vivid now. *Delay is beneficial to you at this stage.* Even your good ideas are half-baked. So let them bake a little longer! Don't mistake your anxiety at being temporarily naked for a new suit. Relax into the vision and release the hold of the past.

Examples

○ J.K. Rowling, while on a train trip from Manchester to London, got the idea for the *Potter* novels, which she said "came fully formed" into her mind.

○ Stephen King was rammed by a van while walking, and spent months in recovery.

○ Teenaged Germaine Greer fled her abusive home.

○ Thich Nhat Hanh was fully ordained as a Buddhist monk.

○ Bono's mother died. He was fourteen.

○ Carl Jung met Sigmund Freud.

○ Miles Davis got his first trumpet for his thirteenth birthday.

○ Mary Cassatt fled her upper-class Pennsylvania family to paint and study painting in Paris.

○ Walt Disney conceived *Snow White*, the first full-length animated film.

○ Frida Kahlo divorced and remarried Diego Rivera.

○ Thelonius Monk was arrested for narcotics possession.

○ Elvis Presley was inducted into the U.S. Army as a private.

○ Muhammad Ali was convicted on criminal draft-evasion charges and stripped of his heavyweight title for his moral objections to the Vietnam War.

THE LITERAL DARK OF THE MOON

For many years, I took a different tack on the whole question of progressed lunar phase. I now believe that the system I have just presented is more sophisticated, but my older understanding has value and demonstrable reality as well. It focused strictly on the progressed New Moon and the progressed Full Moon, and so is much simpler.

The key to understanding its foundation lies in trusting the obvious messages of our senses. Visually, there is no Moon in the sky for about three nights. Similarly, the Moon appears to be Full for about three nights. It takes a practiced eye to distinguish the "real" Full phase from the night before or the night after.

As we move from the realm of what we actually *see* in the heavens—the realm of transits—to the realm of progressions, everything slows down. Days literally become years. So we could speak of the three *years* of the "visual" Dark of the Moon or the three *years* of the "visual" Full Moon. That would then signify a period that started about eighteen months *before* the exact 0° New or 180 Full aspect was reached and extended eighteen months *after* the exact aspect. Thus, the Dark of the Moon by this standard would embrace what we have been thinking about as the latter part of phase eight and the early part of phase one. It is, in other words, a very different view of lunar phase, and not readily compatible with the main theory I am developing in this book. But it does work pretty well. And the Moon, of course, is not bothered by simultaneous, mutually contradictory truths.

At the visual New Moon, we see nothing. And yet the cycle is beginning. For that reason, we could define the New Moon as *a beginning that gives no evidence of its existence.* Think of a mighty oak, early in its career—it is actually only an acorn, freshly germinated under the mulch. Thinking of an acorn as an oak tree is a little odd, but it is also true. Think of a woman who has been pregnant for seventeen nanoseconds. Something quite extraordinary is occurring, but she may not even be aware of it—her attention is presumably elsewhere. Nature, in other words, abounds with examples of these kinds of subtle and hidden beginnings. Not everything important starts with explosions and fanfare.

As the Moon lines up with the Sun, there is a parallel development in our own personal lives. We, too, are experiencing a beginning that gives no evidence of its existence. To do so successfully, we need to *let the Moon eclipse the Sun within us*, which is to say, to let the heart eclipse the head. We must feel our way forward.

Again, this reasoning applies to a period starting about a year and a half before the technical "moment" of the New Moon and continues until about a year and a half after it.

In the light of the broader theory I am developing in this volume, we can make sense of this second perspective, despite the contradictions with our eight phase system. During the eighteen months or so before the exact New Moon, we are deep inside the Waning Crescent phase. Our consciousness is optimized for releasing the past so that we can receive a new vision. There are two parts to that process, and they are interlocked: *letting go of what we have been* and *receiving the emotional chord upon which the future will rest.* That whole process seems to develop extra intensity and urgency during the final half of phase eight, as the Moon actually disappears from the inner sky, as well as the outer one.

The moment of the exact New Moon comes. By the standards of this present book, we enter phase one. But the Moon remains invisible for approximately the first half of that New Moon phase. We are in a beginning, needing to move forward confidently, at least inside ourselves, with the emerging vision. That is true of the whole first phase, as we learned earlier in this chapter. But during this true "Dark of the Moon," there is an underscored emphasis on the need for patience, silence, and receptivity to the deeper self. As we come out of that three-year period of literal darkness and the Moon actually becomes visible, even though we are still in phase one, there are often more tangible expressions of the new start. We begin to have something to show for the inner work. The acorn sends up a shoot.

THE LITERAL FULL MOON

Our thinking about the progressed Full Moon is essentially the same as our thinking about the New, only backwards. Again, we have a period of about three days in which the Moon is experienced visually as Full. Translated into progressions, that becomes about three years—eighteen months before the technical moment of fullness and eighteen months afterwards. This period embraces the last half of the Waxing Gibbous

Moon and the first half of the Full Moon phase. As per our basic theory, this is a time of maximum engagement with the outer world of people, events, institutions and culture. The fourth phase has that "Beltane" feeling of exciting co-creativity. The fifth phase begins the waning cycle, and so we begin to grasp that we are in a tangled web of our own making. But we are still in Midsummer, riding high on manifest momentum, for good or ill. In this perspective on the Full Moon, our vision is maximally visible to others. And inwardly, despite the fanfare, there is often a feeling of anticlimax.

Finding illustrations of this second, more visual approach to the New and Full Moons is easy; it works quite reliably. J.K. Rowling got the basic inspiration for her Harry Potter series in a flash during the three years of her "New Moon" as we are defining it here—it actually came to her deep in her Waning Crescent stage. During the three years of her "Full Moon," she broke all previous historical sales records when *Harry Potter and the Deathly Hallows* sold eleven million copies in a single day—and of course kept on selling.

During his "New Moon" three years as we are defining it here, Bono answered an ad in a Dublin paper—Larry, Adam, and Dave were looking for a singer. During the three years of his "Full Moon," U2's album *Joshua Tree* won a Grammy for Album of the Year and, during that same cycle, U2 went on to release another fabled masterpiece, *Achtung Baby*. To many people, this was the height of the band's creative power and impact on the world.

In the three years of his Dark of the Moon, a young Mukunda Lal Ghosh was searching for a guru. At the Full, he was Swami Paramahansa Yogananda, founding the Self-Realization Fellowship.

These two ways of looking at the progressed lunation cycle are not the same, but they are not irreconcilably opposed to each other either. I use them both. The formal way I make sense of the friction between them is fairly simple. *Materially* and *outwardly*, the three year "visual New Moon" period will almost always, at least in retrospect, constitute a significant beginning, while what is begun then will typically "peak" in the three-year "visual Full Moon" period. That is what it looks like existentially and biographically. That, in other words, is what happens overtly.

Meanwhile, *inwardly* and *psycho-spiritually*, our eight-phase system is more relevant. That is what I use nowadays to help people navigate these time periods. That is where the best guidance lies in terms of astrological counsel and self-reflection.

Bottom line, for helping people as an astrological counselor, I would be inclined toward using the eight-phase system that is the heart of this book. For placing the inner process in the context of visible, outward biographical reality, I pay a lot of attention to the second, more visual perspective I have just introduced.

EYES ON THE SKY

Throughout this section, I have been presuming the "three nights" of the Dark of the Moon. That is a practical statement, not an absolute one. Just think of how hard it is to tell if the Moon is really Full—half the time when we believe that is what we are seeing, it is actually the day before or the day after the actual moment of technical fullness. Muslims start their holy season of Ramadan with the first sighting of the waxing Moon, and so for well over a thousand years they have been making a diligent effort to detect it as early as possible. They routinely beat our "three-day" mark. Islam uses a lunar calendar and the timing of Ramadan floats through the seasons from year to year, but it is always linked to the beginning of the ninth lunar month of the year, which is timed to the first sign of the Waxing Crescent.

Technically, it is possible to sight the slim sickle of the emerging Moon as soon as about fifteen hours after the actual Sun-Moon conjunction. Everything has to be just right for that to happen—the precise moment of the New Moon occurring late in the wee hours, so that the slim Crescent just sneaks out of the Sun's glare fifteen hours later, around sunset. Binoculars can be a real aid in this quest, but beware—that is a blood sport. The Moon would of course be very close to the Sun, perhaps only 7° away. One wrong twitch and you've got the Sun in the binocular field. That might well be the last thing you ever see in this world, as it can literally blind you.

For practical, experiential purposes, saying that there are three days of Dark and three days of Full is a good approximation. One insight we can take away from all this is that our three years are not meant to be taken rigidly, to the day. Unlike the eight phases, they refer more impressionistically to a ragged period of time without a clear start or finish.

LUNAR RETURNS

On another note entirely, the progressed Moon helps us address one more of life's big riddles: *the psychology of aging*. With its cycle of twenty-seven years and four months, it follows that shortly after anyone's twenty-seventh birthday, he or she will experience the progressed Moon conjunct the natal one. We do not need to know anything at all about the person astrologically to be sure of that. All we need is the age. That is one lunar cycle, universally. After sixty minutes, the minute hand of your clock will be back where it started. The logic here is exactly the same. And of course, by the same logic, we know that when somebody completes two of those same cycles, the progressed Moon will once again be back where it started. That works out to an age of fifty-four years and eight months. And—you guessed it—we can take it one step further: At age eighty-two, it happens a third time. Many people live to see that third *lunar return*—and a rare few live to experience a fourth one at the tender age of one hundred nine.

In practical terms, we can think of life as being divided into three Moon cycles, with the twenty-seventh and fifty-fifth birthdays as the approximate dividing lines. The majority of us check out sometime near the end of the third cycle. One way to understand those periods is to view them through the lens of archetypal feminist psychology: a woman is first Maiden, then Mother, then Crone. With modest imagination, men can make appropriate translations there. We might more neutrally think of *Youth, Midlife*, and the *Cycle of the Elder*.

There are universal, core issues at each lunar return, and that is what we will explore in the next few pages. For each one of us, however, the lunar returns have specific and unique signatures. Which house and sign does the natal Moon occupy? What phase was the Moon in at birth? And where are we presently in terms of the lunation cycle?

The astrology of the aging process is complicated. We cannot reduce it to the Moon's progressions alone, even with these details added to the mix. In contemplating the astrology of the life cycle, most astrologers would start out thinking of *Saturn returns* rather than progressed lunar returns. Saturn's cycle is just a little longer, at about twenty-nine and a half years, so we all have a lunar return, then a Saturn return shortly thereafter. The first lunar return could be viewed, Moon-fashion, as an *inward, psychological initiation* into midlife, and the first Saturn return a couple years later as a more outward one—and of course few people face their thirtieth birthdays without considerable "outward" fanfare from their friends. Turning thirty is a big deal. Saturn is concrete in its action and nature; it manifests visibly and publicly what the Moon has already created inwardly and privately.

Similarly, the second lunar return in our mid-fifties is an inward, private initiation into elderhood, while the second Saturn return about four years later calls for more social recognition of the event. In everyday life, the second Saturn return basically translates to "turning sixty," and of course everyone gets embarrassing presents and comments from their friends at such a time—Viagra, rubber pants and so forth. One irony is that astrologically and psychologically we "turn sixty" when we are fifty-nine, so the sixtieth birthday itself typically feels anticlimactic. On the street, people would explain this phenomenon by pointing out that unless we were truly abysmal at mathematics, when we turn fifty-nine, we can see what is coming. The deeper reality is that sixty is just a number with a zero at the end of it, so it looks important. Fifty-nine however reflects an organic cycle—and, more subtly and inwardly, so does the lunar return at age fifty-four years and eight months.

A full analysis of the complex astrology of the life cycle is beyond the scope of this volume. I cover it in some detail in Chapter Six of *The Changing Sky*, taking in the cycles of Jupiter, Uranus, and Pluto as well. I might like to tackle the subject again now that I have, shall we say, a "broader perspective" on the aging process. But in any case, the full subject is beyond the scope of this book. Here, I want to focus strictly on the meaning of the progressed lunar returns.

THE FIRST LUNAR CYCLE

The first lunar return, twenty-seven years and four months after our birth, marks the end of youth. During the first lunar cycle, running from birth until this moment, our *instinctual self is optimized for dreaming*. In saying this, I do not mean strictly to refer to night-dreams, although they are often strong, meaningful, and compelling in these early years. I am thinking more about "dreaming up" a future for ourselves. To be happy, to take care of ourselves well during the first lunar cycle, we must let our imaginations range widely over our possibilities. We need to feel our way into our futures. We are naturally idealistic, tending toward big answers. In essence, we are trying to discover ourselves.

Ask a six-year-old what he wants to be when he grows up and he might say "Batman!" And, at age six, that is an excellent answer. Of course he will not actually become Batman, but, in the context of that mythic metaphor, the kid is planning on becoming a powerful force for good in his community, capable of taking care of people about whom he cares, and generally stepping up to the plate. At age six, Batman fantasies are a good neurological rehearsal for adulthood.

A sixteen-year-old who says "Batman" worries us. As we advance in the first lunar cycle, our dreams need to start converging with reality. Try this: A sixteen-year-old says he wants to fly interceptors for the Air Force. As adults, we know that his actually succeeding in doing that is a long shot, but we like that the young fellow has a big dream—and unlike becoming Batman, he actually has a chance of it coming true. It would be a sorry adult indeed who said to him, "That will never happen. You should stop thinking about things like that and concentrate on getting a real job."

The point of all this is that during the first lunar cycle, consciousness is trying to upload the vision that will guide the person toward a meaningful life. At first the messages are mythic and generally overblown. As the cycle advances they should become more concrete. And at the first lunar return, those dreams begin to collide with reality—a process that reaches a concrete crescendo at the Saturn return. We feel the finitude of life closing in around us. We feel our limits and our impossibilities. But, if we have done a good job of "dreaming" during the first cycle, we have also held onto a kernel of inspiration and direction. We can recognize our path in life and begin to make it real.

THE SECOND LUNAR CYCLE

The second Moon cycle of life runs from age twenty-seven up until the second lunar return just short of our fifty-fifth birthdays. Obviously, there is a lot of difference between the natural psychology of a thirty-year-old and that of a fifty-year-old. But there are also common denominators. The mood of midlife is about *bringing the dreams and visions of youth into concrete manifestation.* To be happy, we need to be accomplishing something that feels significant and meaningful to us. Dreaming youth's big dreams is no longer enough. Emphatically, these accomplishments do not need to be in a career category. That is not everyone's path. They might just as easily be creative or familial or spiritual. The birth chart as a whole will address the question of the natural orientation of those dreams in eloquent detail. It describes the life we were born to live. At the first lunar return, we must begin to bring that vision to fruition. Our psycho-spiritual health during the entire second lunar cycle depends simply upon *making it real.*

Since the timing of these cycles is universal, it follows that we do not need to be astrologers to understand them and to feel them in our bones. Being human and reflective is sufficient. Forgetting astrology, just imagine for example a twenty-five-year-old who is not yet sure of her career path. Or one who breaks up with her boyfriend because she is not yet clear about whether he is really "the one," or about whether she wants to have children. Most of us would not be terribly bothered or worried about her. She is still young, only twenty-five. It still seems right for her to keep her options open if that is what she feels like doing. But if she is forty and reporting the same uncertainties, we tend to be less comfortable. She is in the midst of the second lunar cycle; she should have a vision for herself by now. She should be ready to make her stand in this world. We are no longer so tolerant of her uncertainty and confusion. We may not say these things out loud, but we feel them inwardly. She is older; the rules underlying sanity have changed.

THE THIRD LUNAR CYCLE

When we come to our second lunar return, we are in our mid-fifties. About that time, our mailbox fills with literature from organizations for senior citizens or retired people. My own mailbox brought a cheery opportunity to "Win a Pre-Paid Cremation!" We start getting discounts. People toward whom we might feel a little zing of attraction start addressing us respectfully as "sir" or "ma'am." If we are female, there is a good chance we are noticing some significant changes in our bodies— and that is true in a slightly more subtle form for males as well. Nature and society, in other words, are teaming up to send us a message.

But what is the message? Try a little thought experiment. First, imagine a library that contains every word that has been written in the past century on the subject of the psychology of infancy and childhood and its implications for our adult lives. That library would be the size of an aircraft carrier. Now imagine a library that contains the complete literature on the psychology of the final third of life. That is definitely a smaller building. Now try this: the psychology of the end of life—how to die, in other words. That library is maybe one wing of the second building.

Aging scares people, and death terrifies them. That is of course not universal, but as a cultural observation, it is real enough. Yet we cannot understand the third lunar cycle without facing these late-life realities squarely. In a nutshell, *in the third cycle, we are making our preparations to exit this world.* We are not necessarily thinking specifically of death and dying all that time, but it is time for us to begin to *disentangle ourselves from our creation.* Given the enormity of death as a psychological and spiritual event, what a mercy it is that our psyches naturally are inclined to take three decades or so preparing for it—and what a tragedy that our cultural norms do their best to undermine that natural, instinctual preparation and actually allow death to surprise people.

In the first cycle we build the vision; in the second cycle we manifest the vision, and in the third cycle we release the vision.

One part of what that means is that we begin to pass on the torch. At a more interior level, we become much less motivated by outward rewards and vastly more drawn to the treasures we actually *can* take with us. In a materialistic culture, it is easy to see why the third lunar cycle is dreaded—the only things we have been taught to value either become more slippery or begin to lose their savor. In a spiritual culture, the potential for an older person's calm, clarity and relative freedom from the grips of compelling appetites are treasured.

At the simplest level, think of someone becoming a grandparent. To such a person, what could be more delightful than spending time with the grandchildren? "Grandma, can you teach me how to bake a cake?" "Grandpa, can you show me how to fish?" Imagine such a scenario unfolding. Who is happier, the kids or the grandparents? In the third cycle, there is *joy in generosity.* Whatever we have accumulated, materially, intellectually or spiritually, becomes our gift to the rising generations.

Much of our happiness lies in having that gift received.

Shortly after I passed into this phase of life myself, I had an experience that epitomized it for me. I was speaking at an astrological conference in which several of my students were also speakers. They had established themselves, built practices, written books and articles, individuated. I was feeling like the proud grandpa. Here's the edgy part. I attended their talks, and I heard many of them not only saying things I had taught them, but in some cases using my own words. I had a moment of pique. They were "stealing my act"! And then, of course, I laughed at myself. Wasn't that really the *point* of all my teaching? I settled into feeling gratified that the flame would keep on burning after I was gone. *I began to learn the fine art of being a happy ghost.* And I reflected gratefully on my own astrological and spiritual "grandparents" and the debts I owed them. I knew that I had devoured their gifts rather obsessively during my first lunar cycle; they had fed my "dream." I knew that I had made those gifts my own, turning them into books and lectures, during my second lunar cycle. And that now it was time to begin releasing them, letting others carry on the traditions in their own way and with their own fingerprints.

Life is kind in some ways. If I live a normal span of years, and *if I follow the good instincts of the third lunar cycle,* I will have three decades or so to try to disentangle myself from this sticky world before the good angels punch my ticket home.

20

☽

PLANETARY PHASE ANGLES

The Sun and Moon are a natural pair, forever linked through their opposing natures. They represent logic and intuition, the head and the heart—and what traditionally were called masculine and feminine, back in the days when men were Suns and women were Moons. As opposites, neither one can exist without the other, not any more than we can contemplate "dry" without considering the idea of "wet."

As our thinking becomes more sophisticated, we realize that opposites do not necessarily "oppose" each other in the sense of being irreconcilable enemies. Sometimes they complement each other too. In competition, opposites might destroy each other—or bring out excellence in each other through challenge and striving. In complementing each other, they might both become stronger—or slip into dark collusions that weaken and compromise both of them.

This hermetic dance, specifically as it manifests between the Sun and the Moon, has been the theme of this book. The previous several chapters have been an attempt to provide a detailed map of this cyclical gyre of interactions between the solar and lunar principles. But the template of understanding that we have created here is archetypal, and not limited to our comprehension of the lunation cycle. We have, for example, already explored its *doppelganger* in the seasonal cycle of the year, where the opposites are not solar and lunar, but rather the annual breathing of light and dark, of the length of day and the length of night. The same template worked there too, and our ancestors encoded it for us in their cycle of eight natural holidays.

Might there be other astrological applications of this template?

PLANETARY PAIRS

Certain planets are naturally paired through their quality of being linked opposites, just like the Sun and the Moon. Two such complementary links are almost universally recognized among astrologers—the pairing of Venus and Mars and the pairing of Jupiter and Saturn. Venus is still often related to the feminine and Mars to the masculine. I do not think that wording is very helpful nowadays with gender roles in such flux, but we can eternally see the opposition of attraction and aversion, of love and hate, of affection and anger—of Venus and Mars, in other words.

Similarly, expansive, optimistic, speculative Jupiter naturally exists in oppositional tension with contractive, pessimistic, concrete Saturn.

I believe a similar case can be made for Uranus and Neptune, with Uranus representing the full flowering of ego in the form of true, freely-expressed *individuality*, while Neptune indicates states of consciousness in which mind is *no longer identified with ego* at all. More simply, the Uranian need for radical selfishness exists in oppositional tension with the Neptunian need for surrender. Sometimes we need to stand our ground, while other times we need to give ground.

What happens if we consider the *cyclical relationship between these natural planetary pairs* against the backdrop of our solar-lunar phase theory? In everyone's birth chart, for example, Mars and Venus are in some kind of angular relationship to each other. There is no reason that we cannot read that angle as a phase relationship, exactly as we do with the Sun and the Moon.

NUTS AND BOLTS

The Moon moves faster than the Sun, so we think of it as forming the phases as it races out ahead of the Sun, swings around through the Full Moon, and wanes back down to catch up with the Sun at the New Moon. The Sun is, of course, also active in all this, moving along at its slower pace. We apply the same style of thinking to these natural planetary pairs. With Venus and Mars, for example, we know that Venus is the faster of the two. In a sense, it then plays the role of the Moon, forming a conjunction with Mars, then moving out ahead and eventually catching up with Mars again from behind. During that cycle Venus forms all the possible aspects with Mars. Another way to express that same idea is that Venus and Mars pass through our familiar eight phases—New, Waxing Crescent, First Quarter and so on, exactly as do the Moon and Sun.

This Venus/Mars cycle, by the way, is quite chaotic. Sometimes the conjunctions form only weeks apart. Other times it might be as long as a couple of years between them. And both planets make stations, turn retrograde, and cycle around to direct motion again, further complicating the picture. On a given day, it is quite possible that Mars would be moving faster than Venus. With retrograde motion involved, it is also possible that someone could be born with Venus and Mars in New phase, and that they would then progress into the Waning Crescent relationship—it would happen "backwards," so to speak. The planetary cycles, in other words, are not quite the same as the lunation cycle. But the basic principles still hold.

Faster Jupiter and slower Saturn do the same thing, only at a much more leisurely pace and in much more clockwork fashion. The period between their successive conjunctions is about nineteen years, ten months—or exactly 7,251.81 days. With Uranus and Neptune, the cycle of phases takes 171 years to make it all the way around, and so there, we would see a more "generational" signature on the phases, with whole populations born under each phase and the mark of that energy left on a period of cultural history.

To determine the phase relationship between any of these planetary pairs, you reason the same way as you do with the Sun and Moon. Start with the slower planet of the two and let it be the "fixed" point, then see how many degrees the faster planet lies ahead of the "fixed." If, say, Mars is in the middle of Libra and Venus is in the beginning of Libra, remember that Venus has gone all the way around the circle and is about to overtake Mars—it has come to something like 345°—and it is definitely in the Waning Crescent or "Balsamic" phase.

The phase cycles of these three planetary pairs could easily be the topic of another book. They are rich in meaning and they add tremendous depth to the conventional theory of astrological aspects. Despite what most texts indicate, a waxing square of Venus to Mars, for example, is a different kind of puppy than a waning square. The same two archetypes are there and they are still relating to each other in a tense way—that much remains constant. We can say helpful things to a client based simply on that information. But, as you will see, we can take it much further if we know whether it is a waxing or a waning square that links them.

The three planetary pairs we have mentioned are "matched opposites," and so possess a natural analogy with the Sun and Moon. That makes them easier to use against the backdrop of our lunation cycle template. But there is no ultimate reason why we could not consider, for one illustration, the phase relationship between Mercury and Pluto. That would deal with the constantly shifting dialogue between what we see, think and believe (Mercury), and the sometimes contradictory information accumulating in our unconscious minds and distorting our perceptions (Pluto). Similarly, we could pair any two planets, and consider their interaction from this kind of perspective.

A further attraction of this phase-angle approach to planetary aspects is that it could be effective in helping us to understand the interactions of planets which, from a conventional astrological point of view, have no aspectual relationship at all—say, Venus in 4° Aquarius and Saturn in 13° Pisces. In that case, the planets are 39° apart. There is no commonly-used aspect there, but we can confidently know that Venus and Saturn are in Waning Crescent phase—and that therefore certain ancient vows of fidelity (Saturn) in relationship (Venus) are, on one hand, coming to an end and, on the other, requiring completion in this incarnation (Waning Crescent).

In what follows, I want to explore the phase relationships of Mars and Venus, of Saturn and Jupiter, and of Neptune and Uranus. I will do that briefly, with just a few words about each particular phase. As advertised, this volume is primarily a book about the Moon's phases. I do not want to get too far afield, so we will just take a short "salad course" detour down this intriguing exit ramp from the main highway. Perhaps you will want to visit it again someday, and stay a little longer. If you do, you will almost surely discover insights and perspectives that I have missed entirely.

VENUS-MARS: THE CYCLE OF SEX

We have all felt the pull of purple passion. And we have all felt the tender, romantic call of gentle affinity. Most of us have made love. And most of us have . . . how shall we put it? I'd like to quote Tina Turner here and ask, "What's love got to do with it?"

Partnering love between two people really needs both of these expressions—tenderness and passion, chemistry and friendship. Meeting both needs, finding the balance between them, and making interesting mistakes in navigating all the attendant mirages—this is so much the story of our real lives, especially in the first half of life. The phase relationship of Mars and Venus casts light on what is going on behind the romantic dramas.

Phase One: Venus 0° - 45° ahead of Mars

New soul contacts being made. Innocence. Naiveté. Sexual charisma—often unrecognized by the person who possesses it. The freedom to establish new erotic and romantic patterns—patterns which will later bind us, but which we enter voluntarily. Claiming one's sexual autonomy and confidence.

Venus and Mars in "New" Phase

In the previous graphic, Venus has advanced ahead of Mars by 43 degrees and 10 minutes, putting the two planets just inside the limits of the New phase, about to enter the Waxing Crescent phase.

Phase Two: Venus 45° - 90° ahead of Mars

Emerging sexual identity and sexual confidence. Ability to charm, engage and fascinate. Potential difficulty seeing others in three dimensions; people become symbolic. We are genuinely confused by their behavior. Legitimate need for breadth of sexual experience. "Finding oneself."

Phase Three: Venus 90° - 135° ahead of Mars

Sexual drama. Clash of autonomy versus commitment. Facing the consequences of one's sexual actions and choices. Getting serious. Attracting particularly challenging partners or relationships. Physical distance. Scandal as the price of love. "How bad do you want it?"

Phase Four: Venus 135° - 180° ahead of Mars

Sexual renaissance. Enthusiasm. Unabashed vitality. Fascination with "the Other." High romance; the big love story. Soulful gazing. A bee flitting from flower to flower. Hunger for spiritual fulfillment via relationship. Asking for a lot. Sexual compulsiveness.

Phase Five: Venus 180° - 225° ahead of Mars

Consummation. Commitment. Actual marriage. The long haul. "Going all the way." Romantic complications. Can't-stay-and-can't-leave. Feelings of fated love. Children and family. Emotionally prominent in-laws. Staying together for the children. Accepting reality.

Phase Six: Venus 225° - 270° ahead of Mars

Mature perspectives on love and sexuality. Learning to accept and appreciate the imperfect. Marriage as the bond between two flawed human beings. Getting past illusions. The creative couple, active in the community. Breaking bread together after conflict.

Phase Seven: Venus 270° - 315° ahead of Mars

A poignant feeling of the preciousness of each moment. Tender caring. Genuine selflessness in love. Radical supportiveness. Self-sacrifice. Resignation. "Yes, dear." Forgiveness. Acceptance. Learning not to judge or to assume. Ritual, repeated behaviors. Robotic predictability. Relationships which must be let go.

Phase Eight: Venus 315° - 360° ahead of Mars
Mystical feelings of connection. Sacred sex. "I feel like I have known you before." Finishing karmic business. The spiritual relationship. Platonic connections. Completing the work. Revisiting the past. Release. Endings. Forgiveness. Tragic romance. Loneliness and despair.

JUPITER-SATURN: THE CYCLE OF AMBITION

We envision a beautiful garden in our backyard, lush with flowers, fountains, and mysterious nooks: an earthly paradise, only awaiting construction. Welcome to Jupiter.

We get halfway through digging the first hole for the first five-gallon flowering plant. We realize how hard this project is going to be. Perhaps we reassess our attempt to re-create Versailles. Welcome to Saturn.

Big visions always collide with reality. But without big visions, how drab reality would be! And without realism, hard work, and compromise, would humans ever produce anything beyond advice, hot air, and the empty recommendations of yet another committee? When are we being too ambitious and when are we selling ourselves short? "Doubt nothing except your limits." It is an encouraging sentiment, but I fervently doubt, were I to set out to be the first person to swim to Hawaii, that I would make it. Some limits are real, and we can learn that the easy way or the hard way.

The phase-relationship between Jupiter and Saturn tells us a lot about what our souls are learning in terms of unraveling this tangle between our big dreams and objective reality. Because of the principle of synchronicity, it also casts light on the kinds of circumstances—both in terms of opportunities and resistance—that our ambitions are likely to encounter.

Phase One: Jupiter 0° - 45° ahead of Saturn
Big dreams. Learning how to aspire. Visionary experience. Inner accomplishments, unseen by the world. Learning to honor the invisible and unmanifest. Creativity. Futurism. Contagious enthusiasm. Utopianism. Leadership. Breakthroughs and new beginnings. Ideas ahead of their time or for which "the

technology does not yet exist."

Phase Two: Jupiter 45° - 90° ahead of Saturn

Pioneering. Boldness and audacity. Fresh perspectives on old problems. Leadership and inspiration. Ungrounded, untested methods. Reinventing the wheel. Betting the house. The journey of a thousand miles starts with a single step. Faith. Pigheaded unrealism.

Phase Three: Jupiter 90° - 135° ahead of Saturn

Putting it out there. Challenging authority. Questioning and breaking rules. "You can't make an omelet without breaking a few eggs." Enemies. Competition. Rivalries. Consequences of actions and choices. Daring. Blow it up and start all over again. Let the chips fall where they may.

Phase Four: Jupiter 135° - 180° ahead of Saturn

Co-creation. Engagement with teams. Joint efforts. Serendipitous conversations. Teamwork. Surprise. Openness. Holding half the cards. Cooperative efforts. Shared excitement. Recognizing talent in others. Loss of vision "in committee."

Phase Five: Jupiter 180° - 225° ahead of Saturn

Manifestation of vision. Offering a gift. Responding to the needs of the community. Reading the spirit of the Zeitgeist. Having a tiger by the tail. Politics. Responsibility to the team. Being defined by one's work. Monumental stuckness and institutional paralysis. The person of the hour.

Phase Six: Jupiter 225° - 270° ahead of Saturn

Mature, proven expression. Mastery—or going through the motions. The tour de force. Becoming an institution. The copyright runs out; the work enters the public domain, its creator forgotten. A legend in one's own time. Caught in the past. Calcified institutions. Dinosaurs. Generosity. Group mediation and reconciliation.

Phase Seven: Jupiter 270° - 315° ahead of Saturn

Passing on the torch. Accepting apprentices. Finishing what we have started. Endgames. Anticlimax. The mature technology. Seeing it through. Conserving the good things of the past. Living in the past. The finishing touches. Recognizing failure to be part of the cycle.

Phase Eight: Jupiter 315° - 360° ahead of Saturn
Letting it go. Losing ego-investment in accomplishment. Release and surrender. Graceful endings. The has-been. Inspiration. Not being recognized. Intimations of future possibilities. Prescience. "Today's science fiction is tomorrow's reality." Compassionate gifts.

URANUS-NEPTUNE: THE CYCLE OF MYTHIC RENEWAL

Uranus takes eighty-four years to get around the Sun. Neptune takes one hundred sixty-five. They come together every one hundred seventy-one years. Obviously you don't want to hold your breath waiting for their phases to form! As I will demonstrate below, we can see the mark of the phase-relationship between these two outer gas giants on history and on generations. Its fingerprints are indelible in individuals too—to dismiss it as merely "generational" misses the point. The real point is that, while this cycle touches the lives of all the members of a generation very deeply and personally, often they are not aware of that impact until they are old enough to compare themselves with the newly-rising generations.

Neptune correlates with the "myth of the world." What that means is that for each epoch of history, there are distinct metaphors, attitudes and assumptions underlying its view of life. These manifest in religion, in art, social customs, and in all the other products of the human imagination. Uranus, meanwhile, promotes rebellion, innovation, and individuation. So, with this cycle, we see a new vision (Uranus) of the myth of the world (Neptune) passing through the familiar eight stages of development.

This is a truly gigantic subject, and in keeping with my intention to restrict this chapter to a small part of the book, I am going to deal with it in a very cursory way. Richard Tarnas in his masterful *Cosmos and Psyche* deals with some of these same subjects brilliantly and exhaustively. It would be an interesting exercise to reread his book in the light of the phase theory I present here.

Note that the dates I give below for each phase are approximate. The two planets typically dance back and forth across a phase line for at least a couple of years due to their retrograde and direct motions. For births or historical events near the transitions, check the computer or the ephemerides. The years I give here are for the first instance of an entry into a new phase. In every case, there was at least one subsequent retreat into the previous phase.

There is an ambiguity that is inherent in all these Uranus-Neptune phases, the descriptions applying in two slightly skewed ways. First, they bear on the historical spirit of the times in which that phase-angle actually existed between Uranus and Neptune in the heavens. And secondly, over a longer term, they are reflected in the attitudes and natures of the children born under that phase—children who will leave their mark on the arts, institutions, and politics of the world for the next several decades as they grow up and flower into adult creativity, responsibility, and temporal authority. If we live a normal span of years, we all live through phases that are different from the ones under which we were born.

Phase One: Uranus 0° - 45° ahead of Neptune
Years: 1821-1845 and 1993-2017

A new vision emerges out of the collective unconscious. It insinuates itself almost unnoticed into the fabric of belief. Geniuses are born or flower. Often their power and the implications of their work are only understood much later. The children born in this phase seem different from us; their minds operate according to a distinct logic. We enshrine them in fear, worry, judgment or grandiose deification—all symptoms of our inability to grasp the assumptions upon which their reality is based.

1821-1845. The birth of the age of electricity and fossil-fuel driven technology; in a sense, the birth of modernism. Mary Shelley writes Frankenstein—*a story about science creating a monster whose consequences can neither be foreseen nor controlled. There's a metaphor! And again, 1993-2017. The global Internet; the global economy; possibly the collapse of the myth of nations as autonomous actors. "Indigo children."*

Phase Two: Uranus 45° - 90° ahead of Neptune
Years: 1845-1868

The new vision continues to grow, often generating excitement and hope, but without yet seeming substantial enough to be a threat to the pre-existing myth. Charismatic figures who embody the spirit of the new vision are born and flower. We experiment with practical expressions of the new vision. Many of these experiments fail, too Utopian or ungrounded, and yet we learn.

Phase Three: Uranus 90° - 135° ahead of Neptune
Years: 1868-1887

The new vision clashes overtly and dramatically with the old structures. Rivalries and tensions abound. The Rubicon is crossed. Breakthroughs of a practical nature assert the "arrival" of the new vision. There are accusations of the "immorality" of the present countered by mockery of the past. Anger flares. Judgments are hurled. Generational tension. Caricatures, both living and in print, abound.

Phase Four: Uranus 135° - 180° ahead of Neptune
Years: 1886-1906

A period of free-flowing cultural creativity. A sense of boundless possibility. Ideas are connecting with ideas, exploding exponentially. Geniuses and their inventions trigger each other. The old guard has either died off or retired, leaving the field to the new mythic order. The new vision is now the collective assumption about "the way things obviously are."

Phase Five: Uranus 180° - 225° ahead of Neptune
Years: 1906-1931

The vision that was born back in phase one is now manifest everywhere. The past that came before it almost a century ago—that is, prior to the outset of the present cycle—seems hopelessly remote and backwards, almost incomprehensibly foreign. The old guard has died out completely. There is a feeling of being in a world that was "destined to be." (The last time around, it was mythologized as "the modern world.") Triumphalism arises. But cracks are beginning to show, if we look for them. Certain impossibilities and contradictions, long ignored, unknown, or swept under the carpet, begin to show signs of their existence. The worm is in the apple.

Phase Six: Uranus 225° - 270° ahead of Neptune
Years: 1931-1954

Elements of discontent arise. Distinct evidence appears for the errors, tragedies and insufficiencies of the existing way of life. Some try to deny it and to defend the present order; others embrace dissent. This division often manifests along generational lines. Service calls, reflecting a gnawing search for meaning. Transcendent spirituality offers some solace for the discontent. Those born in this phase carry a sense of alienation, of having been born into a world which offends, misunderstands, and opposes them.

Phase Seven: Uranus 270° - 315° ahead of Neptune
Years: 1954-1972
That the old vision is hopelessly flawed, hidebound, and doomed to eventual collapse is increasingly obvious to an ever-larger portion of the population. Again, this attitude tends to be more evident among the young—those born in this phase or those entering maturity in its atmosphere. Less obvious is the reality that no one really has any clear idea yet of any positive alternatives to the old vision. Art and spirituality prosper. Those born in this phase carry a sense of suspicion toward the present world, as if they were distant from it or separate from it. Some take refuge in romanticizing the more remote past.

Phase Eight: Uranus 315° - 360° ahead of Neptune
Years: 1972-1993
An age of nihilism relative to the old vision takes hold. As Yeats put it, "The best lack all conviction while the worst are full of passionate intensity." Irrefutable evidence of the unraveling of the fabric of the world order presses from every direction. Inward, personal spirituality calls loudly. Dreams, meditation, escapism and fantasy fascinate. Religion—for good or for ill—offers solace. Some of those born in this phase carry a sense of cynicism about the past, present and future. Others are the seed-bearers of a new vision.

The Current Cycle of Mythic Renewal

In our own times, Uranus first formed a conjunction with Neptune on February 2, 1993. Thus, we entered the New phase. The last time they had been aligned in the sky occurred on December 3, 1821. In this present cycle, Uranus will attain a point 45° ahead of Neptune on August 11, 2017. From October of that year until June 2018, it will be back in the previous phase. It will return a second time to the New phase from December 15, 2018 through May 1, 2019. After that it will be solidly in the Waxing Crescent phase until 2039. Thus, in broad terms, humanity entered the New phase of the Cycle of Mythic Renewal in 1993 and will remain in it until 2039.

The subject is too vast for me to address here in more than this sketchy fashion. As I write today, in 2010, in a time of collective fear and apocalyptic worry about the immediate future, I have just one thing to say: *Trust the children. Trust the children not yet born. And trust their children too. Deep in their astrological DNA, they carry the seeds of a new world.*

21

☽

NODAL PHASE

The cycle of the Earth's seasons and endless gyre of the Moon's phases are entirely distinct astronomical phenomena. They have different causes and different lengths. From a mechanical perspective, they simply have nothing to do with each other. And yet from the astrological point of view, they are twins—fraternal rather than identical twins perhaps, but twins nonetheless. They are organized according to the same principles. Their phases run in parallel. If we comprehend the Earth's seasons, we have found the key to understanding the phases of the Moon. That serendipity has been one of the major structural bones of this book. The eight natural holidays of the year have provided us with a template for a deeper understanding of the lunation cycle.

In the previous chapter, we extended that reasoning a step further. We realized that a third layer could be added to the cake: *planetary phase*. As the seasons of the year and the Moon's phases are objectively independent of each other, similarly the cycle of Jupiter in relation to Saturn is independent of both of them, and the same can be said for Venus and Mars and for Uranus and Neptune. Yet the same principles unite them.

The eight-phase system is, in its ultimate essence, an archetypal structure that is more fundamental to the structure of reality than any single one of these specific astronomical phenomena.

The eight phases probably work perfectly well in other star systems in other galaxies, just as would $E=MC^2$ or $C=\_D$. Likely, nine-feet-tall alien astrologers with blue skin and fetchingly long tails have discovered it too, and for the same reason: It pervades the nature of reality. The cycles we have been studying are merely three-dimensional, earthly reflections of this primeval principle. Presumably, if we look, we will see it everywhere.

Before we come to the end of this book, I would like to aim your awareness at one more manifestation of our eight-phase mandala: *nodal phase*. What we will be considering here is the relationship between the position of the Moon and its own south node. This will bring us into deeply metaphysical territory: karma, reincarnation, and the evolutionary future. As always with this kind of material, the facts are more slippery, at least regarding the specifics of prior lifetimes. What is not slippery at all, but in fact completely testable in the present tense, is the relevance of these insights to the present life.

THE NODES OF THE MOON

The plane of the Moon's orbit around Earth is tilted about 5° relative to the ecliptic. What that means is that as the Moon circles us, half the time it is north of the ecliptic and half the time south of it. The point where the Moon's orbital plane crosses to the northern side of the ecliptic is the *north node*. Where it crosses heading south is the *south node*. These lunar nodes themselves "orbit" the Earth, taking about 18.6 years to retrograde once through the zodiac. That works out to about a year and a half in each sign.

Symbolically, the south node represents the past and the north node the evolutionary future. The south node pulls us into old, familiar patterns, and the north node beckons with remedies and new possibilities. Astrologer Michael Lutin once quipped, using a metaphor from Alcoholics Anonymous, that "the south node is the bottle and the north node is the meeting." I am in awe of Michael. In typical fashion, he said in thirteen words what it once took me an entire book to say—plus he brought the house down with laughter. Written in a popular style for a mainstream publisher, his book *Sunshines* contains in thinly-veiled fashion quite a lot of pithy material on karma, reincarnation, and the lunar nodes.

The book of mine to which I referred is my last volume, *Yesterday's Sky: Astrology and Reincarnation*. If you find yourself drawn to more metaphysical approaches to astrology, you might have a look at it. In this chapter, I will summarize its principles briefly as needed, but exploring the whole realm of reincarnation as evidenced in the birth chart is a rich and complex undertaking. It really does require its own volume. I would also happily refer you to David Railey's *The Soul Purpose: Attaining Fulfillment and Security with Astrology*, Patricia L. Walsh's *Understanding Karmic Complexes*, Elizabeth Spring's *North Node Astrology: Rediscovering Your Life Direction and Soul Purpose*, and Maurice Fernandez's *Astrology and the Evolution of Consciousness*. Evolutionary astrology is getting to be a large field, and there are undoubtedly worthy books and authors I have not mentioned here, out of ignorance. My apologies to them.

For our purposes, suffice it to say that the south node of the Moon carries the essence of the prior-life karma that has *ripened* for you in this present lifetime. That means it will make itself felt, for sure. Maybe you will resolve it, and maybe you will simply repeat it. But it will crystallize somehow in your experience.

The phase relationship of the Moon to its own south node says something about your *optimal emotional relationship* to that karma and the best strategies for resolving it. As ever in astrology, it also warns of traps, illusions, and soul-cages.

THE TECHNICAL DETAILS

Everyone has a south node. Everyone has a Moon. While the two phenomena are related astronomically, they are actually free to be in any possible geometric relationship with each other. The south node, in other words, could potentially be anywhere in your chart. Ditto for the Moon itself. Another way to say it is that all the astrological aspects are possible between them. Every one of the eight-phase relationships is available to the Moon in relation to its south node.

As with the Sun and Moon themselves, and also with planetary phases, we take the slower-moving point as the anchor and see how far ahead of it the faster-moving point has moved. In this case, the south node becomes the anchor, and we measure how many degrees ahead of it the Moon lies.

VISUALIZING THE NODAL PHASES

To get a visual sense of the nodal phase relationship between the Moon and the south node, take a look at the two charts that follow. In the first chart, you'll see an example of the **New nodal phase**. In this example, the Moon is in Virgo, about forty degrees ahead of the Cancer south node. This means that the Moon is in New phase relative to the south node.

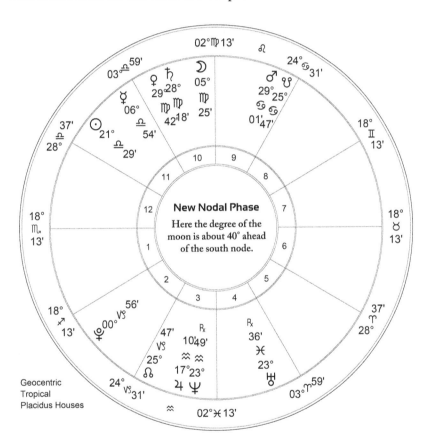

If the distance between the south node and the moon were greater than 45°, the phase relationship would no longer be New, but would then be in the Waxing Crescent phase.

In the next chart, for a date about seventeen days later than the previous chart, the south node has retrograded just a short distance—remember, it is always retrograde. It is still in about the same part of Cancer. But the Moon has now swung around into Aries, about 257° ahead of the south. So, relative to the south node, the Moon is now in the Waning Gibbous nodal phase.

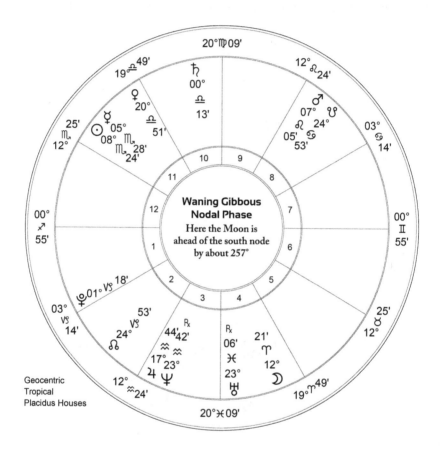

Note that we are no longer describing the Moon's phase in the usual lunar phase sense! The Moon's lunar phase is about the relationship between the *Sun* and the Moon, using the slower-moving Sun as the anchor-point. For the nodal phase, we are measuring from the **south node**, not the Sun. The nodal phase is an entirely different thing, with a different meaning.

WHY THE SOUTH NODE, NOT THE NORTH?

Most astrological ephemerides and computer programs default to showing only the Moon's north node. Generally, if you want to see the south node too, you have to ask for it. The standard explanation is that the south node is opposite the north, so you only need to know one of them. That feeble argument breaks down with the use of the increasingly popular "true node." The "true" north node is not, as many assume, directly opposite the "true" south node—as is the case with the mean nodes, although many astrologers act as if it were. (For a full investigation of mean vs. true nodes, see Chapter Five of *Yesterday's Sky*.)

What is going on here? Why is the south node ignored? Northern hemisphere bias may play a linguistic role, but mostly I think it comes from the fact that the lunar nodes in general have not been very well understood. In my view, the south node is actually the more charged point. It literally carries the momentum of lifetimes of habit, whereas the north node is basically little more than a most excellent suggestion. In any case, the south node, with all its rich karmic implications and its demonstrable influence upon our lives, is the natural anchor-point for nodal phase work.

WHAT NODAL PHASE MEANS

The brilliant Southern novelist William Faulkner once said, "The past is not dead. In fact, it's not even past." There are many levels of meaning to those two short sentences. Faulkner might have been referring to the way the complicated history of the American South has shaped its present culture. And of course any psychologist understands that one's childhood lives on in the adult personality. At the most metaphysical level, we can understand Faulkner's lines as a reference to the power of karma and how the unresolved issues of our prior lifetimes live on in the present. Our challenge is to stop "getting on with the past."

Some people are uncomfortable with the idea of reincarnation. One can understand the Moon's south node in a variety of other ways. It can be your ancestral past. It can be your DNA. It can be "how God made you." Or, if you are open to the idea of past lives, it can be your karma in the Buddhist, Hindu or probably Druid sense. In this chapter, I am going to assume reincarnation, but please feel free to translate if you are more comfortable in a different theological framework.

We can postulate a phase relationship between any two points in an astrological chart. But the Moon and the Moon's south node obviously have a close connection; the node could not exist without the Moon. Their phase relationship immediately emerges as a potentially rich area of investigation. How can we understand it?

Phase cannot exist unless we are talking about the *relationship* between two points. With the Moon we are always contemplating *mood, attitude*, and a *set of underlying subjective assumptions*. With the south node, we are contemplating a karmic predicament and the emotional logjams implicit in it. Putting two and two together, in nodal phase we are exploring a mood, an attitude, and a set of assumptions regarding the mostly-unconscious elements of our unresolved past-life issues—and of course, as Faulkner reminds us, "past" does not mean "over and done." These unresolved issues are "reincarnated" in our present situations and challenges.

Both the Moon and the south node relate to the power of *attitude* and *assumption* as they flavor our perception of reality. (Illustration: Bold people often do not see dangers. Depressed people often do not see encouraging possibilities.) Therefore, when these two symbols come together, we understand another element in their phase relationship—a strong reference to the *potentially blinding impact of underlying beliefs*.

While lunar phase does not reveal a person's age, we have found all through our explorations that the earlier lunar phases resonate with the natural psychology of youth and the later ones with life's second half. We might similarly expect that nodal phase would reveal some sense of where a soul might be in a cyclical context relative to its own karma. *Emphatically, this does not tell us how "advanced" the soul is in general, but rather where it is in relation to the resolution of a particular set of issues.*

Going further, evolutionary astrology is fundamentally prescriptive rather than merely descriptive. It makes suggestions about how to go forward, rather than simply painting a static picture of "your personality" or "your situation." Implicit in those suggestions are warnings about the consequences of not making an effort. In the case of anything involving the Moon's south node, those consequences boil down to the endless, futile repetition of past patterns. Down that road, we fulfill Mr. Faulkner's prophecy by continuing to "get on with the past." More uplifting is the realization that nodal phase also offers insight as to the most effective attitudes and strategies when it comes to advancing our own evolutionary agendas.

Putting all this together, we can frame three critical insights into the meaning of the phase relationship between the Moon and the south node:

○ It reveals the most *effective attitude* that we might apply to resolving our own evolutionary predicaments; thus it speaks to us of *productive strategy.*

○ It warns of attitudinal *loops and blind-spots* that can potentially trap us in the endless repetition of old, dead-end patterns.

○ It implies something about *how far along* in the evolutionary process *relative to these issues* the soul finds itself. And even though "further along" might sound like the superior condition, each stage has its unique traps as well as opportunities, as we will see.

About that final point, it is both imperative and encouraging to note that no one needs to go methodically through all eight of these processes before resolving a particular karmic pattern. The system is not that rigid or formulaic, and, as ever, consciousness is in the driver's seat. Implicit in *each* phase are methods that can trigger breakthroughs and "graduation" then and there. Handled correctly, any one of them can be a launching pad into liberation.

If you have internalized the elements of this book so far, much of what follows will feel like familiar territory. It should be! The eight phases are an archetypal system, translatable into all cycles in the world of nature. Here we are simply applying recognized principles in a new way.

WAXING AND WANING

When the Moon is "waxing" outward from the south node—thus 0° to 180° ahead of it—the spirit of the karma is "forward." The soul's instinct, and generally its correct strategy, is simply to bring the energies into manifestation. *To put them out there*, where they can be seen and experienced directly, and where one can work on them.

There are dangers in this approach, of course—naiveté, insensitivity, and foolishness. These are the familiar follies of youth and of the waxing natal lunar phases in general, and—while a soul in this nodal phase emphatically should not be labeled as unevolved—its relationship with these particular issues *is* in fact relatively un-evolved. As is the case with any young person, often its best strategy is to just go out there and make some interesting mistakes. Think of someone who has lived six lifetimes celibate in a monastery. That person may be quite evolved in terms of inward matters, and yet when it comes to relationship choices, we will detect the fingerprints of innocence and inexperience. Time to kiss a few frogs.

The current Dalai Lama provides a fine illustration of this broad point. No one would mistake him for an unevolved being, and yet his nodal phase is in the first quadrant. After many lifetimes as the ruler of a stable nation, he has found himself from an early age in this incarnation having to improvise an entirely new role.

What about the waning nodal phases? Here the Moon has swung out into "Full" relationship with the south node, and beyond. It lies 180° to 360° ahead. The spirit here, in common with that of the waning lunar phases in general, is more reflective and contemplative. The aim is to release the past, something often easier said than done. The higher self presses the personality simply to *get disentangled* by whatever means necessary—to finish the business, to unbind, to face the music, to pay the debts, to forgive. Liberation can be achieved here through *insight* and through *surrender*. There is not the same need to "jump in" as we saw in the waxing phases. Reflecting on what might happen if we *did* jump in might be sufficient.

In the four waning nodal phases, we might speculate that the soul has been contemplating these issues for a while. This is probably not its first lifetime on this particular "project," so to speak. Once more, this does not equate with a higher evolutionary state—that ultimate state is not something that can be detected at all in a birth chart, in my opinion. What it suggests is only that *within the context of the predicament revealed by a full analysis of the south node*, this soul has been working on it for a while. Both Jung and Freud, born with the Moon in the third nodal phase quadrant, illustrate this notion. Each one was ready to sit back and contemplate the mind and its condition rather than hurling himself outward into improvisation

Reflexively, the waning condition might seem more desirable than the more naive, "starter" realities of the waxing cycle. The sobering key here, however, is to realize that having worked on something for a while is not an iron-clad guarantee of success. In the waning nodal phases, we see the familiar dangers and soul-cages of midlife and old age: *despair, tiredness, a sense of defeat, hopelessness*, and *cynicism*. Those are the Shadow manifestations of the waning nodal cycle. We might just give up. We are now quite possibly "skillful" at staying stuck, and have maybe lost faith in any other possibility. Adolph Hitler, with his Moon in the eighth-nodal phase, is a classic illustration.

DARK AND BRIGHT

We explored the bright/dark distinction in detail in Chapter Seven. There we learned that the bright half of the Moon's cycle corresponds to *manifestation* and *incarnation*. It is engaged, co-creative, and communal. It thus runs the risk of losing itself in its entanglements with the world—and that risk goes far beyond mere materialism or blind ambition. Even more commonly, it is linked to *relationships* and the web of practical, ethical, and affectionate bonds they create.

The dark phases of the Moon, on the other hand, are more inward and self-sufficient in their natures. They are archetypal in orientation, potentially spiritual, and concerned with principles and ideals. They risk being ungrounded. They are so inward that they can be curiously disengaged from "normal" human feelings of affection or empathy, not so much out of meanness as from a quality of being gauche or clueless.

Translating these observations about *lunar* phase into *nodal* phase is straightforward. When the Moon is in the bright phases relative to its own south node—that is, between 90° and 270° ahead of the node in the zodiac—the tendency is for the karmic pattern to be revealed concretely in the circumstances of the life. It typically takes the form of various kinds of entanglement. More often than not, these are *interpersonal* entanglements. Conversely, when the Moon is in its dark phases relative to the south node—within 90° on either side of the conjunction—the karma is expressed less concretely. Its hold is more upon the *mind* and the *attitude*. Its fingerprints on the outer biographical life are typically somewhat less direct.

THE EIGHT NODAL PHASES

Let's look at each of the eight-phase relationships between the south node and the Moon. In what follows, I will emphasize the positive, practical bottom line about what kinds of attitude, decision-making, and values best serve the evolutionary needs. We will also from time to time get some hints regarding the Shadow expression of each one.

I will not rehash the theoretical underpinnings, as they are nearly identical to material we have already covered throughout this book. Your understanding of each phase will be deepened if you reflect upon its place in the waning and waxing cycles, along with where it lies in the cycles of darkness and brightness—the material we have reviewed in the last few pages.

For the deepest available astrological understanding of nodal phase, it is necessary to understand the specific nature of the person's karma as symbolized by the south node in its planetary context. This complex theoretical terrain, as I have mentioned, is explored thoroughly in *Yesterday's Sky*. Here, I will simply refer to "the karma" and leave it at that. But please remember that karma comes in a lot of flavors! One with a karmic pattern of explosive anger will react differently to each of these phases than will one with a karmic pattern of simmering resentment, despair, addiction, or laziness. A person who was subjugated by a repressive spouse in another life carries different latent potentials than one who was subjugated by a repressive government or social system. One who carried the social burden of sainthood has different trigger-points than one who "was only following orders."

In all cases, the karma indicated by the south node has "ripened," to use Buddhist language. That means it will surely manifest in this lifetime. As it does so, consciousness has the opportunity to work with it—or to be temporarily extinguished by it. Hopefully, the upcoming guidelines will help tilt the table in a beneficial direction.

It is difficult to fit a lot of nuanced philosophy onto a coffee mug or a T-shirt! That is basically what I am attempting in the next figure, which reduces a lot of theory down to eight words. Each one is a simple exhortation that sets the tone for the most effectively supportive attitude for people born under each of the eight nodal phases.

Read on for the deeper perspectives.

NEW NODAL PHASE

With the Moon 0° to 45° ahead of the south node, the evolving mind-stream is beginning something new and fresh. It is as if a chapter has ended and new one is about to begin. I often get the feeling that people born with this configuration have been out of embodiment for a while, sort of "on sabbatical" from this world. One way of saying it is that they were having "a moment of rest upon the wind," as Kahlil Gibran put it so memorably in *The Prophet*. We might equally envision an "in-depth discussion with their guardian angels" on the other side of the veil.

In any case, the mountain that now lies before such souls may be steep, but there is a freshness of inspiration and faith in them. They have recently had a long pep talk with the Divine. They will surely make inter-esting mistakes, and probably earn substantial insights from them. They are on fire with a new soul-impulse, but one that needs to be tempered in the cauldrons of experience. Negatively, they may be full of themselves, lit up with a zealot's confidence. Meanwhile, their karma is deeply seated in their reflexive attitudes and assumptions, which may blind them to the fresh path that they actually need to follow. Remember that this is a very early stage in a long path. Their soul intention is to recognize and over-come all those reflexive attitudes and assumptions. They must eradicate them, and focus on the remedy which is symbolized by the north node of the Moon. Otherwise they may zealously set out to solve problems they do not actually have, all the while ignoring the real issues.

The dilemma, encapsulated, is simply that fresh inspiration and old patterns are quite knotted up at this point in the nodal cycle. There is a tendency to do the right thing for the wrong reasons, or the wrong thing for the right ones. At this juncture, such people are torn between explo-sive evolutionary fire and their old routines. Keeping the faith relative to that higher aim is essential—and even harder is remaining mindful of it in the face of the tendency to let the habitual patterns of thought and action take over. There is great freedom and possibility here, but with freedom comes uncertainty, tension, and the prospect of running off the rails. A great virtue here is simply *expecting to be surprised*. Another great virtue is a willingness to "blow it up and start all over again."

Our exhortation is "Believe!"

WAXING CRESCENT NODAL PHASE

With the Moon 45° to 90° ahead of the south node, I am reminded of the famous scene in *Star Wars* when Luke Skywalker hears the spectral voice of Obi-Wan Kenobi encouraging him to take off his targeting helmet and instead to "trust his feelings" and to "feel the force." Counterintuitive, to be sure, but consider: while thinking is often useful, it requires that we have accurate data. At this early stage of the nodal phase cycle, a person's life-data is still very much distorted by traces of old karma. It is not very good information, in other words. What is beneficial here is a kind of purity of unpremeditated action—a willingness to dive into the soup, trusting the kind of intuition that comes to us in a flash or a blink. We are trying to bypass the old patterns of cognition, and instead to trust a kind of fresh, elemental soul-impulse. The notion of trusting your first instinct has great relevance here. So does a taste for breaking up old patterns and trying new approaches.

Won't this get a person into trouble? Yes indeed—and that, paradoxically, is a big part of the point. *Recall that in the entire waxing half of the cycle, the aim is to bring karma into manifestation, not to avoid it.* In this pagan frame of reference, being wholly alive and open to "the full catastrophe" is a positive evolutionary method. The laboratory in which we are working it out is not in our heads, it is in the world. If we are too cautious, we will never even *see* the karmic questions. Instead they will haunt us as vague fears and the ghosts of roads not taken. Better to go ahead and put it all on the table, and not overvalue safety and caution or the desire to be perceived as "right."

Our exhortation is, "Act!"

FIRST QUARTER NODAL PHASE

With the Moon 90° to 135° ahead of the south node, we cross the line into the bright hemicycle. This, as we have seen, is a far more social and external frame of reference than are the dark phases. The upcoming four bright phases have to do with community and relationship. They have to do with people. In all of them, the soul-contract involves meeting a great many other beings with whom we have unfinished business. Those "fated" meetings begin here in this third phase—with a bang.

As you may recall, the First Quarter is our "Easter" phase. While it does not mean you are scheduled to be nailed to a cross, it does suggest some element of *confrontation* and *tension*. Those other souls whom you are destined to meet in this incarnation were often problematic for you in prior lifetimes, even if the relationships began sweetly back then—or begin sweetly this time around. Ultimately they constituted obstacles, heartbreaks and vexations. Perhaps there was war or rivalry. Maybe you folded up before them. Maybe you destroyed them. Only a full nodal analysis can cast light on those kinds of specifics. But in any case, in this First Quarter nodal phase, it is time to step up to the plate and deal creatively, effectively, and honestly with conflict—conflict that will often feel inexplicably familiar even though you "just met." Directness is essential. Martyrdom, and all its seductive dramas, is optional.

With all that said, we must also recognize that a certain fanaticism and blindness to other perspectives is characteristic of this third nodal phase. Hitting a wall at ninety miles per hour may be painful, but it certainly gets one's attention! In this phase, there may well be such wake-up calls about one's deepest assumptions, especially about people and relationships. Nothing for it except to dive in.

Our exhortation is, "Challenge!"

WAXING GIBBOUS NODAL PHASE

With the Moon 135° to 180° ahead of the south node, one's karma still carries the "forward" quality of the waxing cycle, mixed with the "engaged" quality of the bright hemicycle. These same two qualities are also combined in the prior phase. There, they often manifest as conflict or rivalry. Here, in phase four, they tend to manifest in friendlier fashion. Most of the rawness leaves the mix and is replaced by a delicious fascination with other people. In its core, there is an intent in the Waxing Gibbous nodal phase to solve our karmic dilemmas through allowing others to fertilize our own imaginations and understandings. We need them to impact us, to mess with our beliefs and our self-image. With Beltane symbolism in the background, human sexuality serves as a kind of template for our understanding here. As all couples know, love-making can equilibrate people's energies, bringing them back into harmony after a conflict is faced and new contracts have been drawn. Meaningful, and perhaps varied, exchanges of sexual energy can be a helpful part of this fourth-phase process, but it is salutary to realize that many other kinds of non-sexual creative exchanges are desirable here as well: *creative partnerships, conversations*, and *constructive debate*. In practical terms, these latter kinds of interactions are even more common.

In the previous phase, we often meet people with whom the nature of our unresolved karma is conflictual or competitive. It is *aversive* karma, in other words. Here in this fourth phase, we are more likely to encounter people with whom the karma is connected more to *attachment* and *desire*. In *Romeo and Juliet*, for example, the relationship between the young lovers was aborted by death before it could be explored realistically. What happens when "Romeo" and "Juliet" meet again, as they surely will? *We do not know!* All we know for certain is that they will again meet, and that all their unresolved and unrequited desires toward each other will be re-ignited. They will pick up where they left off, and from there enter an unpredictable future.

A core point is that we all need help. We need to let ourselves be touched and affected by others. Probably in our effort to resolve karma in this co-creative way, we are also creating some new karma. So close to the Full phase, we are now far from the "pure" world of the beginning of the cycle—and remember that, with the nodal cycle, that earlier "purity," while brash and confident, was based significantly on error. Here, we are learning from other people. We have to accept shades of gray. If you get two steps forward for the price of one step back, you are doing fine.

Our exhortation is, "Link!"

FULL NODAL PHASE

With the Moon 180° to 225° ahead of the south node, in Full phase, the underlying soul intention is the *maximal material and existential manifestation of the karmic dilemmas*. This might seem counterintuitive until we contemplate the alternative: to keep the karma carefully hidden, never to be seen or explored. That gets us nowhere. As Ram Dass once quipped,

"One thing I can't stand is a horny celibate." The aim, in other words, is to put it out there. Be real and deal with the results.

In the Full nodal phase, we must try not to give fear or shame too much power. We must not fear our imperfections. We benefit from being fully human. There is no evolutionary advantage at all to be had from the slightest "spiritual" posturing. Any good actor can fake that for a week or two. As Yeats put it in his poem, *A Coat*, "there is more enterprise in walking naked." Be careful, though—this is not a general license for laxness and misconduct! Instead, it reflects a commitment to accept the realities we create, to follow through on them, to face them squarely and to reckon with the results. We aim to finish what we have started, and to take responsibility, even if we are temporarily unhappy or frustrated. Done right, it feels more like good psychotherapy than some self-righteous meditation group.

Remember: this fifth phase always has a "midlife" feeling. It's more about "marriage" than about "dating," in every possible sense of those words, literal or metaphorical. It's about actually doing the work rather than dreaming about utopian ideals. In fact, to get this phase right, we must abandon all hope of perfection, replacing it with a hunger for degrees of advancing clarity, increasing truth, and incremental motion toward completions. There is a "warts and all" feeling about it. Entanglements arise and can be difficult to sort out. Sometimes, rather than sorting them out, we must *ride them out* instead, and try to act with integrity in complex, nuanced, "grown-up" situations.

Our exhortation is, "Accept!"

WANING GIBBOUS NODAL PHASE

With the Moon 225° to 270° ahead of the south node, we enter the last phase of the bright hemicycle. Therefore, although we are still very much in the soup of karmic manifestation, we are also getting thoroughly tired of it—and, hopefully, fairly advanced in resolving it. In living gracefully within the context of the evolutionary realities represented by this nodal phase, it is helpful to recall the words of the Tibetan saint and folk hero, Padma Sambhava. He said, "If you want to know your past life, look into your present condition." What you are experiencing now—all the "random" blows of destiny, all the "dumb luck," all the slings and arrows of outrageous fortune—are the crystallized consequences of choices you made long ago. In this sixth phase, in other words, your karma is showing up quite concretely, and it *feels* like karma. *Déjà vu* runs rampant.

In working with this sixth phase energy, it is helpful to remember that even in situations that seem unbalanced and unfair, there is an underlying justice. Karma has momentum; it carries forward into the present life. That is always true for everyone, but it is particularly vivid and obvious in this phase. There is often a great desire to be finished and to move on—and yet in this Waning Gibbous nodal phase, the actual way forward requires patience. Certain debts simply must be paid. It is best to cultivate *forbearance* and *generosity*, and to strive to *lose one's self-importance*. Better to turn the other cheek than to get even. It is, in fact, *by* turning the other cheek that you actually *do* get even.

Opportunities to help other people with their various dramas and transitions are likely to abound. Be the Good Samaritan when you can. Do not expect the appearance of balance; you will not see much of it. But do be mindful of the easing of a sense of burden within yourself as you offer kindness without requiring or anticipating any reciprocity.

Others are in the same pickle with you, caught up in the passion play too. Don't try to escape them or even to analyze them too much. Instead, help them out as much as you can. Assistance, not diagnosis! If they will not accept help, cultivate compassion toward them. They may be suffering from pigheadedness, but let the accent in your mind be on their suffering.

Our exhortation is, "Help!"

LAST QUARTER NODAL PHASE

With the Moon 270° to 315° ahead of the south node, the circle is closing. We have now re-entered the dark hemicycle, where the whole nodal gyre had its birth. But, in the familiar words of Joni Mitchell, we look at it from "both sides now." We possess the perspective—and the emotional pitfalls—of maturity. Along with calmer wisdom, it is also true that cynicism, resignation and despair can loom. We must fight them. There is still evolutionary work to be done. Avoid the tempting belief that you have everything figured out! The aim in phase seven, in a nutshell, is to put as graceful and harmonious an *end* to things as possible. People must be let go—and blessed as they leave. Torches must be passed on, apprentices designated and empowered. As in the tales of the old Taoist sages, we are invited to turn our backs on the glitter and glory of the emperor's court and disappear into the wilderness to cultivate our quiet bean fields—and, ideally, this retreat is not felt so much as a sacrifice as a positive choice. It is a relief. Goodbye to all that.

Art and ritual can be very helpful in this phase. Maybe we do an abstract expressionist painting full of bold swaths of red and black and orange. No one would call it pretty, but we find ourselves obsessed with the process of creating it. We are blasting Metallica's *St. Anger* as we paint. It is not even the kind of music we like, but we play it anyway. Something deep inside us is telling us not to think too much. For weeks afterwards, we feel a kind of unaccustomed serenity. We do not know it consciously, but a "demon" left over inside us from a horrible, unfair death in the French Revolution has been excised from our souls. Maybe later, in the grips of an instinct we do not comprehend, we burn the painting. These are the kinds of dramatic, cathartic mysteries—and powers—we can access in this seventh nodal phase.

Old karmic friends appear now to sing a final chorus of *Auld Lang Syne*. Maybe we sleep together. Maybe we don't. Maybe that energy is not even in the air. The connection—and the implicit poignant good-bye—is what matters, not the form it takes. Old adversaries might appear too—and the aim is less to "settle" things than it is to realize that we have moved beyond the need for anything to be settled. We might think of the familiar line from the twenty-third Psalm, "Thou preparest a table before me in the presence of mine enemies." Here, as we determine truly to be done with a cycle of karma, we *forgive*. We relinquish our claims. We surrender. We bow—and thus know the deepest spiritual mysteries of victory—and we simply walk away.

Our exhortation is, "Release!"

WANING CRESCENT NODAL PHASE

With the Moon 315° to 360° ahead of the south node, the cycle comes to a close. Ideally, the karmic pattern is being finally and fully extinguished. This is not to be confused with Enlightenment—it is only the notion that a particular pattern of habit, drama, and attachment, as revealed in detail through a full analysis of the south node and its planetary correlates, is potentially almost played out. In this nodal phase, we might come to a kind of spiritual graduation. It is time to move on. Perhaps we are on the verge of a fundamental elevation of consciousness, a kind of quantum leap beyond the scope of our present imaginations.

In claiming those lofty hopes, we speak of the higher possible meaning of this nodal phase. As always, there are lower possibilities too. They are all connected with succumbing to a sense of defeat and resignation. Think of the broken drunk who gives up on any notion of ever achieving sobriety. Nothing now stands between him and the bottle but free-fall. Think of the compulsive shopper who knows that shopping will never fill that hole inside her, but who is shopping anyway. She is now immune to all insight. Such *depressive resignation* is the Shadow in this last nodal phase, and it is formidable.

The higher ground lies in surrender and faith. Ideally, the melodrama is over. The passion play has ended, and it feels as drained of emotion as do the memories of petty teen-age rivalries to a wise ninety-year-old. All is forgiven. The emotion is leached out of situations that used to press our buttons. Detachment arises. We start to understand the faraway, almost blissful, look in the eyes of those suffering, martyred saints in medieval paintings. They know with absolute certainty that heaven is just around the corner. All worldly pain is trivial in comparison. Angels, guides and spirits draw close at such a time. A person born under this nodal phase may very well sense such benign interventions from "the other side."

Consider a romantic heartbreak you suffered in the ninth grade. How do you feel about it today? Still seething with angst and judgment, ready to pluck out the fingernails of your rival? Or does it seem more like a half-forgotten movie you don't care if you ever see again? Is the memory almost sweet, now that time has worked its magic? If you can relate to the second perspective, you understand the eighth nodal phase. The tears and the drama are over. There is nothing left now but the neutral truth itself—that, and a sense that something new and unimaginably rich, but as yet undefined, is just around the corner . . .

Our exhortation is, "Forgive!"

The Eight Nodal Phases

CONCLUSION

)

A TRICK OF THE MEMORY

Every time I smell honeysuckle I am brought back to a summer night in a park in Larchmont, New York. I must have been about ten years old. The air was heavy with humidity, but pleasantly temperate after the heat of the day. My little sister Jan and I were scampering on the coastal rocks while the waves of Long Island Sound broke docilely against the stones below the paved pathways. Saltwater smells mixed with the land-locked perfumes of an August evening. Sailboats were lying tranquilly to their moorings in the harbor. Just a dozen paces back from the water, the tangles of honeysuckle vines began. My mother and my father were walking together not far away. I remember them holding hands. I am not sure if that is true, but that is how I remember it.

I loved that park, but at the time I thought it was because of the tide pools and the "pirates' cove" my sister and I discovered. Now I realize it was something deeper: a sense, however illusory, of having found a safe niche in time where family-feelings could dance with the adventurous promise of rocks and the open water forever. That is a wavelength to which my own Moon is naturally tuned. That is why the images of that evening sunk so deeply into me, and why they sunk into me in that exact way, just as a thief might remember an unlocked door or a painter the color of a sunset.

I can imagine that in a future incarnation, I might be hypnotically regressed to a prior lifetime. Suddenly, in my trance, I might smell hon-eysuckle. I might glimpse the rising Moon reflected in a tide pool. I might see my mom and dad in the distance. *And then I might remember being kidnapped by pirates and swept into a swashbuckling life of adventure...*

Above, my guardian angels would, of course, get yet another laugh out of me and my "memories." But that is how recollection works—and not just in terms of remembering prior lifetimes. Our more immediate memories are also subject to various distortions. Wishes and fears become confused with facts.

Prior lifetimes—when we reflect on them, it is not difficult for most of us to add a requisite grain of salt. Naturally, with our at best fleeting impressions of past lives, we allow for uncertainty. It is far more disconcerting to realize that our memories of our present lives might be similarly distorted. The police, for example, view "eyewitness accounts" with caution. Half the time, they vary widely. According to the Innocence Project, the misidentification of perpetrators of crime by eye witnesses is "the leading cause of wrongful conviction in the United States." The facts are hard: Three-quarters of the unjustly-jailed people later exonerated by DNA testing were convicted on the basis of such "eyewitness" evidence.

Less dramatically, I suspect my sister has different memories than I do of that seaside park in Larchmont. We grew up in the same family, but our natures and our storylines are not the same. Her Moon would filter it all very differently.

Objectively speaking, you cannot really believe your eyes, in other words. Nor can you trust your memory of what you believe your eyes saw. As George Santayana put it, "Memory itself is an internal rumor." Feelings, needs, and fears interact with mood, prejudice, and our arbitrary emotional priorities. That is the tricky lens through which we peer into the past. Rather literally, the Moon gets in our eyes.

Astrologically, we might helpfully distinguish two types of memory: the *Mercury memory* and the *Moon memory*. My telephone number as a child was MO7-6030. Off the top of my head, I can tell you that the speed of light through a vacuum is 186,282.3 miles per second. If someone asks me to define the Fibonacci series or to talk about the Black Plague, I can do that too. Those are Mercury memories. Facts, in other words. But the smell of honeysuckle and the resultant rush of images of that seaside park half a century ago—that is a Moon memory. It rides a wave of emotion.

Like delicate antique porcelains, we treasure these sentimental heirlooms from our past. And yet in their very slipperiness they seem fragile. Nothing could be further from the truth. Memories that become enmeshed in our emotional lives may be particularly subject to factual distortions, but they are also extremely robust. Bottom line, we remember feelings far more vividly and far longer than we remember facts. That remains true whether we are talking about last year or another lifetime. Everyone's emotional memories "reincarnate," both day to day and lifetime to lifetime. The boy who was sexually abused by a priest in 1974 is mistrustful of religion today as a man, even though he may have repressed the experience—his Moon remembers, even though he has no Mercury memory of the violation. Similarly, the woman who died in childbirth in a prior lifetime may not literally remember that hard death today, but there is an excellent chance that the thought of pregnancy will fill her with dread.

Another way to say this is simply that while emotional content distorts facts, it also electrifies them, fixing them in our memories. Ask a long-married couple about their first date. Think of your first day in kindergarten or your first experience of sexual intercourse. What is the bravest thing you have ever done? What is the most frightened you have ever been? Recall the first time you truly felt love. Ever lose a partner or a best friend to some terrible disease? How did that feel? (As Renaissance philosopher Michel de Montaigne said, "Nothing fixes a thing so intensely in the memory as the wish to forget it.") What is the worst thing another human being has ever done to you? Positive or negative, these are all examples of emotionally-charged happenings. In almost every case, the details come flying like banshees out of the memory banks, regardless of how long ago the events occurred—but let us note soberly that in every case, the other people involved would presumably hold to significantly different versions of those happenings.

Now think of the first time you ever opened a book on the subject of algebra. Think of preparing your 2007 tax returns. Think of a dull lecture at a conference you attended six years ago.

Can't remember, huh? Me neither.

These charged Moon-memories have a particular anatomy. They contain "Mercury" facts and they also contain a lunar matrix of mood, affect, and feeling in which the factual memories are embedded. As if they were friable sandstone, time often gradually erodes the facts, leaving only the granite outcroppings of the emotionally-charged memories. Sometimes that loss occurs within the context of a single lifetime as Mercury memories simply fade or as more dire afflictions arise in the ageing brain. But that erosion of factual memory becomes nearly absolute as the physical brain dies and the mind stream passes into the mysteries beyond death. Then most of what remains to us is Moon memory.

The point of all this is simply that the Moon, with its vast baggage of internal, subjective biases, is the true ruler of the only thing any of us can reliably keep or take out of this world: *the core, underlying moods and attitudes that our memories have generated in us.*

Resisting pressure to write his autobiography, Carl Gustav Jung, in the last three or four years of his life, wrote,

> "... all memory of outer events has faded, and perhaps these 'outer' experiences were never so very essential anyhow, or were so only in that they coincided with phases of my inner development. An enormous part of these 'outer' manifestations of my life has vanished from my memory ... Yet these are the very things that make up a sensible biography: persons one has met, travels, adventures, entanglements, blows of destiny, and so on. But with few exceptions all these things have become for me phantasms which I barely recollect and which my mind has no desire to reconstruct, for they no longer stir my imagination."

In the words of Aniela Jaffé, who worked closely with Jung eventually to produce his autobiography, *Memories, Dreams, Reflections*, "I often asked Jung for specific data on outward happenings, but I asked in vain. Only the spiritual essence of his life's experiences remained in his memory, and this alone seemed to him worth the effort of telling."

Even the great Carl Jung forgot much of his life. Our own memories are not very reliable either. Should we be worried about this? Much human effort is wasted on solving problems that we do not actually have. I picture a Sagittarian woman born in 1867 struggling to become "more ladylike." I picture her Cancerian brother, embarrassed by his strong emotions, struggling to become "more manly." Both of them feel they have problems. Neither one actually does. When social training and nature are at odds, we must at least consider the idea that nature could represent the profounder truth. Have we simply been trained to imagine that the "objective facts" about "what really happened" are more valuable than the honeysuckle perfume they leave in the mind after the facts are forgotten?

Carl Jung presented Aniela Jaffé a serious challenge as his biographer: He claimed he could not recall his life! But let us contemplate that "problem" from a more encouraging perspective. Maybe we only think there is an issue with this kind of "forgetfulness." Nature seems to incline us toward it, especially as we age. We joke about "senior moments." But maybe Carl Jung, in instinctively releasing all attachment to his Mercury memories and only holding onto those of his Moon, demonstrated a fundamental wisdom.

Most of us believe that the purpose of our being here in this world has something to do with the evolution of consciousness. People might call it self-improvement or salvation or realization, but it always comes down to something positive happening invisibly in the nonmaterial dimensions of our beings. As poet David Whyte eloquently tells us, "To be human is to become visible while carrying what is hidden as a gift to others." In almost every religion or metaphysical framework, the assumption is that, unlike transitory money, fickle fame, or even our memorized educations, these deeper accomplishments are carried forward beyond physical death. They are what is precious about us. They are perhaps our only truly meaningful gift to others.

In what specific form might they be carried forward?

A child is born, and right away we sense something special about her. There is wisdom and kindness in her eyes. Fifty years later, she is an extraordinary herbalist, held precious by her community. No surprise there. *And five hundred years earlier,* in a different body, she was a Lakota medicine woman, playing a similar role in that society. You look into that baby's eyes today and a kind of *emotional summary of the entire history of her soul* is gazing out at you right there, thirty seconds after her birth. That mood is what has been "carried forward." With that infant, you do not know "the facts" behind what you are seeing, but you feel their essence.

Nearing the end of his days on the earth, Jung likened the outer events of his life to phantasms he had no wish to reconstruct. As he released his attachment to these Mercury memories, was he riding the wave of a healthy instinct? Was his psyche skillfully packing its bags for the next world, taking only that which he actually *could* take? Jung said, "All memory of outer events has faded, and perhaps these 'outer' experiences were never so very essential anyhow, or were so only in that they coincided with phases of my inner development." Had all the outward experiences of Jung's illustrious life been nothing more than grist for his soul's mill? Was everything he manifested in life—his writings, his relationships, his legacy—all secondary to the evolutionary process of feeding "what is hidden"? Did everything he accomplished and experienced serve only to *feed the Moon*? In the light of our mortality—and in the light of what we see in that newborn baby's eyes—how could we possibly come to any other conclusion?

In her book *Animal Dreams*, Barbara Kingsolver writes, "Memory is a complicated thing, a relative to truth, but not its twin." How much of what you remember really happened in your life the way you remember it? And how much of it is only "a relative to truth"? This is the question with which we have been wrestling—and it is actually a slippery one. Much pivots on exactly what we mean by that elusive word, "truth." What are the distinguishing qualities of genuine truths? How do we discern them? One familiar answer might be that *real truth is eternal*. Even science lays only a tenuous claim on that prize. For all eternity, energy will probably equal mass times the speed of light, squared. But what about other scientific assertions? One hundred and fifty years ago, scientists assured us that time, space, and mass were constants. That assumption was absolutely basic to all scientific thinking before the theory of Relativity. Fifty years ago, scientists assured us that homosexuality was a psychiatric disorder. As late as 2003, scientists told us that Vioxx would improve your health—and now we realize that was only true if you did not mind the occasional heart attack or stroke.

Real truth stands the test of time. *And what part of our memory does in fact stand the test of time?* It is not, as we have demonstrated, the memory of outward facts. It is their emotional meaning. What survives is the internal, lunar distillation of all the experience we have truly digested.

Even before he died, Carl Jung had begun to forget the material details of his outward life. He is not unusual in that. Many people become more forgetful in old age. Winston Churchill apparently suffered either from Alzheimer's disease or some other dementia-inducing disorder in his final years. Did the disease that erased his memories also erase his great soul?

We are entertaining several perspectives simultaneously here. I am saying that honesty and humility compel us to recognize that the version of our biographies that we carry in our memory banks is, to a significant degree, objectively unreliable—that it is only "a relative to" what actually happened in our lives. I am also arguing that this does not matter very much, that it is not "the facts" that survive or feed the evolution of the soul. The concrete facts of our outward lives are trivial things anyway—short-lived, unreliable, and soon forgotten and dissipated. What remains to shine out of our eyes in our old age and in any future births is the Moon memory: an amalgam of reactions, fantasies, wishes, and fears, all flavored with dim impressions of half-remembered realities, "smelling of honeysuckle."

We die. Many metaphysical teachers assure us that we are reborn. In between, we occupy a very mysterious state—one with strongly lunar overtones. How we navigate them has a huge bearing upon our experience there and also upon the quality of our next birth. Dzogchen Ponlop Rinpoche, in his *Mind Beyond Death*, writes that in our experiences following physical death, "we are very susceptible to intense emotional states, to overwhelming moments of panic and fear. So learning how to work effectively with our emotions now is regarded as crucial training for these later bardo experiences." Translated into astrological terms, he is of course talking about maintaining an honest, healthy connection with our Moons in this lifetime. We can do it now while it is, relatively speaking, easier—or we can face unalloyed extremities of fear, rage, and despair in that time of transition.

I explored past-life territory pretty thoroughly in *Yesterday's Sky*—and as Carl Jung once put it, "The mere fact that people talk about rebirth . . . means that a store of psychic experiences designated by that term must exist." Here, in this book, in pursuing a deeper understanding of the astrological Moon, we have taken a different tack. More often than not, we have set the past aside and focused upon what the Moon tells us about how to maintain emotional health in the here and now. But, as Dzogchen Ponlop reminds us, a very significant side effect of our present efforts is the quality of our after-death experience, which bears quite directly upon the quality of our next lifetime.

So what will your issues be next time around? What about your mood? What will shine from your eyes five minutes after your next birth? At first blush, these questions seem unanswerable. But recall Padma Sambhava's simple formula: "If you want to know your future life, look at your present actions." That is the law of karma. If you are always angry today, there is an excellent chance that same anger will still be blazing in your eyes next time you are a baby. If you are loving and gentle today, that mood will tend to reincarnate as well. Karma, most fundamentally, is merely habit. There are deeper waters here, but these simple principles are pivotal—and not really hard to understand because we do not need to reincarnate to see them working. We live them every day. Yesterday's raging bull stands a good chance of being tomorrow's raging bull too.

Solar experience pours into us through the gateways of the five senses. But once inside, it has entered the second world, the realm of the Moon, where we might digest it and turn it into lasting substance in our beings. Here is where we shape the laws that govern the realities not only of our emotional lives, but also of our dreams and our attunement to the realms beyond the material plane. That gradually-accreted inward reality, which we have been calling the "Moon memory," is what nourishes the soul—or potentially poisons it.

Built into the message of the Moon in your natal chart are instructions for making sure that the memories you are building today are nourishing ones. That does not mean anything as simple-minded as being happy and positive all the time, and it certainly does not suggest any attempt to edit unpleasant experiences. Instead, it simply means that there are specific attitudes that genuinely feed and support you in the long run—and they are not necessarily the same attitudes that would be good for me, your Uncle Joe, or the person who shares a bed with you. *There is a mood you are trying to achieve.* Getting there entails a right relationship to grief and despair, which are naturally a part of everyone's life. And it entails a right relationship with happiness and victory too.

Few insights that could be found printed on a greeting card will be very helpful here, in other words. The entire point of astrology's message is that we are all different beings on different journeys. Underlying every word in this book is the notion that there are right moods and attitudes for someone with a balsamic Moon in Scorpio—moods and attitudes which would be unhelpful to someone with a fifth-house Gemini Moon in Beltane-phase.

Whatever your lunar configuration, if you get it right, you are laying down the capricious bricks of memory with the right mortar. You experience immediate benefit. You feel *happy*, for starters. You feel a comfortable sense of well-being. In the longer run, you are setting the inner tone of your later years, regardless of whether or not your physical brain thrives. I suspect you are actually helping to ensure that it will thrive. *Beyond all that, you are also shaping the part of you that will pass through the door of death and rebirth.* You are putting a positive spin on your next birth.

As you age, you, like Carl Jung, might find that your literal memories grow vague. But the moods and attitudes you have created in your heart will remain. That Moon memory will shine out through your rheumy, geriatric eyes, even if your brain fails. It will define much of the mysterious experience you face after your heart stops.

And when, after a moment of rest upon the wind, you have two clear eyes and a child's impressionable heart again, it will shine on.

Steven Forrest
New Year's Day, 2010
Borrego Springs, California

RECOMMENDED READING

Many of the works below were either directly referenced in the present volume or were somehow instrumental to the formation of the understandings underlying it.

Aswynn, Freya. *Northern Mysteries and Magick* (a revised edition of her *Leaves of Yggdrasil)*. St. Paul, MN: Llewellyn, 1998.

Boehrer, Kt. *Declinations, The Other Dimension*. Fortunata Press, 1994.

Bradley, Marian Zimmer. *The Mists of Avalon*. Alfred A. Knopf, 1982.

Busteed, Marilyn, Richard Tiffany and Dorothy Wergin. *Phases of the Moon: A Guide to Evolving Human Nature*. Boston, MA: Shambhala, 1974.

Rosenthal, M.L., editor. *Selected Poems and Two Plays of William Butler Yeats*. Collier, 1962.

Cabot, Laurie. *Celebrate the Earth: A Year of Holidays in the Pagan Tradition*. New York, NY: Bantam Doubleday Dell, 1994.

Eisler, Riane. *The Chalice and the Blade*. Harper & Row, 1987.

Fernandez, Maurice. *Astrology and the Evolution of Consciousness*. Evolutionary Astrology Inc., 2009.

Forrest, Jodie. *The Ascendant*. Borrego Springs, CA: Seven Paws Press, 2007.

Forrest, Steven. *Yesterday's Sky: Astrology and Reincarnation*. Borrego Springs, CA: Seven Paws Press, 2008.

Forrest, Steven. *The Night Speaks*. San Diego, CA: ACS Publications, 1993.

Forrest, Steven. *The Changing Sky: A Practical Guide to Predictive Astrology*. New York, NY: Bantam, 1986. Revised ed. San Diego, CA: ACS, 1998. Rpt. Borrego Springs, CA: Seven Paws Press, 2007.

George, Demetra. *Finding Our Way Through the Dark*. American Federation of Astrologers 2008, 1994.

George, Demetra. *Mysteries of the Dark Moon: The Healing Power of the Dark Goddess*. HarperSanFrancisco, 1992.

Goldsmith, Martin. *Moon Phases*. Whitford Press, 1988.

Green, Jeffrey Wolf and Steven Forrest. *Measuring the Night, Volume Two*. Seven Paws Press and Daemon Press, 2001.

Herring, Amy. *Astrology of the Moon: an Illuminating Journey through the Signs and Houses*. St. Paul, MN: Llewellyn, 2010.

Jones, Prudence and Nigel Pennick. *A History of Pagan Europe*. Routledge, 1995.

Jones, Tristan. *To Venture Further*. Grafton Books, a Division of Harper-Collins, 1991.

Lutin, Michael. *Sunshines: The Astrology of Being Happy*. New York, NY: Simon and Schuster, 2006.

Metzner, Ralph. *The Well of Remembrance: Rediscovering the Earth Wisdom Myths of Northern Europe*. Boston, MA: Shambhala, 1994.

The Mountain Astrologer magazine http://www.mountainastrologer.com.

NCGR, *Geocosmic* magazine. Spring, 1998. (Issue topic: Declinations.) This issue is currently (as of 2010) available online here: http://geocosmic. org/mm5/merchant.mvc?Screen=PROD&Store_Code=A&Product_Code=J-98SPR&Category_Code=

Pagels, Eileen. *Adam, Eve and the Serpent.* Random House, 1988.

Pennick, Nigel. *The Pagan Book of Days.* Destiny Books, 1992, rpt. 2001.

Ponlop, Dzogchen. *Mind Beyond Death.* Ithaca, NY: Snow Lion Publications, 2006.

Railey, David R., *The Soul Purpose*, iUniverse, 2009.

Rudhyar, Dane. *The Lunation Cycle.* Servire, 1967.

Seymour-Smith, Martin. *The New Astrologer.* Collier, 1981.

Spring, Elizabeth. *North Node Astrology: Rediscovering Your Life Direction and Soul Purpose.* Archeon Press, 2009.

Tyl, Noel Jan. *Holistic Astrology: The Analysis of Inner and Outer Environments.* St. Paul, MN: Llewellyn, 1980.

Walsh, Patricia L. *Understanding Karmic Complexes.* Wessex Astrologer, 2009.

Yeats, William Butler. *A Vision.* MacMillan, 1937.

Zeilik, Michael. *Astronomy: The Evolving Universe, Third Edition.* Harper & Row, 1982.

About the Author

Steven Forrest is the author of several astrological bestsellers, including *THE INNER SKY, THE CHANGING SKY, THE BOOK OF PLUTO, THE NIGHT SPEAKS*, and the new classic *YESTERDAY'S SKY*, written with support from a grant by the Integrative Medicine Foundation.

Steven's work has been translated into a dozen languages, most recently Chinese and Italian. He travels worldwide to speak and teach his brand of choice-centered evolutionary astrology – an astrology which integrates free will, grounded humanistic psychology and ancient metaphysics.

Along with his busy private practice, he maintains active astrological apprenticeship programs in California, Australia, North Carolina, and Switzerland. He is a founding member of the Ethics Committee of the International Society for Astrological Research (ISAR).

See his website www.forrestastrology.com for more details.

Praise

In praise of Steven's work, Jungian Robert Johnson says, "You have restored the divine art to its noble status." The musician Sting calls Steven's work "as intelligent and cogent as it is poetic." DELL HOROSCOPE describes him as "not only a premier astrologer, but also a wise man." Callie Khouri, who wrote the screenplay for Thelma and Louise, praises his "humor, insight, poetry, and astute, articulate observations of human nature." O: THE OPRAH MAGAZINE writes, "Forrest's approach... stops the blame game in its tracks...we're warriors fulfilling our turbulent evolutionary paths." Actor Robert Downey Jr. says, "I marvel at the accuracy of Steve's readings. He insists that nothing is so grave as to be beyond repair, and correspondingly that there is no rainbow that won't be evaporated by poor judgment in the now. I can't recommend him highly enough." And astrologer Rob Brezsny simply calls him "the most brilliant astrologer alive."

Learn Astrology with Steven Forrest

Interested in learning more about Steven's unique approach to astrology? For a listing of lectures and workshops that are available in a variety of audio and video formats, go to: http://www.forrestastrology.com/MP3-Audio-Downloads.

Better yet, join the many successful students who have completed **Steven's Astrological Apprenticeship Program,** where he teaches both the specific techniques of interpretation and the style of presentation that have made him one of the most successful and influential astrologers in the world. Steven takes great joy in passing on the teachings and strategies that have worked for him over the years through his Apprenticeship Program.

The Apprenticeship Program presents students with a rare opportunity to learn astrology in a supportive environment of like-minded individuals, who together create a feeling of community and connection, leading to bonds that last throughout life. Some come to the program to train professionally, while others come for personal or spiritual enrichment.

Steven's apprenticeship groups are currently meeting in North Carolina, Southern California (near San Diego,) Northern California (north of San Francisco), Australia, and Europe.

Once enrolled in the program, students gain access to over 10 years of Steven's private teachings, recorded in audio format, and also available as pdf transcripts of select programs.

Learn more at www.forrestastrology.com

CPSIA information can be obtained
at www.ICGtesting.com
Printed in the USA
FSHW020031130519
58077FS